100 YEARS *Young*

ENLIGHTENED MEDICINE
AND THE
SECRETS OF LONGEVITY

GARY COURTENAY ND *and*
KATHERINE JOYCE SMITH DHS
with Jon Eisen & Sue Walter

The information contained in this book was prepared from
sources which are believed to be accurate and reliable.
However, the opinions expressed herein by the author do not
necessarily represent the opinions or the views of the publisher.
Readers are strongly advised to seek the advice of their
personal health care professional(s) before proceeding
with any changes in *any* health care program.

Canadian Cataloguing in Publication Data

Courtenay, Gary, 1939–
    100 years young : enlightened medicine and the secrets of longevity

Includes bibliographical references.
ISBN: 1-896817-01-7

    1. Longevity. 2. Health. 3. Nutrition. 4. Aging.
I. Smith, Katherine Joyce, 1971– II. Eisen, Jon III. Walter, Sue
IV. Title. V. Title: One hundred years young.

RA776.75.C68 1998   613   C98-900281-0

Apple Publishing Company Ltd.
220 East 59th Avenue
Vancouver, British Columbia
Canada v5x 1x9
Tel (604) 214-6688 • Fax (604) 214-3566

Email: books@applepublishing.com

TABLE OF CONTENTS

WHERE IS THE WISDOM?

THE POVERTY OF MEDICAL EVIDENCE

From *The British Medical Journal* October 5, 1991

"Where is the wisdom we have lost in knowledge, and where," asked T.S. Elliot, "is the knowledge we have lost in information?" There are perhaps 30,000 biomedical journals in the world, and they have grown steadily by 7% a year since the seventeenth century. Yet only about 15% of medical interventions are supported by solid scientific evidence, David Eddy, professor of health policy and management at Duke University, North Carolina, told a conference in management last week. This is partly because only 1% of the articles in medical journals are scientifically sound, and partly because many medical treatments have never been assessed at all. "If," said Professor Eddy "it is true, as the total quality management gurus tell us that every defect is a treasure then we are sitting on King Solomon's mine."

What are the implications for purchasing health care when the scientific basis for medicine is really so fragile? Because, as Professor Eddy said, "it is not enough to do the thing right; it is also necessary to do the right thing." The implications for purchasers of the poverty of medical evidence were considered at the Manchester meeting, which was organized jointly by the

British Association of Medical Managers and the resource management unit of the NHS Management Executive.

Professor Eddy began his medical life as a cardiothoracic surgeon in Stanford, California but became progressively concerned about the evidence to support what he and other doctors were doing. He decided to select an example of a common condition with well established treatments and assess in detail the evidence supporting those treatments. Beginning with glaucoma, he searched published medical reports back to 1906 and could not find one randomized controlled trial of the standard treatment. Later he traced back the confident statements in textbooks and medical journals on treating glaucoma and found that they had simply been handed down from generation to generation. The same analysis was done for other treatments, including the treatment of blockages of the femoral and popliteal arteries; the findings were similar. That experience 'changed his life,' and after taking a degree in mathematics at Stanford University he became a professor and one of the consultants most in demand in the United States.

...The weakness of the scientific evidence underlying medical practice is one of the causes of the wide variations that are well recognized in medical practice..."

HOW TO LIVE TO A RIPE OLD AGE IN SPITE OF YOUR DOCTOR

While there are many doctors who carry out the noble tradition of saving lives and healing the sick—and for them we have nothing but respect and admiration—on balance we believe that the medical profession in general has failed both as a science as well as an art.

Medicine has become, in the words of Dr. Robert Mendelsohn—a physician trained in the orthodox school of medicine—'a religion.' It comes complete with its catechism, its hierarchy, and its willingness to excommunicate anyone who dares to deviate from the accepted dogma.

The chances are that if you get sick and see a doctor you will be treated by someone who has not and will not deviate from the accepted dogma. This dogma has been most likely instilled in him/her by a medical school that teaches *virtually no nutrition*—probably the most important factor in maintaining good health and the lack of which is certainly one of the most important causes of the deterioration of good health. Most medical schools established in the US were initially funded by big business interests, and continue to be funded by the same, usually pharmaceutical companies. Most breakthroughs, if they cannot be patented by the drug companies, are ignored, discarded, or disparaged by the medical profession, usually without thorough investigation.

Possible cures for diseases like Alzheimer's, such as the one described in these pages, are usually trashed as 'anecdotal' without the slightest evidence of curiosity. The same goes for Chelation Therapy, probably the most promising treatment for heart disease ever discovered.

There is an old joke which has more than a grain of truth to it: "What is the difference between God and a doctor?"

Answer: "God doesn't think He's a doctor."

As Dr. Mendelsohn wryly observed, the medical profession thinks that all mistakes on its part were made in the past. It has historically been unwilling to countenance mistakes that it could be committing in the present, and for this reason has been notoriously slow in accepting input from outside its own closed fraternity, reluctant to look at anything—witness its narrow-minded attitude with respect to acupuncture until 1972!—That might appear to be a threat to its collective financial well being.

Orthodox medicine has not acted as a collective healing establishment. For example, when Hoxsey's and Rife's promising cancer therapies came along in the 1940s after unsuccessful attempts to buy them out, the medical profession destroyed them—resorting to time worn shibboleths like "double blind studies have never been made" or "it hasn't appeared in a professional medical publication like the *Journal of the AMA*." Yet, the profession refuses to see the mote in its own eye. Procedures in use for decades, like triple bypass surgery, *have never been investigated in any double blind study*. One reason alternative treatments don't get published in orthodox journals is because no one will publish them if they are perceived as an economic threat, whether they are good science or not good science. In fact, only 10–20% of all procedures used by medical doctors have been subject to double blind trial.

This is not to imply that orthodox medicine should have no place in your life. Many of their surgical and diagnostic techniques are sophisticated and effective. Emergency rooms routinely and not so routinely save countless lives; some antibiotics work wonders on bacterial diseases.

But if you are thinking about longevity, we believe that preventative medicine is still the best, and this could mean consulting a qualified naturopath or practitioner of Chinese medicine. If you are interested in effective noninterventionist techniques, homeopathy may be considered; it certainly works for the British Royal Family. Drug-free pain relief and a host of other effective treatments for various conditions can be accessed from your local acupuncturist who practises one of the oldest forms of medicine to be found on the planet, and one of the most sophisticated! Herbal medicine is also of an ancient and noble lineage and there are others as well.

Your health is your responsibility and the more you learn about it and your body, the better off you will be. We in the West have long neglected our health and it shows. Our cancer epidemic is showing no signs of decreasing in its virulence, and our antibiotics are often not as effective as they were only a few years ago. We seem to care more for the 'bottom line' than we do for each other, or even ourselves, and this seems to be a symptom of a spiritual disease in which we have got our priorities wrong.

This book is offered in the hope that it will encourage you, the reader, to begin the valuable and fascinating quest to attain both the knowledge and the responsibility for your own well-being.

May you live to 100—at least!—And enjoy every year, and every moment. And may each year bring blessings on you as you share your love and your knowledge with others, and may you grow in wisdom and grace.

THE TROUBLE WITH ORTHODOX MEDICINE

The trouble with orthodox medicine is the trouble with any orthodoxy. Orthodox behavior relies on what is acceptable to the prevailing group. It therefore respects power and conformity to the dictates of power, whether that power resides in a political tyrant, a religious potentate, a 'traditional way of thinking' as enforced by positive and negative reinforcement from authority figures, or even an internal censor. What it does not respect is individual thinking, creative approaches and novel solutions arrived at independently.

Orthodox medicine has its codex, its rituals, its hierarchy, its initiation rites, its rigid belief system, its 'us' vs 'them' mentality; it excommunicates its heretics and it behaves in an irrational manner when confronted with new facts that don't 'fit in' with its orthodox view of disease and treatment. It has its temples like the Mayo Clinic or Memorial Sloane Kettering Cancer Hospital, its pantheon of gods.

And it is failing miserably. Like the naked emperor, it demands to be worshipped, but the innocent can see that its intellectual cupboard is quite empty. It does not cure our serious illnesses; rather it is in league with the giant multinational corporations that are helping to exacerbate old diseases like cancer and create new ones like AIDS. It relies on greed to fuel itself, and as such is constitutionally incapable of finding cures for diseases like cancer.

For there is no money in cures for cancer—only in the endless search itself, financed by public money and donations from the desperate and the disconsolate. For make no mistake about it, cures for the scourges of our time have been found—cures for cancer and even AIDS, cures for arthritis and heart disease, but you will not find them in your Physicians Desk Reference nor from any orthodox 'specialist' nor from your local family doctor, your HMO, your Group Plan, or your metropolitan hospital. Orthodox medicine has become a juggernaut, uncontrollable and responsible for the needless deaths of millions of people.

This is because modern medicine is based on the orthodox model. That means if you are a cancer research person you cannot get funding for any research project not likely to lead to a patentable drug. That means you do not design your project around herbal medicine, vitamins or nutritional ideas, but search only for a drug that might get a patent and therefore make a 'killing' for your pharmaceutical company sponsor. That is the current orthodox model.

Never mind that the road to optimum health may lie in oxygen therapy, vitamin C, potassium rich foods or liver extracts, Essiac, papaya leaf tea or garlic. It doesn't matter. What matters is that the positive reinforcement—the jobs status and funding—is in drugs; and the negative reinforcement—the FDA raids on your clinic, the lack of funding, the harassment by your peer groups, the loss of job or status—prop up a system that has little if any objective validity. In other words it doesn't cure anybody, or at best a low relative percentage, but it is the system of choice, reinforcing itself even as it feeds on the population. It is little wonder that such a system succeeds when you consider that hospital and doctor visits, and expenditure on drugs counts as part of the Gross Domestic Product. In other words, the sicker we get, the richer we look on the books.

THEY DON'T MAKE OLD AGE LIKE THEY USED TO

Have you ever noticed that some people seem to age faster than others… while some people retain obviously good health their entire lives? And in some parts of the world the life-span is much higher than in other parts of the world? In fact, there are some cultures, like the fabled Hunzas, whose *average life-span is well up in the hundreds!*

Over the past twenty years or so thousands of different studies have proved the connections between nutrition *(and fasting!)*, exercise, positive thinking, free, unimpeded breathing and… increased health and longevity.

These studies have concluded that the common sense correlations between how we treat ourselves and how we are treated by our own bodies are completely accurate. Longevity seems to be connected to enjoyment of life and the love of oneself and others.

This only stands to reason. How we think and what we think, and what we think about what we think, are all important. Thoughts are like magnets, drawing "realities" to them in mysterious but nevertheless very real ways. "I think therefore I am," said Descartes, and it is perfectly true. What you think is literally what you become. The 'trick' (if there is one) is in realizing that you have control over what you think. In other words, if there is something or someone bothering you, **you can change the thought**. This will indeed change the 'reality' and leave you less bothered, less stressed. More on this later.

The body is far 'more' than we realize it to be, and is in fact susceptible to both disease and good health, in part thanks to the thoughts we think and the attitude we have about life itself. This is not some mystical incantation, but is actual quantum physics. We are pure light, pure energy in our essence, and timeless besides.

Which means that in effect we are, all of us, immortal. Our very atoms, everything we're made of is billions of years 'old.' When we consider it from that point of view we have all been around forever, and will go on forever. What makes us 'alive' now is the consciousness that animates those atoms, those cells. Our intelligence is in realizing the free choice of the thoughts that we have at any given moment. We are all of us 'plugged into' that universal intelligence, that cosmic awareness, and we can access it at any moment, at every moment. That place, if indeed it is a place at all, is, quite literally immortal.

They don't make old age like they used to. No longer do people accept obsolete concepts of aging; we are beginning to gain control of our own lives in some startling new ways. We are beginning to sense that we *can control the aging process itself* by determining the extent to which the process can be altered—both biochemically and psychosomatically. Back in the 'old days' we did not realize how people's life-spans were role modelled on the life-spans of their family and peers. Life-spans were often 'hereditary'—not because of any genetic program, but because of suggestion and auto suggestion. People literally talked and thought themselves into predetermined life-spans.

This is still happening today, but with a major difference. We are beginning to learn new ways of consciously monitoring our thoughts and thought patterns to take increasing responsibility for who we are.

This book is our attempt to report on some of the timeless wisdom as well as the newest research into ways of gaining and then maintaining perfect health and well being for our entire lifetime. But it is also a report on some startling new discoveries that open up possibilities of a life-span that is far in excess of what we are used to, and in fact may harken back to biblical life-spans like Methuselah's.

His was reportedly 900 years.

There are some people who believe that the human body is potentially immortal and they have found examples of people whose life-spans are 'unreasonably' long. Leonard Orr, the founder of the rebirthing movement, discovered numerous examples of people who might have lived for many centuries. Whether this is pure speculation or has some factual basis is problematical. But, as Orr is fond of pointing out, *immortalist consciousness never hurt anybody.* Freud theorized that Eros, the life force, was always in battle with Thanatos, the death force. Locked in an endless struggle within each of us, the two forces—the yin and yang of existence—more or less balance each other out. Orr maintains that each of them is influenced by our thoughts, and perhaps most importantly, **we have a choice over what we think at any given moment**—and to what we devote our energy.

When we finally realize this startling fact, whole new worlds of possibility open up to us; and the weight of 'determinism' drops away. No longer are we so inclined to apportion blame—either to ourselves or others—when we realize that blame is just another way of living in the past and retaining an anger that has not produced positive results and is not likely to procure for us the kind of life we really desire for ourselves.

More productive is the experiment of forgiveness, not merely as a concept drawn from some romantic utopianism, but because it is the most likely avenue to take to get the desired results. These results for people eager to embrace a healthy and a long lifetime begin to come naturally—though they are the result of hard work and a willingness to accept love as one's personal friend.

Even though no possible harm can come from embracing the highest wisdom people are strangely reluctant to embrace even the most elemental precepts of a healthy life—honesty, forgiveness, clarity, purity of food and water— and instead operate as though cause and effect did not apply to them. How absolutely Orwellian, but then, this has become an Orwellian kind of world where the dominant institutions no longer deliver accurate or trustworthy information and are seen as self serving. Even (or perhaps especially) our vaunted science, the 'god' to whom people have looked for salvation for more than a century, has become another idol with clay feet, beholden and subservient to the interests that pay for it, and the egos which strive for status within its halls of power.

This book is grounded on the idea that 'positive thinking' can have only positive results. Moreover, given what we are learning about our true potential, perhaps there really are no limits to what we—you, too—can achieve.

"Hold it! We've got some bits left over!"

CHAPTER 1

WHAT IF?

100 Years Young is written with the express purpose of helping you achieve a major consciousness breakthrough to the real possibility of lengthening your life-span to an age you may have wished for but never thought possible.

We have paradoxically called this book *100 Years Young* because it asks the question, 'What if?' What if we stopped thinking that our life-span is only 70 or 80 years, and started *seriously thinking* that our life-span was indeed much longer.

What we think determines our reality. *In fact, it is our reality.* This book reiterates the point that we are conditioned into thinking many things. We are conditioned into believing that we are 'independent thinkers,' individuals to the last. What makes for social cohesion is that we all share a certain consensus about what is 'true' (and therefore acceptable) and what is not. In our ignorance and arrogance we think that our peculiar and particular truths are universal and immutable. This is what makes us so rigid and ill equipped to deal creatively, appropriately and instantaneously with an ever changing universe.

The point is, we think we are merely 'describing' an objective 'reality' while what we are really doing *is creating that reality we think we are describing*.

There are several societies in which a huge percentage of the people live to well over 100. What if you lived in that society from the time you were very young? Would you not begin to accept (create) the fact that you, too, were going to live that long as well?

When you begin to answer this question you begin to understand exactly how this mass hallucination we call reality actually impacts on our *consciousness*. And how we can and do fashion our lives according to how we adapt to the consensus around us.

What if we simply refused to 'buy into' the prevailing longevity paradigm? What kinds of actions would logically follow? The answer to that question is partly what this book is about.

Would we not immediately begin investigating how we treat ourselves (physically, mentally and spiritually) as well as how we treat others? Would we not immediately adopt a philosophy of harmlessness? Would we not begin to see that positive thoughts have positive results and the accumulation of positive results leads to further positive results? Is this not merely *the physics of life, of cause and effect?*

Individually as well as culturally we have been seduced by the shallow rewards of base materialism, not realizing—even in the spasmodic writhing of an entire planet that is literally reeling from the filth and degradation of its human guests—what this materialism has wrought upon the planet and ourselves.

Part of the meaning of that materialism is that we have adopted a posture toward death and dying that is utterly appalling. We have cheapened death as we have cheapened life itself. The result is an ever stronger vortex sucking us into paralysis and possible annihilation. "Thanatos rules, OK?" could be the slogan of a civilization whose great gift to the ages is plastic.

This book urges you to consider 'What if?' it didn't have to be this way. And 'What if?' you could take control of your own life, indeed your own *life force?*

And what if by the time you reached 100 you were still young?

If you think that it's ridiculous to even think thoughts like this one, you should either 1) stop reading this book or 2) ponder on why you think it's ridiculous to even think thoughts like this and then go on reading. Impossible? How can you think that anything is impossible after so many developments in this century alone that started out being impossible and ended up taking pride of place in your living room or waving to you from the moon.

"If you want to get the impossible done," the saying goes, "hire someone who doesn't know it's impossible."

The authors don't know that living to 100 years and still be young is impossible. We don't know *for sure* that anything is impossible. Do you?

This book challenges you to begin the discovery of the wisdom of ancient herbal medicine, homeopathy, naturopathy and all the healing skills and arts of those who have studied widely and who bring to this existence a love of learning and a passion for healing. It urges the reader to seek out those with something positive to share, and to affirm life and forgiveness. We are all of us in this together for better or worse. Therefore the energy you give yourself is also the energy you give to others; give yourself the love you deserve, for if nothing else, we all deserve love.

CHAPTER 2

THE MENTAL COMPONENT

ATTITUDE AND ITS RELATION
TO HEALTH AND AGE

So, you're getting old? On what understanding did you base that assumption?

To begin a chapter with two simple questions may be a little unusual. However they are important questions and your answers will reveal your attitude or social conditioning towards "aging."

Becoming one hundred years young is much more than 'survival.' It is attaining the ability to live life's journey from beginning to completion with the passion of a child at play.

We all remember those times when life seemed so simple and our imaginations ran free as we created our own reality in the games we played and the thoughts we created. As a child, we seldom held on to an idea for long. Change was an exciting part of the adventure. Indeed it was fun! **And then we grew up!**

Age can be viewed from two perspectives. The first is that of the flow of time and is known as Chronological Age.

Through day into night, from season to season, as our sun moves through the heavens and our planet moves through our solar system, change occurs and the perception of time is measured.

The life-span of all things can be measured relative to these movements. For example, a mayfly lives but a few days, whilst the giant California redwood trees live on for 3,000 years. Yet each lives in health for its allotted span, serving its purpose in the great scheme of life. All species have a natural cycle and in general do not suffer from the myriad of problems that beset people living in modern societies. A good example of our potential can be seen in the life of the people known as the Hunzas. Like many others living under ideal conditions, they lived for up to 150 years, often riding horses at 100 years young! Like the Hunzas, the people of Abkhasia also often live up to 165 years. In Abkhasia, people harvest a diet rich in organic produce. They are accustomed to hard work throughout their lives. Consequently, their minds and bodies are strong right up until they leave this planet. Death comes swiftly with little or no illness. If it is possible for them, without the assistance of our vaunted science and technological infrastructure, then surely we should question some of our values and beliefs. They simply lived within the natural order of things.

In the days gone by, when most people lived close to nature, growing their own food and tilling the land, this process was generally accepted without question.

As society changed and city life became the norm, where milk comes from cartons and meat from the supermarket the understanding that we are one with nature's cycles was lost.

In large cities, many children develop their understanding of the world without ever having touched or seen the soil that their ancestors tilled.

Their lives are entwined with the concrete and steel of the buildings and roads they grow up in.

The second perception of aging is the essence of this chapter and is known as biological age.

'Bios' means Life, thus biological age indicates the degree of life activity of the body and its cellular function. Whilst all living things participate in the chronological process, nature has an in-built mechanism whereby regeneration is an ongoing process throughout life. Cells are continually replacing themselves as they become worn out or damaged. This process is continually occurring even at the level of the very atoms that make up the cell. According to the latest findings, the liver replaces itself (its atoms) every 7 days. The DNA is constantly undergoing this regeneration process. In fact Creation is a continuous process, ongoing as long as life exists. In fact, parts of your intestines are never older than three days.

The logical conclusion of this observation is that really there is nothing to 'age'—only changes occurring in harmony with the chronological cycles.

All natural therapies have this understanding as their philosophy. Even in the process of disease, regeneration occurs, as the body endeavors to maintain homeostasis or balance of its systems.

Unfortunately, the attitude of much modern medical practice ignores this and attempts to control or change the symptoms occurring by suppressing them without addressing their cause. Under this system the symptom is seen as the 'enemy' to be overcome.

Nothing could be further from the truth! All life's processes have a purpose.

Theoretically, because of the regeneration process, we should not deteriorate at all!

What we call 'aging' usually is the cumulative effects of poor nutrition and cellular damage caused by chemicals and other toxic substances we ingest daily through the food we eat and the air we breathe. These substances cause **free radical** damage which affects the control mechanism of cell replication. Even the oxygen we breathe can cause such damage, through oxidization, a process similar to the rusting process. This will occur if we do not have a sufficient intake of antioxidants, such as vitamins A, C, E, Kyolic Aged Garlic Extract, Selenium, Green Tea, etc.

Some damage can have a marked effect on the function of the mind and nervous system to the extent that our perception of reality is altered, just as alcohol in sufficient quantities does. The brain and central nervous tissue is affected by the food and substances we ingest. This is observable in many children who react adversely to food coloring and excess sugar.

Toxins may also be produced within the body, from faulty metabolic processes. Some of these occur because the body is deficient in vitamins, minerals and trace elements. Even a small deficiency can often cause dramatic damage as is evident in the case of folic acid. Folic acid is now often prescribed to pregnant women to prevent certain chromosome damage in the developing fetus.

However, one of the major contributing factors in the production of internal toxins is **stress.**

From the time of Pavlov, who proved that under stress the digestive system ceases to work effectively, to the latest studies on the chemical processes of brain function and their relationship to perception and thought and disease, it is evident that "you are what you think." The ancient Greeks concluded that the ideal was "a healthy mind in a healthy body" and that remains appropriate today.

So what is stress and how do our attitudes contribute to its effect upon us?

Simply put, stress is any factor, mental, emotional, or physical, that 'pressures' an individual. The ability to cope with stress largely depends upon the attitudes that we have developed from early childhood. Many of the attitudes that we think are 'naturally' ours, are in fact learned behavior deeply embedded in the subconscious mind to form an automatic response system. This response triggers many chemical and physical reactions, perceived by the mind as necessary for survival. **The level of stress experienced depends on your response, which depends on learned attitudes and values.**

Attitudes are what we are. Our existence and relationship with those around us is totally governed by attitudes. Our response to Life's journey, depends upon attitudes. So what if the attitudes that we have learned from our parents and social consciousness are inappropriate for optimal functioning? What if our cherished Beliefs are false? Remember, it was not that long ago that people believed that the Earth was flat, that some races were 'inferior' to other races and that heavier than air flight was impossible. Perhaps our faith in the experts needs to be reevaluated as well.

Certainly, many of our present beliefs will one day be proven wrong, and one of them may be our attitude to becoming old or aging.

Perhaps these beliefs are incorrect as well:
- too old to learn
- can't teach an old dog new tricks
- we are all getting older
- no one's getting any younger
- I will probably be like my Aunt, Uncle, Mother, Father, etc. and die before I get to 95
- you should act your age
- *you are showing your age*

This chapter began with a look at the child's passion that is diminished over time through social conditioning.

The key to slowing the aging process is to remember the 'child within' and seek to rekindle the passion for everything you do. Attitudes can be changed, the subconscious can be reprogrammed, old and outgrown beliefs **can** make way for new and exciting understanding in the game of life. Learn to identify the difference between the chronological process and the continual creation of life that arises within.

The Mind is the tool for this and you can use the subconscious as your servant. It willingly obeys every command you give it with your conscious mind, which has the power, when used correctly, to analyze and assess new ideas and attitudes. These eventually replace old subconscious memory and become the new patterns from which you will respond to life. Your new-found understanding will reprogram every cell within you to align to your attitude. Your vitality will increase and your concept of aging will change.

Start by using positive affirmations such as:

- "Each day that goes by, I get younger and younger."
- "I love and accept myself at every stage of my journey."
- "Each moment in life is perfect."

All life is a game of self hypnosis. Control that and you control your life. Affirmations are nothing more or less than conscious self hypnosis.

Use your own imagination, rekindle the child within and learn to play the game of life!

CHAPTER 3

THE IMMUNE SYSTEM

In order to maintain good health, protect the body against bacterial and viral infections, and remove ingested chemical or toxic materials, nature has endowed us with our immune system. This system is capable of removing anything that is 'not you.' An example of its function is seen in organ transplants. These succeed only because science has devised chemical ways to effectively stop rejection caused by the natural immune response to a foreign invader.

In a healthy body the immune system has the capacity to defend the body against infectious agents and even remove body cells that have become cancerous *(see chapter on Cancer)*.

The immune system is a complex structure and is capable of selective response, depending upon the needs of the body and the type of invader. This regulatory mechanism is genetically controlled and regulates such functions as the interactions of macrophages, T- and B-lymphocytes, susceptibility to disease agents and the production of chemical mediators that regulate the actions of cells involved in immune responses.

It is not the purpose of this chapter to explain the intricate nature of the immune system. However a brief description of some of the key "players," will assist in the understanding of the powerful ally that cares for the integrity of every cell in the body.

An **antibody** is a Y–shaped protein triggered by an antigen and capable of neutralizing invading organisms and some tumor cells.

An **antigen** is a substance such as a food, pollen or dust particle that can provoke an allergic reaction, specifically the production of antibodies.

Bacteria are one-celled organisms, some living in harmony with us, some disease producing, and a few lethal. Many bacteria assist in our normal functioning.

B-lymphocytes are white blood cells and are capable of transforming into antibody producing cells, called plasma cells. Their role is that of defence against the disease producing bacteria.

The **complement system** consists of 20 distinct plasma proteins involved with the destruction of an antigen.

Helper T-lymphocytes interact with B-lymphocytes in antibody formation.

Lysozyme is a protein found in tears, saliva and nasal secretions, and is capable of breaking down susceptible bacteria. As we are constantly breathing in dust, bacteria and foreign proteins, this is an important defence mechanism.

Enzymes digest or break down ingested matter.

Macrophage cells are the front runners in the defence system and are part of the process of containment by ingestion of foreign invaders including bacteria and viruses.

Stem cells are a bone marrow cell from which most white and red cells arise.

All of these key players, like every other cell in the body, require nutrients for their manufacture and function. There is still much to be learned. For example, the nutritional requirements of the important T-cells has never been studied! However our understanding of the importance of antioxidants, an overall balanced intake of fresh, naturally produced foods, and the avoidance of processed and chemicalized foods and additives, is the result of many years of scientific and empirical observations, which have proven beyond doubt that "we are what we eat."

We are not at the mercy of any and all diseases. We do not need to fear disease, for we have a vast array of specialized cells to protect us. All we need do is to take care of the cells by taking responsibility for our own health.

We do not need vaccines and chemical potions to protect us. This is a very negative approach to disease prevention and one day in the future will be looked upon as being as primitive as blood letting and the use of mercury and arsenic for syphilis, a common practice until relatively recent times.

Natural medicine practices what is termed **probiotics**, which is pro–life, and its function is to support the body's natural immune system and healing capabilities. Antibiotics, on the other hand, are substances designed to kill or injure life, such as bacteria and other organisms. Antibiotic actually means anti–life.

Antibiotics disturb the natural bacterial flora of the body. Probiotics enhance the natural bacterial and immune functions, thereby improving immunity to invading bacteria.

The following are some suggestions on how to approach common health problems.

STRENGTHEN AND MAINTAIN THE IMMUNE SYSTEM

This can be achieved by taking a diet of fresh raw or lightly steamed vegetables, raw fruits, nuts, seeds, legumes, brown rice, grains (millet is the only non–acid-forming gluten-free grain and is ideal for those with gluten intolerance), a little meat, chicken, fish, purified water, fresh fruit and vegetable juices, and a teaspoon of cold pressed oil such as flax seed oil, each day.

Try to buy or grow organically grown food. Eating residues of pesticides and other chemicals used on produce grown for size and appearance only, puts a heavy burden on the liver. In addition chemically altered soil and food is lower in nutritional value and life force or 'prana.' Organically grown food has to meet strict standards, and is generally higher in vital nutrients.

Avoid refined, preserved, processed foods, sugar, caffeine, alcohol and heated fats.

Sufficient exercise promotes the circulation of lymph fluids but it need not be strenuous. Yoga, tai chi or walking oxygenates the body.

Massage stimulates lymph drainage.

Obtain sufficient rest and sunshine.

Practice meditation and correct breathing *(see Breathing, Chapter 6)*.

Foster good creative outlets *(see Relaxation, Chapter 6)*.

Keep the liver cleansed and functioning well *(see below)*.

IMMUNE SUPPORT PRIOR TO WINTER

The following supplements will help to give your immune system the boost it may need to cope with the winter flu season.

Pro-biotics in supplement form include:

Vitamins A, C, E: these are the most important.

Beta carotene, selenium, zinc, garlic, iodine are also useful in supplement form because our diet may not supply the quantities needed in our modern world. These may be taken individually although the orthomolecular form of synergistically prepared formulas can be superior. For those who usually suffer ill health through winter some of these formulas are available from a health shop. For those whose immune systems are chronically weakened, a registered natural therapist would be able to prescribe special orthomolecular preparations to boost the immune system and general health throughout winter.

The herbs chamomile, echinacea, garlic, ginger, ginseng and goldenseal may also be used to boost the immune system. These can be taken in tea form or can be purchased in supplement form from a health shop.

THE LIVER

The liver is the master organ of the body—and the master organ of the immune system. It weighs about 4 lbs. and is the largest organ in the body. It is the only organ that will totally regenerate itself when part of it is damaged. Without this capacity, the human race would not have endured the onslaught of the chemical invasion of our ecosystem.

Why? Because **every** chemical or drug, including prescription medicines, taken into the body must be processed by the liver, neutralized and eliminated. If the liver is unable to neutralize a toxic chemical, it will be stored in the body's fatty tissue, where the chemical will do minimal damage to cellular function.

Take a moment to ponder the endless toxic substances we ingest daily, from exhaust fumes, to the additives in our water supply, preservatives in foods, insecticides, herbicides, etc.

Toxins are also produced by the normal metabolic processes and oxidation which allow food to be converted to energy within our cells. These "home grown" toxins must be detoxified by the liver for safe elimination by the kidneys and colon. An example of this process is demonstrated in the digestion and utilization of proteins and the fermentation of foods in the intestines. This produces ammonia which must be detoxified by the liver and eliminated via the kidneys.

Of all the foods we eat, the intake of protein is the most vital. Proteins are building blocks for the body. In order for the liver to regenerate after being damaged by exposure to chemicals, it needs an ample supply of amino acids —the building blocks of protein. Ten amino acids are termed 'essential amino acids' because the body cannot manufacture them itself. It is vital that the daily diet contains all of these essential amino acids, since if just one is missing, the body is unable to synthesize the others.

Low protein diets can lead to liver damage, among other health problems. This makes it essential for vegetarians to take care to ensure that their diet contains all the essential amino acids.

The liver has many functions, the most important of all being the production of bile, which is stored in the gall bladder. Bile is necessary for the digestion of fats and protein. It also plays an important role in the synthesis of 'essential fatty acids' from amino acids and carbohydrates, for the production of cholesterol and lipoproteins etc. It also aids peristalsis which prevents constipation.

Cholesterol has gotten a bad name for itself, however, cholesterol is necessary for the proper functioning of the digestive system, enzymes, and forms the raw material for the synthesis of many hormones. It is the most powerful antioxidant produced by the body, and can be found in the brain, nerves, liver, blood and bile. A healthy body produces the same amount of cholesterol that would be found in 4 lbs of butter!

There are two types of cholesterol thus far identified. The 'good guy' is called HDL—High Density Lipoproteins—and 'bad guy' is called LDL—Low Density Lipoproteins. The production of oxidized LDL is partly precipitated by free radicals and our modern diet, especially excessive sugar intake.

The liver produces GTF—Glucose Tolerance Factor—from Chromium and Glutathione which is required for insulin to maintain blood sugar levels and energy.

Excessive sugar or carbohydrate eaten is stored by the liver as glycogen in the muscle and fatty tissues of the body. When glycogen or blood sugar is low, e.g.: Hypoglycemic, the liver will convert this stored food back to blood sugar to be used as energy. This happens every night while you sleep. An adequate level of blood sugar is necessary for proper brain function.

After digestion, food is absorbed through the wall of the small intestine into the bloodstream and transported to the liver where nutrients, including the fat-soluble vitamins A, E, D, K, essential fatty acids, as well as iron and the B vitamins are extracted and stored.

Such is the function of the master organ. You are not just the result of what you eat, but also of what the liver is able to do with the digested food it receives via the bloodstream through the portal vein. Hence, you are what you absorb.

To care for your liver, eat only natural foods which are easily digestible. Avoid preserved foods, and those laden with chemicals. Eat a balanced diet of fruit, vegetables, grains and protein. Consume natural fats—those that are found in avocados, flax seed oil, cod liver oil and butter. It is important to avoid **all** processed fats, especially the hydrogenated, partially hydrogenated or heated ones. Drink plenty of **pure** water daily.

Remember your liver's task, and **avoid** putting unnecessary toxic substances into it, and it will serve you well for your journey through this life.

SPECIAL NUTRIENTS FOR LIVER CARE

Herbs:

- **Silymarin**: This herb, a type of thistle, has a special protective action towards the liver. It has even been used to avert the deaths of people who have consumed excess amounts of psilocybin mushrooms which can cause fatal liver damage.

- **Dandelion**: The humble dandelion is a traditional remedy for liver and gallbladder problems. Use a few young leaves in salads or with other steamed vegetables. To make a tea, take two teaspoons of dried leaves for one cup of boiling water, steep for 10 minutes. Take one or two cups daily for liver congestion. Your local health store should stock a selection of dandelion products.

- **Garlic**: Test tube studies have shown that Aged Garlic Extract and its various constituents can protect liver cells from toxic compounds. A major study has shown that Aged Garlic Extract and its constituents, S-allyl cysteine mercaptocysteine (SAMC), and S-propyl cysteine completely suppressed the cytotoxicity (cell killing power) of the liver toxin, carbon tetrachloride, whereas four control drugs were found to be less effective at protecting the liver cells.

- **Turmeric**: Curcumin, the yellow pigment contained in turmeric has been shown in laboratory tests to help protect against liver damage. One teaspoon of dried powder per day may be added to fruit or vegetable juice. In India, this herb is revered as a healer. *Caution: Turmeric does have anti-clotting properties, so consult your health practitioner before using it.*

Amino Acids: The most important amino acids to take for the liver are Methionine and Cystine (500 mg of each) and Glutathione (100 mg). Take three times daily between meals.

These amino acids should be available from your health store as part of a lipotropic formula to aid liver regeneration.

Lecithin: Take up to one tablespoon granules or powder before meals or capsules as directed by your health professional.

B Complex Vitamins: These are also necessary for healthy liver cells. Take as directed on the packaging.

CO Enzyme Q10: This is essential for the oxygenation of liver cells. 30-90 mg daily is considered a effective dose.

Vitamin C: This is necessary to neutralize toxins and protect against free radical damage. Take 1000 mg one to five times daily—or use the 'bowel tolerance' method. See the section on vitamin C, in the chapter "Nutrition and Health."

Vitamin E: This vitamin improves circulation and tissue repair, and is also an excellent antioxidant. A supplement of 400 IU daily is recommended for liver protection. But please see caution in Nutrition and Health chapter if you have high blood pressure, rheumatic heart disease or take anticoagulant drugs. Consult a health practitioner.

Fasting: Taking regular three-day fasts or other cleansing regimes on freshly made juices will assist the liver to detoxify itself. Carrots, beets, cabbage, celery and apples are all suitable.

THE COMMON COLD AND INFLUENZA

Both these illnesses are of course caused by viruses—a class of organisms that are only capable of reproducing in a susceptible living cell. A virus can be likened to a 'bit of information' copied on a 'computer floppy disk' of a cell. They are crystalline in nature and are incredibly small. For example, the HIV or AIDS virus is only 0.1 micron in size and it would take more than 20,000 HIV viruses to cover the head of a pin!

Most people have experienced a viral infection. In order for this to have occurred, there must have been a suitable environment for the virus to reproduce. Natural medicine suggests that this environment is often simply a toxic condition of the body tissues.

The common cold is often caused by infections to the upper respiratory tract by common rhinoviruses and coronaviruses. However colds can also be toxicity related. A tired sluggish body, often with a congested liver, trying to deal with too much 'dead' food like bread, pastry and pasta, rebels and induces a time of spring-cleaning where all of its elimination organs go into top gear. By their very nature, colds often dictate that we take less food and more fluids. You have an intelligent body: a cold is a time to help it. The usual symptoms of a cold are excessive clear nasal secretions followed by nasal and head congestion, difficult breathing, coughing, sneezing, fever, headaches, swollen lymph glands and general aches and pains. Many of these symptoms are brought about by the immune system's acting to destroy and rid the body of infected cells. Swollen lymph glands are caused by the proliferation of white blood cells ready to combat viruses. Mucus should be allowed to flow—since this is your body's way of eliminating toxins. Over-the-counter medications that suppress symptoms by shrinking blood vessels, or drying up secretions, only impede the immune system.

Influenza is caused by the more contagious and virulent influenza virus which attacks the membranes of the nose, throat and lungs. It causes more work for the immune system because it is clever enough to keep changing its type, and evading many of the antibodies sent to destroy it. Its symptoms are usually worse than a cold's and may also include severe aching of the body and general weakness, shivers, nausea and extreme tiredness. Rest should be taken so that the body has maximum energy to deal with it.

Doctors may be reluctant to prescribe antibiotics for the general unwellness caused by a cold or influenza because it can induce more resistant bacteria. However in the frail and susceptible, secondary bacterial infections can occur especially in the lungs. Therefore heavy or continuing congestion in the lungs is serious and can result in pneumonia. Your registered naturopath or doctor should be consulted. Yellow or green mucus is often an indication that an infection has developed. A tight dry feeling in the chest may also indicate a chest infection.

NATURAL TREATMENTS FOR COLDS AND INFLUENZA

Bacteria are attracted to dry mucus membranes so fluids are required for this reason and to help detoxify the body. They should be taken in the form of mixed or diluted vegetable juices such as:

Carrot juice, which is a very rich source of beta carotene. It also contains vitamins B1, B2, C and 12 essential minerals. It is a blood purifier and its high alkaline level makes it ideal for people suffering from acidic illnesses. Carrot juice is available from the health section of some supermarkets and from health stores *but it is best when you make it fresh yourself.*

Celery juice is rich in organic sodium, magnesium and iron, and is helpful in preventing excess calcium from being deposited in the veins and arteries.

Cabbage juice is high in vitamin A and contains other water soluble vitamins and minerals. It is useful for stomach ulcers. For colds and flus, mix with other juices.

Beet juice is a traditional folk remedy for liver problems. It helps the liver to process fats and detoxify. It is rich in vitamin A and organic sodium and potassium. It tends to taste a little earthy, so mix it with other juices.

Cucumber juice is nature's supreme diuretic helping with the elimination of toxic wastes.

Additionally, **lettuce, spinach, parsley, radish, tomato** and **watercress juice** may be used, especially if you have a juice extractor. *(Use watercress in juice or in salads only if you are confident about its source. Watercress growing wild in streams could be infested with various larvae.)* A centrifugal juicer will remove some of the vitamins and allow the juice to oxidize, so drink it soon after you make it. Alternatively grate the vegetables and squeeze the juice through a muslin cloth, or fine sieve, into a bowl.

Spirulina powder mixed into juice is a good green drink supplying many nutrients including beta carotene and all the amino acids, the building blocks of the body. Take a teaspoon twice daily in a glass of apple or vegetable juice. Shake well and drink.

Kyo-green is a pleasant tasting, live green powder made from wheat and barley grass, chlorella, brown rice and kelp. A study conducted by Dr. Benjamin Lau, of Loma Linda University, proved that taking one to two teaspoons stimulates a positive immune response.

Sugars should be limited or congestion will continue. Fruit sugars are alright taken in moderation because fruits also contain vitamin C necessary for combating colds. Furthermore whole fruit contains all the enzymes necessary to digest and metabolize the sugars, whereas refined sugar is only an extract from the sugarcane plant. Any excess sugars in the body will impede the immune system because they compete with vitamin C for transport to the white blood cells, which are the army of the immune system. *One teaspoon of white sugar can interfere with the immune system for a whole hour.*

Both home made vegetable broths, and the fabled chicken soup, make nourishing meals for those with congested systems not able to digest full meals.

Herbs are medicines in their natural forms. Plants have some powerful properties—some toxic if used incorrectly—and are generally safer in their dried form. The essential oils of plants are highly concentrated and can be harmful so as a rule should only be ingested in minute amounts—1 or 2 drops—under professional direction. The herbs in this section are suggested for medicinal or short-term use *(if in tea form up to 2 cups daily)*. Although they are generally safe in their recommended quantities, the extended use or overuse of some herbs may have side effects. *(Tea and coffee are both herbs with healing properties but when used excessively become dangerous)*. Consult a qualified herbalist or registered natural health practitioner for extended use or for mixed preparations which are very effective. Herbs, like pharmaceutical medicines, may cause reactions in some people. If rashes or diarrhea occur, discontinue use and consult your herbalist or naturopath. Some herbs may not mix well with pharmaceutical medicines, so check with your doctor or inform your herbalist if you are taking any prescription or over-the-counter medications.

Garlic is the supreme herb for colds and flus. A couple of finely chopped cloves made into a paste with honey can be swallowed slowly, to kill any bacteria which may have taken up residence in your throat. Similarly, a strong tasting tea may be made from chopped raw garlic, honey and lemon juice. Before drinking this powerful beverage, the vapor may be inhaled to relieve congested lungs.

For those who like to enjoy the benefits of garlic, without smelling like it, Kyolic Aged Garlic offers the powerful immune system stimulating properties of garlic without the odor. If you can feel the flu coming on, taking two capsules an hour of Kyolic Formula 103 with Astrorgulus which combines 250 mg Kyolic Aged Garlic with 200 mg of non-acidic Ester C. This may be enough to prevent the 'flu from taking hold.

Pau d'arco tea has a natural antifungal and antibacterial action and is available in health stores.

Echinacea is an immune boosting herb. Two teaspoons of root material for a cup of water may be simmered 15 minutes and then drunk or used as prescribed on the packaging of a commercial preparation.

Boneset (Comfrey) stimulates the immune system to destroy minor viral and bacterial infections. Use less than two teaspoons of dried leaves to a cup of boiling water. Steep 15 minutes and drink. This is also available in capsule form.

Goldenseal is a traditional North American Indian healing herb. Its chemical property berberine (also found in barberry) stimulates macrophages and it can kill the bacteria causing diarrhea and amoebic dysentery. It is an effective gastrointestinal medicine. However it is quite expensive to buy in capsule form. Use less than a teaspoon of powdered root for a cup of boiling water and steep for ten minutes and drink. This tea is very bitter—and will also stain clothing or furniture. *Goldenseal should never be used during pregnancy since it is a uterine stimulant, and may cause miscarriage.*

Licorice root is controversial because it acts on the adrenals. However, it is generally safe to use, except by people who have elevated blood pressure. This is because taking licorice promotes the excretion of potassium, and the retention of sodium. For people who have normal blood pressure, licorice is not only safe, but is a very useful remedy for colds and flu. Licorice can soothe a sore throat, and also has the effect of softening mucous membranes, allowing mucous and catarrh to be expelled. This makes it useful for treating coughs. Laboratory tests have shown that it fights the bacteria staphylococci and streptococci. It is very sweet. Just a pinch could be used to sweeten other bitter teas like Echinacea, Boneset and Goldenseal.

Lemon teas are renowned for their effectiveness. They include lemon grass, lemon balm, freshly squeezed lemon juice in hot water, or lemon added to other teas sweetened with honey. To open up the sweat glands (the body's largest elimination organ), add a dash of cayenne pepper to lemon or other teas. But stay warm.

Ginger has traditionally been used for colds and flus in China because it can kill the influenza virus. It was also used by the Greeks and Romans as a digestive aid and to counteract nausea. Use fresh ginger regularly (readily available at produce outlets) in cooking, or steep two teaspoons of powered or grated root for five minutes in a cup of boiling water and add cinnamon, honey and lemon, and drink. This beverage helps to counteract congestion. Taking this tea hot also stimulates both circulation and perspiration which aids in eliminating wastes. Taking herbs such as ginger which stimulate perspiration can be helpful in lowering a fever—however, take care that you don't become chilled. *(Ginger also promotes menstruation, and so should not be used by pregnant women without professional advice.)*

Apple cider vinegar and **honey** also helps with congested digestion. It is also an excellent healing tonic. However, it should not be used by people suffering from candidiasis, because of the yeasts and simple sugars contained in the vinegar and honey. The honey content also makes this beverage unsuitable for diabetics.

Ginseng is renowned for its healing properties. It is a vital tonic for the immune system and has traditionally been used for colds and flus. It also helps the liver to deal with toxic substances. It is available in tea and capsule form at health stores.

Both **Yarrow** and **Camomile** soothe the muscles of the digestive system which may be inflamed during a cold or flu. Use less than two teaspoons of dried herb for a cup of water and steep for ten minutes. Camomile is widely available in tea form from health stores.

Slippery Elm bark is available in powder form. Mix three teaspoons to a paste with a little water, add to a cup of water and bring to boil ten minutes and drink. It is ideal for people with ulcers, helps to keep bowels loose, and is effective for coughs and sore throats either in tea form or mixed with honey and a little hot water. Easily digestible, it is highly nutritious and will often 'stay down' when nothing else will.

COUGH SOOTHERS

Mullein is an ancient ayurvedic remedy for coughs and congestion. Like slippery elm it contains mucilage, a substance which becomes slippery when mixed with water. Use two teaspoons of dried leaves, flowers, or roots in one cup of boiling water. Steep ten minutes.

Oregano is a member of the mint family and contains volatile oils high in carvacrol and thymol which loosen phlegm. Use one to two teaspoons of dried herb in one cup of boiling water. Steep ten minutes.

Peppermint oil contains menthol. Because menthol is a very strong substance straight peppermint oil should not be consumed as more than a few drops may cause nausea. Prepare peppermint tea instead, using less than two teaspoons of dried leaves in one cup of boiling water. Steep 10 minutes.

Eucalyptus tea is used by the aborigines for fever. Russian studies show that it can kill some influenza viruses. Use less than two teaspoons of dried leaves in one cup of boiling water. Steep for ten minutes. As an inhalant put a few drops of the oil or some fresh leaves in steaming water, cover head with towel and inhale the vapors.

Tea Tree Oil, a few drops in hot water, cover head and inhale vapors, or a few drops on hand and sniff.

Horehound was traditionally used in ancient Rome for respiratory problems. It contains the chemical marrubin which loosens phlegm. It's a very strong herb used for serious congestion, coughs and wheezing. Use less than one teaspoon in one cup of boiling water. Steep 10 minutes. A syrup made from green leaves and honey is a most effective remedy for coughs. *People with cardiac problems should avoid its use except under profession supervision.*

Chopped **onion**, lightly simmered and strained makes a useful cough mixture. Add to the liquid a little honey and sip.

Every time you cough, squirt a little liquid Kyolic on your throat and swallow. At night, make a poultice of crushed raw garlic. Apply to the soles of your feet, making sure your feet are well covered with Vaseline before applying crushed garlic. Cover with socks. Repeat for two nights.

Some of these herbs are also available in tincture form from health stores.

HOMEOPATHIC REMEDIES

Homeopathy is an ancient system of healing, dating back to at least the fifth century, BC, when Hippocrates recorded its use. In the 19th century, homeopathy was refined and popularized by Samuel Hahneman. By the early 20th century, homeopathy had become the most commonly practised form of medicine in the United States.

Homeopathic medicines work on the principle that "Like Cures Like." Therefore, patients are treated with a minute dose of a herbal, mineral or animal based medicine, which, if consumed in a large dose, would produce the similar symptoms to those from which the patient is suffering. In homeopathy, great care is taken to choose a remedy that fits the patient's symptom picture as closely as possible, so the patient is questioned closely about both his or her physical and emotional symptoms.

Some homeopathic remedies are prepared from pathogenic organisms such as viruses, bacteria and fungi. In remedies prepared in this way, the pathogenic material is diluted and potentiated. Such remedies are known as Nosodes. They are capable of stimulating the body's immune response against the highly diluted pathogens they contain.

Reckeweg, a large manufacturer of homeopathic medicines in Germany, have conducted controlled studies that prove these medicines do in fact work. Studies published in *The New England Journal of Medicine* corroborate this. They are safe and do not seem to produce the harmful effects which some vaccines can.

To quote the final discussion from a scientific test by their Department of Scientific Research, Feb. 1987, "From these results we can see that natural homeopathic nosodal complexes can be effective treatment for bacterial infections. This system works with the natural immune system to prompt its attack on the micro invaders."

Nosodes include: Influenzinum for flu, and Rubella for measles.

Homeopathic medicines are available from homeopathic practitioners—and are now available in some health stores. Practitioners will have charts and knowledge of correct homeopathic remedy use. For example, No.9 (NatMur) Biochemic cell salt is used for settling the stomach, digestion and liver, while No.11 (Nat Sulph) Biochemic cell salt is ideal for nipping the early sniffle symptoms in the bud. In many people, the cell salt balances are upset, and remedying these can have good effects on general health.

SUPPLEMENTS

The most important supplement for a developed cold is Vitamin A. Its safest form is beta-carotene. Take as directed.

Vitamin C is needed but is more effective taken in large doses before, or just at the beginning of, a cold, and can often weaken the effects of the virus. For more information about taking vitamin C to combat viral infections, see the section on vitamin C in chapter 4, "Nutrition and Health".

Because colds more often develop in dry intestines, take a teaspoonful of cold pressed oil high in vitamin A, like halibut, liver oil, flaxseed, vitamin B complex, or unsalted food yeast (brewers yeast) if not suffering from candidiasis. Add vitamin E, 400 IU, unless you have high blood pressure or other cardiovascular problems.

In chronic illness other orthomolecular supplements may be given under guidance of a naturopath.

Rest as much as needed. Try to get some natural light and sunshine during the day. If you are able, a little exercise stimulates the circulation and elimination of wastes.

As one third of the body's wastes are secreted through the skin, gently scrubbing the skin with a good sea sponge or natural bristle brush when showering or bathing, stimulates lymph drainage and elimination of toxins through the skin.

CASE STUDY

Mr.— sought naturopathic treatment in November 1993 at the age of 68. He was suffering from a laboratory diagnosed multiple chemical sensitivity syndrome.

He had been ill for 17 years and his symptoms were spontaneous bruising, pain below the ears and jaw, sore eyes, impaired hearing and vision, aches all over, tingling of skin and heart palpitations. His face and skin demonstrated allergies with a red rash, itching and burning.

He had undergone a detoxification program with some improvement. However, he was still susceptible to a relapse if he came in contact with insecticides, pesticides etc.

His diet was quite good, so only minor changes were needed to assist the removal of candidiasis that was also evident.

His treatment began with a 'liver support' supplement to assist the liver to improve its function and to protect it against chemical damage. (Where there are allergies present the liver should always be addressed first).

The main therapies used in his treatment were orthomolecular, homeopathy and homeo-botanical. (Homeo-botanical remedies are made from potentiated diluted herbal extracts. They are not nearly as dilute as homeopathic remedies, so they retain some of the biochemical properties of the herbs, as well having the energetic quality of homeopathic medicine).

As the condition of his liver improved, vitamins A, C, and an antioxidant formula were added to his treatment to neutralize and remove chemical residue in body tissues. He soon showed further signs of improvement.

Additional tests indicated a zinc deficiency (zinc is important for enzyme formation and the integrity of the digestive system mucosa). His digestion and assimilation improved after a zinc supplement was included.

By March 1994 most of Mr.—'s symptoms had disappeared and he was feeling great. He is now enjoying an active retirement.

CHAPTER 4

NUTRITION AND HEALTH

As citizens of 'developed' countries in the last decade of the 20th century, we have the choice of a panorama of different foods. Some of them will provide our bodies with good nourishment, others will not. Since we depend upon the foods we consume to provide us with energy for our daily activities, as well as to replace the millions of cells in our bodies, it is important that we optimize our nutrition.

There are several principles to consider when we select the foods which will nourish—or fail to nourish—our bodies.

1. Firstly, every person in the world is unique, and can therefore be expected to have different nutritional needs. Hence, there is no ideal diet for all people, just a broad selection of choices which reflect the needs of our collective human biology.

2. Eat organic, pesticide and additive free foods because the first nutritional need of our human bodies is for pure, unadulterated foods. As a species we humans have been evolving for millions of years for the most part eating a diet of organic foods, coaxed from the cultivated soil by careful husbandry, or collected from the wild. In the last 50 or 60 years, traditional, organic—and sustainable—management of the land has been largely replaced by an agricultural technology dependent upon chemical fertilizers and pesticides.

As a result most foods are now lower in important nutritional components, especially trace minerals. Even worse, toxic sprays used to protect plants and animals from pests and disease can contaminate our food. These are chemicals to which we have as a species had no time to develop a resistance.

Many of these sprays are considered "probable carcinogens", and some have been shown to cause birth defects as well. Since these chemicals have been introduced into our environment, human fertility (as measured by sperm count) has halved, and cancer has become a leading cause of death. Therefore, for the sake of your physical health—and our environment's—buy organic foods where possible. If you have a limited income—or even if you haven't—growing your own food organically can also be satisfying.

As well as being free of pesticides, the foods you choose should not have chemical adulterants added during processing. Avoid artificial additives and artificial sweeteners. None give your body good nutrients and some are known to be harmful.

3. Eat a balanced diet. The typical Western diet is unbalanced, tending to emphasize animal protein in relation to vegetables, fruit and grains. An excessive consumption of animal proteins leads to putrefaction in the colon which can lead to arthritis and a lot of other ailments. A further problem with animal protein foods is that they tend to be high in fat.

Many cultures who follow a traditional lifestyle include animal foods in their diet, ranging from the monkey meat eaten by the Indian tribes of South America, to the kangaroo meat and Wichetty grubs eaten by the Aborigines of Australia. These people generally enjoyed good health—at least until they came into contact with the infectious diseases, the sugar, tinned food and the greed for resources of European settlers. A diet rich in protein would also have been important to people living close to nature because of the hard physical labor everyone would have engaged in. On the other hand, the Hunzas—whose longevity is legendary, and whose daily routine includes a lot of exercise—eat a primarily vegetarian diet, with the addition of goats' milk products and eggs.

One indication that foods rich in protein may be a genetic necessity is that chimpanzees, our closest known biological relatives, are also known to seek out insect larvae—as well as eat smaller primates on occasion.

These examples seem to demonstrate that both a vegetarian diet and a diet which contains flesh foods can both support good health. Balance in your diet and in your lifestyle appears to be the key issue. If you decide you wish to continue to eat meat, current research supports eating less red meat, replacing it with poultry or fish. Nor is it necessary or desirable to eat a meal containing meat, poultry or fish every day of the week. Substituting tofu, tempeh or bean dishes for flesh foods, at some of your main meals, adds variety and different nutrients to your diet. (Beans and rice when eaten together make a complete protein.)

If you do wish to continue to eat meat, remember that the reason you eat meat should not be just because you enjoy it, but that it provides your body with valuable protein and nutrients like iron and B complex vitamins. The amount of protein that you need to eat daily is a topic still being debated. However, 100 grams (just under 4 ounces) of meat, fish or chicken is plenty. Eating less than 100 grams of meat may also be desirable. Meat and other flesh foods should always be served with green vegetables. Don't conclude a meal which contains meat with a sugary dessert, either—this can raise your blood triglycerides.

Always choose quality, lean meats that are raised organically so that they are free from pesticide, hormone and antibiotic residues. Avoid grilling or barbecuing meats so that they become black. If you grill meats, make sure the heat source is above the meat, allowing the fat to drain out. Also avoid processed meats that burden your body with carcinogenic nitrites.

IS A VEGETARIAN DIET FOR YOU?

Vegetarians have been found to be less at risk of degenerative diseases such as heart disease and many types of cancer. In addition to benefits to your health when you eat a well-balanced vegetarian diet, there are other good reasons for adopting a vegetarian or semi-vegetarian diet. These include the fact that the raising of vegetable forms of protein—grains, pulses and seeds—requires considerably less land, energy and water than does raising livestock. If everyone were to have a vegetarian diet, the savings in soybeans and grain, which are used to fatten cattle, for example, would be available to feed undernourished people living in less fertile parts of the world. For more information about the environmental costs of meat production, read *Diet For A Small Planet* by Francis Moore Lappe or *Diet for a New America* by John Robbins. The system of raising animals for meat also ignores the fact that they are sentient beings, and that they are often handled roughly and suffer fear and trauma on their journey to the slaughterhouse, and pain as they are killed.

HOW TO REDUCE YOUR MEAT CONSUMPTION

If you want to change your diet from one centered around the traditional Western 'meat and three veg' to a lighter semi-vegetarian or vegetarian diet, it is important to plan your meals so that you receive an adequate amount of protein. Begin by reducing your intake of red meat first. You will probably find the transition easier if you substitute meals containing already familiar protein foods such as eggs, cheese and baked beans (homemade) for red meat, and continue to eat free range chicken or turkey (factory-farmed chicken are fed a lot of chemicals) and fish during this time.

You may also want to start using tofu (soybean curd) or chicken cubes in stir-fry dishes accompanied by brown rice.

Once you have eliminated red meat from your diet, gradually reduce your consumption of both chicken and fish. If you do this, you may well find that these foods become less attractive to you, as your body becomes less accustomed to having to deal with the toxic by-products of digesting flesh foods. If you notice you start to get headaches—or otherwise feel ill—after consuming a small amount of chicken, or fish, for example, you will know that your body is telling you it no longer wants you to eat that food.

Once you no longer eat meat of any kind, you may want to reduce your consumption of other animal products such as eggs or dairy products.

Things to note: You should not expect to be healthy, if as a vegetarian, you continue to eat junk food. Since many vegetable foods are a less concentrated source of nutrients than meat, and other animal products, you may need to eat more of them in order to get the nutrition you need. (This should not lead to weight gain, since most foods vegetarians eat, with the exceptions of high fat eggs, dairy products and nuts, are also lower in calories than meats.) However if you fill up on empty-calorie junk foods, you do risk both gaining weight and developing nutritional deficiencies. Tea and coffee should also be avoided by vegetarians, since they compromise mineral absorption. If you do not have a thorough knowledge of nutrition already, get a good book on healthy vegetarianism to guide you.

Vegetarians are more at risk than meat-eaters of developing deficiencies of B vitamins, iron and zinc, since meat is a major source of these. Zinc deficiency is indicated by lowered resistance to infection, and white spots on fingernails. Iron deficiency anemia is characterized by tiredness and reduced capacity for exercise. A lack of B vitamins can cause energy loss and irritability.

Most of the 'Superfoods' supplements discussed in the next section are good sources of iron and B vitamins.

SUMMARY OF PRINCIPLES OF GOOD DIET

• Eat organic foods wherever possible.

- Eat whole grains. Cooked whole grains such as brown rice are very satisfying. If you eat bread, choose whole grain bread. Read the wrapper carefully—many 'wholemeal' breads actually contain a lot of white flour. If organic bread is locally available, buy it. It will probably be more expensive, but you may well find it more satisfying, and eat less of it.

- Eat a high fiber diet. Eat whole grains and raw fruits and vegetables, as the base of your diet.

- Eat less meat. Substitute range reared poultry, fish or vegetarian protein dishes for beef, pork and lamb.

- Emphasize raw foods in your diet. Aim for 50% of what you eat to be raw fruits and vegetables. These foods have the vitamins, minerals, and enzymes necessary for efficient digestion. Some authorities suggest that 70% raw foods is ideal.

- Emphasize soybean products. These contain valuable vegetable protein, as well as phyto-estrogens which are thought to reduce women's breast cancer risk. Never, however eat raw soy flour as it contains toxic enzyme inhibitors which have to be inactivated by cooking.

- If you eat dairy products, eat products like yogurt rather than milk or cheese which have been pasteurized. Make sure the dairy products you eat are organic, as one half of all antibiotics are added to animal feed. Cow's milk is a perfect food for calves, however most humans have some trouble digesting lactose. Yogurt is predigested and the lactose is transformed into lactase.

The pasteurization process destroys many of the hormones and enzymes which aid calcium absorption. Avoid milk products which have been homogenized (standardized). Children who drink homogenized milk have been shown to have a higher cholesterol level than those who drink milk which is not homogenized. The same is true of adults.

Consuming homogenized milk can also leave you vulnerable to autoimmune disease due to the fact that the fat molecules in homogenized milk are so small that they can be absorbed through the wall of the small intestine before they can be digested. When the undigested fat particles enter the bloodstream in an undigested form, they are recognized by the immune system as a foreign body, and attacked. The result of this action is the immune system tends to cause the inflammation of the body tissues—the hallmark of autoimmune disorders.

- Limit your intake of dietary fat so that no more than 20% of your calories are derived from fat. Foods which contain beneficial types of fat include fish, raw nuts, flax seed oil and seeds which have not been roasted. Fat from animal products should be kept to a minimum. Raw nuts and seeds also have the advantage of containing B vitamins, and minerals such as zinc.

Avoid fats which have been heated since they contain free radicals. Artificially hydrogenated fats such as margarine and vegetable shortening should also be avoided, since they contain unnatural trans fatty acids which are as harmful to the body as saturated fats, if not more so. A major study of US nurses recently demonstrated a strong link between margarine consumption and breast cancer.

Do get into the habit of reading labels for the words 'hydrogenated,' 'partially hydrogenated,' or 'baker's margarine' on labels, and don't buy foods containing these toxic fats. Don't be fooled by margarine manufacturer's claims that their product contains polyunsaturated oils, and is therefore good for your health. By the time these oils have been artificially hydrogenated, they have lost any natural goodness they may once have possessed.

- Avoid refined foods made from white flour, sugar, etc.
- Don't drink water 15 minutes before, during, or for an hour after eating. Drinking additional liquid dilutes the acid in your stomach, and makes digestion less effective.

Do make a habit of drinking an eight ounce glass of water, at least every two hours, in between meals. Keeping your body well-hydrated has numerous health benefits. One of these is creating a sensation of fullness which helps to prevent over eating. If you don't make an effort to drink enough fluids, even a mild state of dehydration will cause your body to save what water it has by making less urine, with the result that less waste is able to be processed by your kidneys. Since a dirty bloodstream is an anathema to your cells, your liver has to clean house harder than ever.

Don't, however, expect to reform a lifetime of poor eating habits overnight. If you have ever smoked, or had any other substance addictions, or bad habits such as biting your nails, you will know just how attractive something which you know is bad for you can be. When it comes to changing your diet, you are changing many ingrained preferences—many of which are for substances which can be quite addictive. Refined sugar, for example, produces a temporary 'high' as it causes your blood sugar level to soar. When your blood sugar drops again, you may find you crave more sugar to recreate the high. As well as the physical components of addiction to harmful foods, the addiction may also have a psychological component, perhaps the fact that, as a child, your parents gave you candy to show their approval for your good behavior, rather than praising you verbally or hugging you, for example.

Start your dietary transition by reflecting on the physical feelings and emotional associations as you eat.

Once you have chosen to change your eating habits, feel confident in your resolve, and treat any binges lightly; backsliding is to be expected. Perhaps the best way to avoid bingeing is to enjoy the occasional treat. Spoil yourself on special occasions!

However, in the case of particularly addictive foods and beverages, such as chocolate, coffee, or cola, make sure the odd indulgence doesn't sneak its way back into your life as a habit.

SUPERFOODS

There are some foods or food supplements which need only be eaten in small amounts to improve your nutrition or immune system considerably.

The 'Superfoods' include:
1) Spirulina
2) Wheatgrass and Barley Grass Juice or Powder, also; Kyo-Green
3) Garlic, especially Aged Garlic Extract
4) Aloe Vera
5) Chlorella
6) Nutritional Yeast
7) Bee Pollen
8) Lecithin
9) Kelp
10) Royal Jelly

1. SPIRULINA

Spirulina is a blue-green algae which is available as a powder which can be taken in juice, or as easy-to-swallow tablets. Spirulina is a particularly valuable supplement for vegetarians since 10 g contains 18 mg of nontoxic iron. Spirulina is also the richest and only reliable vegetable source of vitamin B12 which is great news for people who don't eat animal products. Surprisingly, Spirulina is also a good calcium source, supplying 140 mg of calcium in just 10 g.

Spirulina also supplies an incredible amount of easily-digestible protein for its weight. Spirulina is 65% protein and has a very high digestibility coefficient of 95%. By contrast soybeans contain about 30% protein, beef contains about 20% protein and eggs about 14% protein.

However, Spirulina isn't just useful for vegans and vegetarians who may be at risk of iron or B12 deficiencies or may need a protein supplement. Spirulina is also very useful for those people who eat a more traditional Western diet, as well as those who are hooked on dangerous personal habits such as smoking, since Spirulina contains a very high amount of beta-carotene. Your body can convert nontoxic beta-carotene to vitamin A as it requires this vitamin. **Diets high in beta-carotene have been shown to have a protective effect against cancer**. Another good reason for developing a Spirulina habit is that Spirulina is a rich natural source of the amino acid phenylalanine which sets off a biological chain reaction in your body which suppresses your appetite. Arginine, another amino acid contained in Spirulina, stimulates your body to produce growth hormone which promotes muscle growth and fat burning. Thus Spirulina not only contains an impressive nutritional profile with relatively few calories, but may also assist you to control your weight.

One further benefit of Spirulina which is of particular interest to women is that it contains a high level of gamma linoleic acid (GLA) the same substance contained in evening primrose oil which can reduce symptoms of PMS. A daily ration of 10 grams of Spirulina will supply you with all the nutrients mentioned above as well as 120 mg of GLA.

If you have not yet tried Spirulina, many fashionable or health-food oriented cafes now offer Spirulina smoothies concocted from Spirulina blended with fruit, juice and perhaps yoghurt. Tasting one of these Spirulina delights will let you know whether or not you like the flavor of Spirulina. If you do like it, buy yourself some and you'll find Spirulina shakes make a great breakfast. If you don't like the taste you can buy yourself tablets instead.

2. WHEATGRASS AND BARLEY GRASS JUICE OR POWDER

These are other green superfoods which are well worth taking. Both wheatgrass and barley grass are available in a tablet form, but they can also be easily grown by yourself, which is both a lot of fun and a significant cost saver. The two grasses are roughly comparable, each containing about 25% protein (in a tablet form), although the protein content of barley grass tablets can sometimes be as high as 48%.

Barley grass powder is also exceptionally high in natural chlorophyll. Chlorophyll has been shown to help rebuild hemoglobin (red blood cells) in animals who have been made anemic by hemorrhage.

Another major nutritional benefit of eating both wheat grass and barley grass powder—or drinking the juice—is that the extracts of both grasses are extremely high in pantothenic acid, one of the B vitamin complex which is especially important in boosting your immune response against infections. Smaller amounts of most of the other B complex vitamins are also present.

The mineral composition of both wheat and barley grass is also impressive. Both grasses contain most major minerals in roughly equal amounts, but there are some important differences. Of the two, wheatgrass is the best source of iron, 10 g worth of tablets supply 5.7 mg. The same amount of barley grass, on the other hand supplies just 1.6 mg of this mineral. Barley grass really comes into its own as a supplier of potassium. It contains 888 mg per 10 g in tablet form, making barley grass a good supplement for people who have a yen for salty foods, since the potassium contained in the barley grass should help redress an unfavorable sodium/potassium balance.

Barley grass is also a great calcium source. It contains 111 mg of calcium per 10 g in tablet form, and considering the other benefits of this superfood, definitely worth considering as a bio-chelated form of calcium supplementation for women—and men—who feel they are at risk of osteoporosis.

A convenient way of enjoying the benefits of both wheatgrass and barley grass—as well as chlorella, brown rice and finely ground kelp—is Kyo-Green, an energizing powdered drink mix which combines especially well with spring water and a dash of aloe vera juice.

How to Grow Wheatgrass and Barley Grass

Buy whole wheat berries and barley from your local health food store. Choose certified organic or biodynamic grain if available, since this will be free of pesticides and probably have a higher mineral content.

Rinse one cup of each grain and soak it (separately or together) for about 24 hours, in a glass or plastic container. Then drain and rinse and leave in a container such as a one liter glass jar for another 24 hours. This should be left in a reasonably warm place, such as a window sill, or if the weather is very cold, in a warm cupboard.

Rinse the seeds at least once while they are beginning to sprout. At the end of the 24 hours tiny roots and shoots should be sprouting from the grain. At this stage, your barley and wheat are ready to plant.

Prepare a tray such as a seedling tray with the best organic soil you have, patted down so it is even. Scatter the sprouted grains over the surface of the earth, then cover with a blanket of earth about 1 cm deep. Place the tray(s) somewhere where it will be protected from birds, such as under a sheet of clear plastic. Check progress daily and water as necessary. Depending on the weather conditions, it will take anywhere from 1–2 weeks for your grass to reach the optimum harvestable size. When the grass is 6–8 cm high, cut it carefully with a pair of sharp scissors about 1–2 cm above the level of the soil.

The cut grass should be juiced immediately in a hand or electrical juicer which juices with a masticating action (centrifugal juicers will not juice wheatgrass).

The trays of grass should be allowed to grow again after the first cutting, since they can be harvested again. The second growth is less nutritious than the first but still packs quite a nutritional punch. Drink small amounts diluted with pure spring water for an energy boost packed with super nutritional benefits.

3. GARLIC

Garlic is a healing herb known since antiquity, during which time it has aptly earned itself the nickname the 'stinking rose.' The health benefits of garlic have become part of the folk wisdom of many nations. It has been found to be particularly valuable as an effective home remedy for common illnesses such as colds and the flu. The juice of fresh garlic cloves was also used on many battlefields, where its topical application to open wounds prevented infection—thus saving many lives.

Treating acute illnesses and battle wounds aside, recent research has shown that how much garlic you eat in your daily diet may help to determine your cancer risk.

One study of people in the People's Republic of China compared the death rate from stomach cancer in people living in two different counties of Shandong Province. The researchers found that people in Cangshan County experienced a very low incidence of fatal stomach cancer—with just three deaths caused by this disease for every 100,000 people. The people of Cangshan County's stomach cancer mortality rate was in fact just one thirteenth of the mortality rate from the same illness of Qixia County residents—40 per 100,000 who died of stomach cancer.

An analysis of the diets eaten by people in the different counties found that people in Cangshan County ate an average of 20 g of garlic daily. In stomach-cancer plagued Qixia County, however, garlic was rarely eaten. Cangshan residents were also found to have a lower level of carcinogenic nitrites in their gastric juices—a factor the researchers attributed to the protective effects of consuming garlic.

Other studies have shown that in addition to helping prevent some cancers, garlic can lower high blood cholesterol and triglyceride levels. Another beneficial effect of that garlic has exhibited on the cardiovascular system is that it inhibits platelet aggregation (stickiness) which predisposes to blood clots. There is also evidence that suggests that eating garlic may lower high blood pressure.

Some caution is advisable when eating garlic, however. Eating more than two cloves of raw garlic daily may have a harmful effect by killing the helpful bacteria in your intestines. Raw garlic is also a harsh, oxidizing herb which can burn sensitive mucous membranes. For this reason, it should be avoided if you have a stomach ulcer. Finally, excessive consumption of raw garlic may cause anemia.

Eating cooked garlic is unlikely to have any harmful effects, although some of the beneficial constituents of garlic are destroyed when it's heated.

Perhaps the best way to enjoy the benefits of garlic without undesirable side effects is to take Kyolic garlic. Kyolic is the trade name for a garlic extract which is prepared by being aged in alcohol for 20 months. This has the effect of converting allicin, and the other unstable sulphur-based compounds in raw garlic into safer more effective and valuable stable substances such as the amino acid s-allyl cysteine.

Kyolic Aged Garlic also has the advantage of being an antioxidant which can offer protection against free radical damage. By contrast, raw garlic is harsh and oxidizing.

Kyolic's antioxidant properties are perhaps best shown by its ability to protect cells from damage inflicted by radioactivity. In 1989, garlic researcher Dr. Benjamin Lau and his colleagues conducted tests to see whether Kyolic would protect human lymphocytes (white blood cells) from damage by radiation. The white blood cells in test tubes were exposed to 2,000 rads of radiation and observed for 72 hours. One test tube, containing only lymphocytes served as a control. The other test tubes contained different forms of garlic , and an amino acid, to test whether these supplements provided any protection to the white blood cells.

At the end of the test period, 80% of the white blood cells which had been 'incubated' with Kyolic liquid survived. Another test tube of white blood cells which had been incubated with the amino acid L-cysteine, also enjoyed a survival rate of near 80%.

By contrast, in the control test tube which contained only white blood cells —and no supplement of any kind—only 25% of the lymphocytes survived.

Also included in the experiment was a test tube which contained white blood cells and fresh garlic juice. All 100% of the lymphocytes in this test tube died within 24 hours.

Test tube studies of human cells haven't only shown how Kyolic can protect cells against radiation, however. In 1989, Dr. Lau and his team also investigated whether Kyolic liquid garlic could protect red blood cells against toxic metals. A solution containing red blood cells and the metals lead, aluminum, copper and mercury was placed in test tubes. Contact between the red blood cells and each of the metals caused the red blood cells to lyse—to burst open—turning the solution in the test tube red. However, an identical mix of red blood cells and toxic metals to which diluted liquid Kyolic was added showed no change in color—demonstrating that the addition of Kyolic protected the precious red blood cells against damage by heavy metals.

Kyolic is available in liquid, capsule or tablet form. As well as plain liquid or encapsulated Kyolic, a number of formulas are available for special needs.

Various cell culture studies have suggested that aged garlic extract and its constituents may inhibit the growth of human breast cancer cells, several human melanoma cells, and neuroblastoma cells. Various animal studies have suggested that aged garlic extract may inhibit the growth of breast cancer, bladder cancer, skin cancer, colon cancer, the development of esophageal tumors and stomach and lung tumors. Studies have suggested that the possible anti-carcinogenic effects of aged garlic extract and its constituents may be due to their ability to reduce the rate of activation of chemical carcinogens, and to suppress tumor cell growth through stimulation of immuno-responder cells.

Studies have also suggested that aged garlic extract may be a promising adjuvant to cancer therapy in that it has been shown to reduce side effects such as fatigue and anorexia in head and neck tumor patients on radio- and chemotherapy and to reduce the cardio-toxicity of the potent anti-cancer drug doxorubicin.

Aged Garlic Extract is still being intensely researched by the National Cancer Institute. The following table provides a summary of various cancer studies using Aged Garlic Extract.

Aged Garlic Extract does not directly kill bacteria; however, it has been shown to mitigate infectious diseases through enhancement of the immune system. It has been found to enhance the phagocytic activity of macrophages T-lymphocyte activity, and natural killer cell activity.

The following human study showed evidence of stimulation of the immune system after oral intake of Aged Garlic Extract:

Aged Garlic Extract was found to enhance natural killer cell activity and to improve helper/suppressor T cell ratio in AIDS patients. Further patients in this study noted improvements in diarrhoea, interruption of recurrent cycles of genital herpes, candidiasis and pansinusitis with recurrent fever.

4. ALOE VERA

The healing properties of Aloe Vera have been known for more than 3,500 years—with this venerable herb gaining a mention in the Bible—as well as in the journals of Christopher Columbus.

Aloe Vera is a plant that everyone can enjoy the company of—since it grows happily inside—as well as outdoors in warmer climates. The fresh gel from the Aloe Vera leaf makes an ideal first aid application for burns—after the affected area has been immersed in cold running water. It's also a healing agent for cuts and abrasions.

In addition to being a superb topical first aid treatment, Aloe Vera is establishing a good reputation as a dietary supplement when the inner leaf gel —or juice prepared from the micronized leaf gel—is taken internally.

If you live in a place where Aloe Vera will grow indoors, you may wish to prepare your own Aloe Vera juice. This is simply done by cutting a leaf from the plant and then hanging it so that the yellow sap which contains anthraquinones drains out. *(Anthraquinones are chemical constituents of Aloe Vera and other plants which can have a sharply cathartic effect on the bowels—so it's best to let them drain from the leaf.)*

Once the yellow sap has dripped out, fillet the leaf and scrape out the gel. Then put the gel through a juicer, or place in a blender with a small amount of pure water. The juice you obtain should have quite a neutral flavor, with a slight sharpness. It is best to dilute Aloe Vera juice before drinking it. If you are not planning to drink your Aloe Vera juice immediately, add some powdered vitamin C, citric acid, or lemon juice as a preservative and refrigerate it.

If you don't have the inclination, time or resources to prepare your own Aloe Vera juice, there are numerous brands of Aloe Vera juices and gels to choose between on the shelves of your local health shop.

To receive an Aloe Vera product as close as possible to fresh Aloe Vera juice or gel, look for the words "unpasteurized" and "cold stabilized" on the label. Unpasteurized aloe vera juice is often preserved with citric acid—a naturally derived antioxidant which also lowers the pH of the product which inhibits bacterial growth. Aloe Vera also contains natural antibacterial compounds, so spoilage should not be a problem.

Aloe Vera preparations which are made from juice which has been heated to reduce the water content, or freeze dried and later reconstituted may not offer the same health benefits of Aloe Vera juice which has not been heat treated.

Aloe Vera juice or gel is 90% water by weight, but also contains vitamins B1, B2, B3, B6 and Folic Acid, as well as vitamins C and E. In the mineral department, Aloe Vera juice has calcium, phosphorous, magnesium, potassium, sodium, iron, zinc and copper. It also contains all of the essential amino acids.

Many of the enzymes which aid the digestion of foods are also found in Aloe Vera juice. These include amylase, lipase, catalase, protease and peroxidase. A study which focused on Aloe Vera's effect as a digestive aid found that a supplement of six ounces of Aloe Vera juice a day had several positive effects. The first of these was improved protein digestion. Taking the supplement was also shown to improve the water holding ability of the stool—thus easing constipation. It was also shown to reduce the amount of yeast which could be cultured from the stool—thus demonstrating an antifungal effect.

As a dietary supplement, Aloe Vera has earned itself a reputation as a good 'pick me up.' It also combines very well with green drinks such as diluted wheatgrass juice or Kyo-Green—a powdered drink mix made from wheat and barley grass powders, chlorella, fine kelp and brown rice.

Aloe Vera juice also makes a tangy addition to shakes containing Spirulina and fruit juice.

In addition to the benefits of improved digestion which have been demonstrated by users of Aloe Vera, regular users of the juice or gel have reported that it has improved, or in some cases, completely healed a number of different health problems.

One of these conditions is arthritis. According to anecdotal reports, symptoms of this painful illness have been remarkably reduced or eliminated in some people after taking 1–2 tablespoons of Aloe Vera juice 2–4 times daily. Some people who have tried this treatment experience relief quickly; others have found it has taken two months of consistent use for their symptoms to subside. There remains a need for research to determine how effective Aloe Vera juice is as a remedy for arthritis. Since letting this food be your medicine can only do you good, you may decide it is worth a try.

Ulcers—including both skin ulcers and those in the stomach—have also been known to improve with regular consumption of Aloe Vera juice. If you wish to try Aloe Vera juice as a treatment for any ulcers, you should obviously do it under medical supervision. The people who have had success in healing their ulcers using this herb also report taking 2–4 tablespoons of juice or gel four times daily.

Other people have credited Aloe Vera juice with healing irritable bowel syndrome, colitis, and, in the case of diabetics, reducing the number of units of insulin they need to inject.

Caution: Like almost any plant which may be eaten or applied to the skin, there is a small risk of having an allergic reaction to Aloe Vera. Before applying the gel or juice to a minor burn or other freshly washed injury for the first time, do a patch test by smearing a small amount of Aloe Vera on the underside of the upper arm to test for an allergic reaction. Likewise, when first beginning to take Aloe Vera juice internally, try only 1 tsp, diluted in a small amount of water, and then increase the amount you drink gradually.

5. CHLORELLA

Chlorella is a microscopic green algae about the size of a red blood cell. It is an extremely ancient plant—fossilized chlorella found in Australia has been dated to the pre-Cambrian era of 2.5 billion years ago. These days, Chlorella is generally cultivated commercially in specially-constructed outdoor or indoor ponds.

Nutritionally speaking, chlorella is similar to Spirulina. However, the cell wall of chlorella is tough and indigestible. This makes it necessary for the chlorella to undergo special treatment to break down the cell wall to make the nutrients contained in this algae available as food for people. Various techniques are used to accomplish this, including ultrasound, heat, enzymes, chemicals and a patented process called Dyno-Mill which pulverizes the chlorella cells.

The manufacturers of the chlorella produced by the Dyno-Mill process claim that their Chlorella has a 'digestibility coefficient' of just over twice that of chlorella in which the cell wall was only partially broken.

Processing differences aside, an average sample of chlorella contains 60% protein—comprising 19 amino acids—and 20% carbohydrate. Fatty acids—four fifths of which are unsaturated—make up between 6–11% of the product. Ash contributes a further 4.6% and moisture 3.6%. A sample of Chlorella may contain between 0.2% and 6% dietary fibre.

Chlorella also contains significant amounts of beta carotene and chlorophyll. It also contains small amounts of all the B complex vitamins. Chlorella is a good source of vitamin B12—containing between 50–125 mcg per 100 g.

Chlorella also has a broad spectrum of minerals, including about 200 mg of calcium, between 220–315 mg of magnesium, and between 500 and 900 mg of phosphorous per 100 g of chlorella.

Chlorella also has an impressive amount of the minerals iron and zinc, with between 80 and 170 mg of iron and 1.5 and 71 mg of zinc per 100 grams.

As you can see from the above analysis, there is considerable variation in the mineral and vitamin content of different Chlorella brands. If you plan to try chlorella as a supplement, it would probably be worth your while to look closely at the label of different brands. If the packaging lacks a comprehensive nutritional analysis, ask your retailer to supply you with one, as well as information on what sort of processing was used to break the cell wall.

The health benefits of chlorella include supplying dietary DNA and RNA. The fibrous cell wall of chlorella stimulates the bowel and can help correct constipation. The fiber contained in Chlorella also helps to remove heavy metals and other toxins and other from the intestinal tract. A clinical study in the *Japanese Journal of Hygiene* in 1978 reported that people suffering from cadmium poisoning excreted more of this toxic metal after beginning to take a supplement of Chlorella.

The clinical experience of doctors and natural therapists in Japan and the USA has shown that chlorella supplementation can assist in healing or controlling infections, peptic ulcers, cancer, AIDS, as well as problems with blood sugar levels such as diabetes and hypoglycemia.

Other studies have shown that chlorella supplementation can improve intelligence. A common observation by people who take the supplement, whether sick or well, is that they have more energy.

Chlorella is available in powder, tablet, liquid or granular form. Chlorella powder, tablets and granules contain whole chlorella algae. Chlorella liquid, on the other hand is prepared by using hot water to extract the nucleus of the chlorella cells. This liquid is rich in nucleic acids, a peptide complex and polysaccharides.

6. NUTRITIONAL YEAST

Nutritional yeast is a useful food supplement. It contains 50% protein and useful amounts of most B vitamins. One hundred grams of nutritional yeast provides 370 kilocalories (1550 kilojoules). *As a yeast product, it is not suitable for people who are allergic to yeasts, since it can provoke reactions in sensitive people. Nutritional yeast should not be taken by people suffering from candidiasis.*

Nutritional yeast is available in tablet form, or as a powder, the latter offering better value for your money. A savory, flaky variety of yeast is also commonly sold. However, this may be too high in sodium for many people. The yeast is most palatable if taken in relatively small amounts at first, since some people find it an 'acquired taste.' Half a teaspoon or more as you become accustomed to the taste can be added to juice, or blender creations. It can also be sprinkled on food.

7. BEE POLLEN

Bee pollen is an extremely rich supplementary food—an average sample containing 20% protein on a dry weight basis. Bee pollen is also a good source of B vitamins, especially nicotinic acid. Minerals make up about five percent of pollen. It also contains DNA and RNA, as well as enzymes and coenzymes that aid in metabolic reactions in the body. It also contains an antibiotic substance which is active against E coli and Proteus.

Although bee pollen is not a particularly rich source of iron, it has been shown that people suffering from anemia who have supplemented their diet with bee pollen experience an increase in the number of red blood cells. Other benefits of bee pollen demonstrated by studies include helping to boost academic performance in school children, as well as improving the memories of forgetful adults.

Another study has shown that consuming bee pollen may lead to a normalization of blood sugar and triglyceride levels in some people. This may be partially due to its high content of nicotinic acid.

Perhaps some of the most exciting research about bee pollen relates to its properties as a food which may help delay or prevent the onset of cancer and also as a remedy to help minimize the side effects of some cancer treatments.

The ability of bee pollen to delay the onset of cancer—at least in cancer-prone mice—was demonstrated in laboratory tests in the late 1940s. Investigator William Robinson of the Bureau of Entomology published the results of his research on mice in the October 1948 edition of the *Journal of the National Cancer Institute*.

The mice he used in his experiment were C3H mice which had been selectively bred to develop mammary tumors at an average age of 33 weeks. Robinson divided his mice into two groups, the first of which were given regular mouse food and regularly examined to discover whether they had developed palpable tumors. This group of mice, which acted as a control group, developed breast cancers at an average age of 31 weeks.

The second group of mice were fed ordinary mouse food which was supplemented with bee pollen. The amount of pollen the mice received was not great—just one ten thousandth part of their daily diet. This pollen supplement was meagre, considering that other experiments have shown that it is possible for several generations of mice to enjoy healthy lives, eating a diet composed exclusively of pollen. However, even just the small amount of pollen added to the food of the second group of mice in Robinson's experiment caused these C3H mice to experience an average increase of 9.8 weeks longer of tumor-free life. Instead of developing cancers at 31 weeks— the mice who had consumed the supplement of bee pollen developed cancer at an average of 41.1 weeks.

The researcher concluded his report on this experiment by saying that bee pollen contains an 'anti-carcinogenic principle.'

Bee pollen has also been used successfully to reduce the side effects experienced by people undergoing radiation or chemotherapy treatments for cancer. A study conducted at the University of Vienna found that women being treated with chemotherapy for inoperable cancer found that those who received bee pollen experienced a number of beneficial changes in their health that were not experienced by those who took a placebo. The advantages conferred by a supplement of bee pollen included: increased production of antibodies; an increase in hemoglobin; an increase in immune system cells. The women who took bee pollen also suffered considerably less from nausea, and didn't lose as much of their hair.

Another European study, this one from Yugoslavia showed that women taking radiation treatments for gynecological cancers who were given a proprietary mixture containing bee pollen and royal jelly in a base of honey experienced considerably less nausea and fatigue than those women who did not take the supplement. The appetite of the women who took the supplement also improved.

Bee pollen is available in natural granules, or it may be powdered and encapsulated. A particularly tasty way of enjoying bee pollen is to buy a spread made from pollen blended with honey, in which the honey adds extra sweetness, as well as acting as a natural preservative. So where to get bee pollen? It should be available from your health store. However, in order to retain its full potency and not become rancid, bee pollen should be refrigerated or in vacuum sealed packaging. If you can't buy pollen which has been stored properly, you may be able to buy direct from a manufacturer.

Caution: Since it is a floral product, bee pollen may cause an allergic reaction in some people. Although this is rare, be cautious when beginning to take bee pollen and take half a teaspoon or less on the first occasion, to check for a reaction.

8. LECITHIN

Lecithin is a fatty component of many natural foods such as soybeans and nuts and seeds. Lecithin is available as a food supplement in the form of a granular powder, or in capsules. Granular lecithin offers the best value for money, and it has quite a pleasant slightly sweet flavor. Lecithin granules may be sprinkled on foods or added to milk shakes or juice smoothies.

The major nutritional value of lecithin is that of the large proportion of polyunsaturated fatty acids that it contains. Linoleic acid and linolenic acid are essential fatty acids (EFAs) which cannot be manufactured by the body and must be eaten as food. Granular lecithin contains 58.9% and 7.0% of these two EFAs respectively. These fatty acids aid in the transport of excess cholesterol to the liver where it can be metabolized safely, instead of being deposited on the inside of the arterial walls.

Your body can manufacture all the cholesterol it needs—people who eat a vegan diet free of animal produce, for example, don't become deficient in cholesterol—therefore foods which contain cholesterol such as most dairy products, eggs, meat and some sea foods can be thought of as adding cholesterol surplus to your body's requirements. Luckily your body is very intelligent, and if you regularly consume these foods, your body will lower its own production of cholesterol to compensate. However, eating a teaspoon of lecithin with every meal or snack in which you consume cholesterol rich foods makes good sense as a simple prevention measure against hardening of the arteries.

Lecithin is, however, like all fatty foods, high in calories—supplying 700 calories in 100 g, or 35 calories per 5 g teaspoonful, perhaps a good inspiration for the weight conscious to cut down on the other fatty, high calorie cholesterol-rich foods which make frequent use of lecithin advisable.

9. KELP

Kelp is available as powder, granules, and also in capsule form. It is most valuable as a supplement because of its high content of natural organic iodine, which is necessary for the proper functioning of the thyroid gland.

Kelp powder also contains a spectrum of other minerals from the sea, including organic sodium, and a significant amount of potassium. Also important, is the fact that kelp has been shown to reduce the uptake of radioactive strontium 90 between 50% to 85%—vital protection in our radioactive era.

Kelp powder can be sprinkled on food, or stirred into vegetable juices. A small amount of kelp powder can be stirred into dishes such as spaghetti sauce, or soups, while they are cooking. It doesn't do to be too heavy-handed with kelp powder, however, since in excess it can lend a gel-like consistency to liquids it is mixed with! Kelp granules are best used in cooking, since they soften and lend a subtle flavor to food without appreciably altering the texture of the dish.

10. ROYAL JELLY

Royal Jelly, which is made by worker bees, is the food of all bees for the first three days of their lives, after which only one larva, chosen to become Queen, receives the food. As a result she grows 40% larger and 60% heavier than her less well-nourished sisters, who become worker bees. Although the Queen Bee lays 2,000 eggs each day on her personal superfood diet, she lives for 4 or 5 years, while the worker bees live for just 40–60 days. It is her superior nutrition which is responsible for her impressive fertility and also longevity.

Royal Jelly has enjoyed a long history of use as a food supplement. It contains 12% protein, including all the essential amino acids, as well as ten nonessential amino acids. It is also a rich source of nucleic acid, a substance which is necessary for the proper nutrition of the DNA and RNA cellular components responsible for your body's cell division and growth.

Royal Jelly is also noted as a rich source of the B vitamin pantothenic acid, needed for proper immune function. It also contains smaller amounts of the other B complex vitamins, including vitamin B12. Just under 3% of royal jelly is comprised of an unknown substance which has never been satisfactorily analyzed.

Research on royal jelly published by the Pasteur Institute of Paris in 1984, indicates that the use of royal jelly as a dietary supplement can have a number of therapeutic benefits. One of these is the normalization of elevated serum cholesterol levels. The Pasteur Institute's Dr. Saenz's survey of world literature relating to the medical use of royal jelly to treat arthritis and senility met with positive results. A "satisfactory remission of Parkinson's Disease" with a "marked reduction" in trembling for the person concerned was also documented in Dr. Saenz's paper.

SUPPLEMENTING YOUR DIET

If you're eating what you consider to be a 'balanced diet', you may wonder whether you actually need to take any food supplements, or additional vitamins and minerals. There are several reasons why supplementing a good basic diet with food supplements and/or vitamin and mineral preparations makes sense.

First of all, unless all the food you eat is fresh, organically grown, and from good soil, it will probably be significantly lacking in trace minerals. Further vitamin and mineral losses are likely to occur during transport, storage and during food preparation—especially cooking.

Unfortunately, even organically grown foods could be deficient in one extremely important trace mineral—selenium. This mineral has an antioxidant function and a selenium deficiency decreases immune response, and has been linked to increased risk for both heart disease and cancer.

Secondly, as inhabitants of planet Earth, as our civilization approaches its third millennium, we need sufficient nutrition to provide our bodies with energy and the necessary components for everyday bodily repair, and also to protect ourselves against a host of environmental pollutants our bodies were not designed to handle.

We are all affected by pollution of many kinds—from the pesticides sprayed on most of our foods, to the various poisons emitted in car exhausts, to the electromagnetic pollution from our home television sets and VDU screens in the work place. Some of these pollutants are known to have a greater effect upon people whose nutritional status is suboptimal. The heavy metals, lead and cadmium, for example, are known to be more easily absorbed by people who have deficiencies of the protective elements calcium and zinc.

Unfortunately, we can not accurately measure the nutrient composition of our foods at the time which we eat them. Nor can we confidently assess the multitude of environmental toxins which, over the years, can have a detrimental effect on our health. Therefore, it seems wise to make sure that your diet is supplemented with nutritionally concentrated foods—the 'Superfoods' discussed here—or vitamin and mineral preparations to guard against possible sub-nutrient deficiencies which may make your body more vulnerable to disease than it should be.

A BRIEF GUIDE TO VITAMINS AND MINERALS

It would take an entire book to inform you fully about the various subtle effects of each vitamin or mineral, the signs of their deficiency or symptoms of toxicity. The information below is designed to make it easier for you to pick one of the better vitamin and mineral products on the market, and not waste money on those which may be ineffective. It will not make you an expert on orthomolecular nutrition. To become better informed some of the references listed at the end of this book may be helpful.

Until you are well informed about the benefits and potential hazards of supplementation, use the products you buy strictly as directed. Do not exceed the recommended daily dose as there is a potential for toxicity with many nutrients which are helpful in small quantities, including, selenium, vitamin A and vitamin D, among others, but in larger dosages may be harmful. The packaging of some brands of vitamin and mineral supplements can be most unhelpful, with instructions such as "Take one or more tablets daily." *If this is the case, take the one tablet and forget about the "more"—unless you have professional advice to the contrary.* Companies which produce labelling this misleading are obviously thinking more about their profits than your well being.

Vitamins are chemical constituents of food which our bodies require in small, but nonetheless, very necessary amounts for our well being. Most of the vitamins found in multivitamins/mineral preparations are laboratory synthesized.

There are two main subgroups of vitamins—those which are fat soluble, and those which are water soluble. The fat soluble vitamins are A, D, E and K. Water soluble vitamins include the B complex vitamins as well as vitamin C.

Vitamin A has one particular form which lives somewhere between the two groups—Beta Carotene—a water soluble compound which your body can convert to vitamin A as it is needed.

In general, any excess of water soluble vitamins can be excreted in your urine, so the likelihood of toxicity from an inappropriately large dose is reduced. The fat soluble vitamins can be stored in the liver, but not excreted easily. Therefore there is a greater likelihood of developing a toxicity problem if large amounts of these vitamins are taken on a long term basis. Vitamin A is primarily used in the body to protect eye function and maintain immunity. Most multivitamin mineral preparations contain no more than 10,000 International Units of vitamin A. This is the maximum recommended dose for pregnant women since an excess of vitamin A (more than 100,000 mg daily) may cause birth defects. Toxic effects in non-pregnant people have been noted at 30,000 IU taken daily over several months. A supplement containing beta-carotene (also called provitamin A) may be more useful than vitamin A as a scavenger of free radicals and cancer preventative.

B Complex vitamins are particularly important for maintaining your energy level and also mental function. Deficiencies may cause subclinical depression, or if severe, mental illness. Since the B vitamins act synergistically, it is rare for a deficiency to develop in just one of the vitamins, except sometimes in B12 which is not present in most vegetable foods, with the exception of Spirulina. There is some evidence to suggest that vitamin B12 may be manufactured by the intestinal flora of a healthy bowel. However, if you rarely or never eat animal products or Spirulina—the dietary sources of vitamin B12—you should take a supplement of this vitamin.

A deficiency of vitamin B12, known as pernicious anemia, can affect some older people even though they eat a diet which contains the vitamin. This is because nutrient absorption can become compromised as people age. This happens when the mucosa of the stomach lining degenerates and no longer produces the "intrinsic factor" necessary for the assimilation of vitamin B12 from the intestines. If this is the case, regular injections of vitamin B12 are needed to maintain good health.

A severe deficiency of vitamin B12 can manifest in psychiatric symptoms which may be mistaken for senility. Anyone suffering from poor mental health should have their B12 level checked.

Vitamin C is needed to maintain general immunity. The acidic form of vitamin C—ascorbic acid—has also been shown to increase the absorption of iron from foods. However, many people would find this form of the vitamin too acidifying to take in large amounts. Calcium ascorbate is gentle on the stomach, and many people find it is a useful home treatment for viral illnesses such as colds and the flu when taken according to the bowel tolerance method which is explained below. Calcium ascorbate powder makes a useful daily supplement—it can be mixed with fruit or vegetable juices—or even water if you don't mind the slightly bitter taste. For the long term treatment of serious illness, a mixture of ascorbates may be more appropriate. Consult with your nutritionally-aware health professional.

Taking Vitamin C—The Bowel Tolerance Method: The bowel tolerance method of taking vitamin C is used to determine how much vitamin C is needed by an individual to combat a viral or bacterial infection, or a condition possibly worsened by vitamin C deficiency, such as AIDS, cancer or arthritis.

The principle behind this method is that the amount of ascorbate (non-acidic vitamin C) needed by the body to saturate body tissues, will be the amount which has a laxative effect which loosens the bowel movements, but does not cause diarrhea. In general, the sicker the person is, the more vitamin C will be required before the person experiences the laxative effect. People with arthritis may need from 1–10 g per day. People with cancer may find they need more than 10 g on a daily basis. Once the required bowel looseness is obtained, the dose should be lowered slightly to avoid diarrhea. When the person has recovered, he/she should *gradually* reduce the dose of vitamin C.

How to take Vitamin C: When using the bowel tolerance method, it is cheapest and easiest to use an ascorbate powder dissolved in water rather than to buy tablets. There are two methods which work well:

Powder in a Glass Method: Put half a teaspoon of ascorbate powder in half a glass of water or diluted fruit juice. Drink and repeat the same dosage every 2–3 hours until bowel looseness occurs. Then repeat at a slightly lower dose so that bowel looseness is maintained but diarrhea is avoided. Continue treatment around the clock if suffering from a severe infection.

Powder in Bottle Method: Use a clean milk bottle—or other bottle with the 600 ml level marked—and put 6 heaping teaspoons of ascorbate powder in it. Add enough water or diluted fruit juice to reach the 600 ml level and then shake to dissolve powder. Take one-sixth of the mixture every 2–3 hours, or if suffering from a severe infection, hourly. When the appropriate bowel looseness is achieved, reduce the dosage slightly, making sure the bowel looseness is maintained.

Warning: Although vitamin C is generally safe to take, caution is needed if you are taking hormonal medications such as the Pill or Hormone Replacement Therapy. Studies have shown that taking 1000 mg or more of vitamin C per day increases the availability of oestrogen. This could have the effect of transforming a low dose contraceptive pill into a high one and may increase side effects caused by high estrogen levels. Women taking hormonal medication should therefore limit any supplement of Vitamin C to 500 mg daily.

Vitamin D is primarily used in the body alongside calcium for bone growth and renewal. Vitamin D is unique among the vitamins since it can be synthesized by skin which has been exposed to sunlight.

Vitamin D deficiency is most likely to develop in people who do not receive enough sunlight during a cold cloudy winter, or those who are institutionalized. The use of sunscreens inhibits the body's ability to synthesize vitamin D. The vitamin D synthesized on the skin surface needs time to be absorbed by your body. Washing, especially with soap and warm water, can wash away the oils at the skin surface and prevent the absorption of the vitamin.

For people at risk of developing vitamin D deficiency—which in adults can be characterized by bone pain and tenderness, a waddling gait, muscle weakness and deafness—a supplement of 400 IU daily is recommended. People who have impaired kidney or liver function which prevents them from absorbing fats efficiently need a specialized form of vitamin D.

Warning: It is thought that due to the chemical similarity of both lead and calcium, taking vitamin D can increase the absorption of the toxic metal lead. If you have lead poisoning seek professional advice before taking this vitamin. (See chapter on Chelation Therapy to learn how to rid your body of this toxin). People who do not have lead poisoning, but who live in an urban environment where significant exposure to lead is likely, should make sure that their intake of calcium and magnesium is adequate before taking additional vitamin D.

Vitamin D should never be taken by anyone suffering from sarcoidosis, except under professional supervision.

A traditional source of vitamin D has been cod liver oil. One teaspoon (4 ml) of cod liver oil supplies 368 IU of vitamin D as well as 3,680 IU of vitamin A. However, there is some concern that the fish from which the oil is obtained may themselves have a significant body burden of heavy metals such as mercury. Therefore, check with the manufacturer of any cod liver oil preparation you intend to use to find out if possible contaminants have been checked for and identified.

Vitamin E exists in nature as a group of fat soluble chemicals called mixed tocopherols. *D-alpha tocopherol* is the form of vitamin E which is most biologically active in the body. When you look for a supplement you should look for one which is naturally sourced (usually from soy or wheat oil) unless you are allergic to these foods. The vitamin E you choose should state its potency as 'X' hundred IU of this chemical. If the supplement contains other tocopherols, the label should state that these are in addition to the d-alpha tocopherol component. A supplement need not contain the other tocopherol to be valuable, for most purposes d-alpha tocopherol on its own is sufficient.

There is one form of vitamin E you definitely should not buy—synthetic vitamin E acetate—which is poorly absorbed by your body.

Vitamin E has many therapeutic uses from menopausal problems to arthritis and poor circulation. As a potent scavenger of harmful free radicals, taking a daily supplement of vitamin E is thought to be a prophylactic against cardiovascular disease and cancer.

Caution: No one who is taking anticoagulants drugs should take vitamin E except under professional supervision. Likewise, people with high blood pressure should not take vitamin E except in small doses under professional supervision, since it can cause a temporary rise in blood pressure. People who have heart damage because of rheumatic fever also need professional supervision when taking this vitamin. For healthy people, a daily supplement containing 200 IU per day is considered safe.

Vitamin K is the name given to a group of fat soluble compounds which play a crucial role in the body's blood clotting processes. Vitamin K is obtained through dietary sources such as green vegetables, cabbage, cereals and lettuce. It is also synthesized by the microorganisms which live in the small intestines. This process can be disrupted by antibiotic use. If you have to take antibiotics to cope with an infection which has not responded to less drastic forms of treatment, be sure to eat yogurt (or Kyo-Dophilus capsules) after you have completed the course of antibiotics since the acidophilus and bifidus cultures help to restore intestinal flora.

Unless you have a problem with hemorrhage, supplementing your diet with vitamin K is probably not necessary.

Minerals. The minerals which are needed to maintain proper bodily function are generally divided into two groups. These are the macrominerals which form part of bones and other body structures, as well as metabolic activities. These include: phosphorus, magnesium, calcium, potassium, sodium and chlorine—which the body requires in amounts of several hundred milligrams each day.

The second major group is the trace elements which take part in important metabolic reactions. These include: zinc, manganese, copper, chromium, iodine, selenium, cobalt, molybdenum and sulphur. These are needed in a few milligrams or less daily.

Two further groups of minerals are the ultra trace elements, and the research elements. Ultra trace elements are elements which have been proven to be needed by the body in tiny amounts. The research elements are those about which there is still uncertainty as to whether or not they are needed by the body.

Calcium is most commonly recognized as being the mineral in the body most needed to build (and maintain) strong bones and teeth, but it also has important metabolic functions. Post menopausal women may need 1,000–1,500 mg of calcium daily. This can be difficult to obtain through diet alone, so supplementation may be necessary.

When considering calcium absorption, the ratio of calcium to the other macro minerals phosphorus and zinc is important. The ideal dietary proportions of calcium: phosphorus and magnesium are thought to be 1,000 mg of calcium for every 1,000 mg of phosphorus and 500 mg of magnesium.

In the Western diet, milk products have been traditionally seen as the major dietary source of calcium. Dairy products are currently being promoted by the various Dairy Producer Associations as the ideal way to increase calcium intake and prevent osteoporosis. However, even for people who are not allergic to them, milk products have significant disadvantages as a major calcium source.

Firstly, milk is significantly higher in phosphorus than in calcium, and is also extremely low in magnesium. This may inhibit calcium absorption, unless magnesium-rich foods are also eaten at the same meal. Young children who drink a lot of milk can easily become deficient in magnesium.

The second major disadvantage of milk products as a calcium source is that most of them are pasteurized. The heat involved in this process destroys hormones and enzymes necessary for the proper absorption of calcium. If you do eat milk products, choose raw or cultured products over pasteurized ones. While raw cow's milk can be difficult to find, raw goat's milk is often still available.

If you analyze your dietary intake and find it to be deficient in calcium, you should choose a supplement carefully. The best supplements contain calcium and magnesium in a 2:1 ratio. The magnesium should be in the form of magnesium oxide, magnesium aspartate, magnesium orotate or amino acid-chelated magnesium. Magnesium gluconate and magnesium chloride give less satisfactory results. (It is not usually necessary to take supplementary phosphorus, since this is amply supplied in many foods including dairy products, meat, whole grains, legumes and eggs, making a deficiency unlikely.)

As well as looking for a supplement which contains twice as much calcium as magnesium, the form of calcium you buy is important. Many supplements contain calcium carbonate (also known as limestone or chalk!) which, unless you have incredibly strong stomach acid, is poorly absorbed by your body, making the supplement a waste of money.

The most readily absorbed forms of calcium are calcium apatite and calcium citrate. Amino acid-chelated calcium and calcium orotate are also good, as are calcium lactate, gluconate and sulphate.

Bone meal and dolomite are traditional forms of calcium which are of questionable value. Bonemeal has a high phosphorus level and may be contaminated with heavy metals and pesticides. The absorption of dolomite is uncertain, and there have been reports that dolomite, from at least one source, is contaminated by heavy metals such as mercury and lead.

Dosage: Check the dosage of calcium supplement carefully. It may say "1,000 mg calcium gluconate" for example, but since only 10% of the calcium gluconate is calcium, the supplement contains just 100 mg of calcium. The label of the better supplements should say "1,000 mg calcium gluconate, equivalent to 100 mg **elemental** calcium." If the supplement doesn't specify how much elemental calcium and magnesium it contains, don't buy it.

Magnesium is a mineral which, as we have seen above is particularly important in the proper absorption of calcium. Food sources which are high in magnesium include all green vegetables. Magnesium is a component of chlorophyll, as well as nuts, shrimp, whole grains and soya products.

Magnesium deficiency can be caused by eating a diet which contains large amounts of foods in which the calcium:phosphorus:magnesium ratio is unbalanced. Eating excessive amounts of dairy products and meat are primary culprits.

A daily intake of 400–800 mg (from foods) is considered adequate for a healthy adult.

Supplemental magnesium could be most useful for people who have the following health problems: heart disease and high blood pressure. Magnesium deficiency has been postulated as a possible cause of the latter, as well as contributing to premenstrual syndrome and diabetic complications.

Taking a supplement of magnesium along with vitamin B6 has also been shown to prevent kidney stone formation.

Iron is perhaps the most important of the trace elements, since it forms the centre of the hemoglobin molecules which transport oxygen inside our bodies. Although iron deficiency anemia is relatively rare—one Canadian study reported that clinical anemia was present in just 2% of the population they studied—subclinical iron deficiency is much more common. The same Canadian study reported that 19% of people studied had a lower than optimum iron level.

The symptoms of iron deficiency include: cracks at the side of the mouth, tiredness, concave nails, and sometimes nails with washboard ridges. People who manifest the symptoms of poor thyroid function, but whose diagnostic test for thyroid problems is normal, should have their iron level checked, since animal tests have shown that those who are anaemic cannot convert one type of thyroid hormone to another.

The best food sources of iron are egg yolks, parsley, organ meats, shellfish and legumes. The superfoods wheat and barley grass and Spirulina are even better sources, Spirulina supplying 15 mg of organic bio-chelated iron in a single tablespoon.

Molasses is often mentioned as a good source of iron. It does have a good supply of this mineral, but unfortunately, it often contains pesticides from the sugar cane, so caution is recommended. At the time of writing, organic molasses is mostly unavailable.

If you are looking for a multivitamin/mineral preparation to boost your intake of this mineral, choose one which specifies that it contains amino acid-chelated iron, or ferrous fumarate. Avoid preparations containing ferrous sulphate. Iron in this form is difficult for your body to absorb, and can cause constipation. This form of iron, made available on prescription to pregnant women, is associated with miscarriages, since it destroys vitamin E in the body. Since vitamin E is such an important free radical scavenger, it makes sense to conserve your investment and take any supplement containing large amounts of vitamin E early in the day, and any iron containing supplement at least 8 hours later to reduce biochemical antagonism.

The ratio of iron to zinc in a multivitamin should be 1:1, or at the most 2:1. If the proportion of iron is increased above this amount, it could impair your body's ability to absorb zinc.

Taking a high dose of calcium at the same time that you take iron may prevent you from absorbing the iron that you need. It is probably best to take any iron containing preparations in the morning, vitamin E at least 8 hours later, and calcium/magnesium supplements at bedtime. Calcium is reputedly better absorbed when your body is at rest.

Zinc plays an important role in the maintenance of general immunity. It is important also in maintaining good eyesight, and properly functioning reproductive organs. A zinc deficiency, along with magnesium, also seems to have an effect of people's mental health. A study done in Great Britain showed that people admitted to a psychiatric hospital had lowered levels of plasma zinc and magnesium, compared to controls who were not suffering from mental illness.

Common signs of zinc deficiency include: immune deficiencies, impaired taste and smell, loss of appetite, infertility in women and low sperm count in men, hair loss and skin problems. Perhaps the most obvious pointer is white spots on fingernails.

If you have white spots on your fingernails and take a supplement containing zinc, you should find that the spots disappear. Zinc supplements are best absorbed at night but do not take them at the same time as a calcium supplement, since the calcium may impair the absorption of the zinc. If you are in the habit of taking a nightly calcium supplement, then cease taking the calcium in the evening and take it earlier in the day until you have treated the zinc deficiency.

Amino chelated zinc is probably the best supplement, followed by zinc gluconate. Zinc sulphate is adequate for short term use. Some forms of zinc may cause nausea.

Selenium is a most important supplement, since much of the soil in many countries is notoriously low in this important antioxidant element. Selenium deficiency has been linked to an increased risk of cancer, as well as cardiovascular disease, the primary killers in industrialized nations.

The average adult requires 200–250 mcg of selenium per day. Analysis of a typical diet suggests that most people's intake is only about 50 mcg per day. A supplement containing 150–200 mcg daily is recommended to protect against the possible consequences of deficiency of this mineral. *This supplementation level, however, should not be exceeded, since in higher doses, selenium can be toxic. People who regularly use selenium containing shampoos such as "Selsun" and "Lenium" which contain selenium sulphide should have their selenium levels checked, since, although it is a rare occurrence, enough selenium can be absorbed from the shampoo to create a toxic body burden.*

The form of selenium grown on yeast seleniomethionone is the most easily absorbable form of selenium. It may however cause a reaction in yeast sensitive people. *If you are allergic to yeast you should take a supplement containing sodium selenite, or selenate.*

Chromium is an important trace mineral lost during the processes in which carbohydrate foods are refined. Eating refined carbohydrates, which in themselves are low in chromium has also been found to increase the likelihood of a developing chromium deficiency.

Since the effects of chromium deficiency include impairing the body's ability to metabolize glucose, leading to elevated blood sugar and loss of sugar in the urine, as well as atherosclerosis (hardening of the arteries) preventing or correcting any deficiency is important.

Whole wheat bread, cheese, wheat germ and calf's liver are good dietary sources of chromium. Brewer's yeast which is high in chromium is also useful. Not all brewer's yeasts are high in chromium, so check that the brand you purchase does contain this mineral.

Supplementing chromium is especially important for diabetics. *(See chapter on*

Diabetes for more information about choice of supplements).

Sodium and Potassium Of all the minerals supplied in the typical diet of a person living in a modern industrialized country, the elements sodium and potassium are probably supplied in the worst proportions in relation to each other. Sodium, generally in the form of common salt or sodium chloride, is added liberally to almost all processed foods because of its properties as a preservative and a flavor enhancer. Almost all breads, crackers, breakfast cereals, pastries and canned foods contain added salt (sodium chloride). Another compound which contains sodium is monosodium glutamate, or MSG. A suspected carcinogen, MSG is used as a flavor enhancer in instant noodles and soup mixes, as well as in Chinese food. It is estimated that the average person consumes about 3,000 to 6,000 mg of sodium per day—perhaps 10 to 20 times more than our bodies need. An estimated daily intake of potassium is 2,000 to 4,000 mg daily. Most natural foods except some meats contain more potassium than sodium.

Consuming foods which are high in added sodium causes an unhealthy ratio of sodium to potassium to develop in the body. This is exacerbated by the fact that when potassium rich foods such as potatoes and most other vegetable are cooked in water, the potassium contained within them leaches out into the cooking water, and is generally thrown away. Many people also add salt to the water their vegetables are cooking in, and once their vegetables are served, add additional salt to them from the shaker.

One of the possible consequences of consuming an excessive amount of sodium and an insufficient amount of potassium is high blood pressure. Significantly for women, consuming an excess of dietary sodium also reduces the availability of calcium for use in the body, which may eventually result in the weakened bones of osteoporosis.

The idea that too much salt was also linked to cancer was advanced by Dr. Max Gerson. The successful cancer therapy Dr. Gerson developed included potassium (and iodine) supplements, as well as potassium rich juices to aid the recovery of the cellular support systems of the body. Salt was strictly forbidden. Eighty percent of the people who have early to moderate stage cancer who go to the Gerson Clinic in Tijuana, Mexico, (which was set up after Gerson's death to continue his treatment) experience an improvement in their condition. More remarkably, 40–50% of the patients who arrive at the Tijuana hospital who have been diagnosed as having terminal cancer also experience an improvement in their condition.

Further information about Dr Gerson's therapy is published in *Suppressed Inventions and Other Discoveries,* edited by Jonathan Eisen. (Avery Publishing Group 1997.) Dr Gerson's own book: *A Cancer Therapy: The Results of Fifty Cases,* is widely available.

So if an excess of sodium and an insufficiency of potassium can be linked to raising your chances of developing hypertension (high blood pressure) as well as osteoporosis and cancer, how do you reduce your salt consumption?

The easiest way to do this is to throw away your salt shaker and don't add salt to foods while you are cooking them. If you miss that familiar salty flavor, you can add very small amounts of naturally brewed MSG-free soy sauce. If you are avoiding fermented foods, Bragg Liquid Aminos makes a good substitute for soy sauce. A squeeze of lemon can add a nice tangy flavor, as can very finely chopped raw or lightly sauteed garlic or onion. Adding a sprinkling of kelp powder to your savory foods also supplies a slightly salty taste, some organic sodium as well as other essential minerals from the sea such as iodine. Your health food store will also have a selection of different sea vegetables which you may well find delicious sprinkled over food, or added into soups or stews.

It is important to remember that both sodium and potassium are essential minerals. Sodium is needed in order for your body to create hydrochloric acid essential for good digestion, and regulate blood pressure—too little can cause low blood pressure. After vigorous exercise, sodium lost in sweat can cause nausea, dizziness, cramps and heart failure in extreme circumstances. Potassium is needed inside every cell of your body, and plays an especially important role in the proper functioning of the heart and nervous system.

CHAPTER 5

HERBS FOR LONGEVITY

There are many herbs which have been used throughout the ages to promote long life. In general, these herbs are known as adaptogens, meaning that they have several properties which increase the user's ability to adapt to changing circumstances, and have been observed to contribute to longevity.

Adaptogens must be nontoxic at normal dosages so that they may be used over long periods to prevent illness. They also raise the body's nonspecific resistance to disease, and have the ability to normalize the functions of the different organs of the body—and even overcome illness.

Below is an alphabetical list of herbs which are classed as adaptogens:

- American Ginseng
- Asian Ginseng *(Panax)*
- Astragalus *(Huang Chi)*
- Eucommia Ulmoides *(Du Zhong)*
- Gotu Kola
- Lycii Berries *(Gou Qi Zi)*
- Poria Cocos
- Suma

- Angelica Sinensis *(Dong Quai)*
- Aswaganda
- Condonopsitis *(Dang Shen)*
- Garlic
- Holy Basil
- Polygonum Multiflorum *(Ho Shou Wu)*
- Schizandra Berries *(Wu Wei Zi)*
- Siberian Ginseng *(Eleutherococcus senticosus)*

PANAX GINSENG

Of all the herbs known to the Western world, Ginseng has one of the best reputations as a longevity herb. According to Taoist philosophy, the power of Ginseng lies in the herb's ability to concentrate the earth energy (ch'i) and the energy of the five elements within its root. These energies are then available to replenish the energy of the person who eats or drinks a preparation of the herb.

From the perspective of Western medicine, the most important constituent of Ginseng is believed to be more than 28 saponins which have been dubbed 'ginsenosides.' Research on Ginseng has shown that these saponins have anti-inflammatory, analgesic, anticonvulsant, and hypotensive properties. The herb is also recognized as being helpful in blood sugar regulation, as a digestive aid, and as having anti-psychotic properties.

The other constituents of Ginseng include long chain polysaccharides, panoxic acid, minerals and B vitamins. Ginseng is also reputed to moderate serum cholesterol levels.

Caution: In the case of Ginseng, as with almost any nutritive substance, it is possible to have too much of a good thing. Traditional practitioners advise taking Ginseng in accordance with the packaging instructions, or on a herbalist's advice, since some of Ginseng's constituents are similar to steroids and may cause side effects when too much is taken.

EUCOMMIA ULMOIDES (*Ta Chung* or *Du Tsong*)

Eucommia Ulmoides is a tree which has been used medicinally by Chinese herbalists for 3000 years. Research undertaken by investigators from America, China, Japan and Russia has shown that *Eucommia* has anti-inflammatory, anti-hypertensive, diuretic, and tonic as well as sedative properties. In Chinese medical terms, *Eucommia* is said to "enhance the vital energies" and "conserve the essence." *Eucommia's* Chinese name refers to a Taoist monk who was believed to be immortal. In Japan, this herb is valued as a sexual tonic.

The combination of *Eucommia, Ginseng, Schizandra, Astragalus and Ho Shou Wu (polygonum multiflorum)* were reputedly the secret longevity formula of Moo San Do Sha who lived for 142 years.

POLYGONUM MULTIFLORUM *(Ho-Shou-Wu)*

Polygonum Multiflorum has a number of properties which make it one of the most useful herbs in the Chinese pharmacopeia. The root of *Polygonum Multiflorum* is said to accumulate large amounts of energy or c'hi in a similar way to Ginseng. In fact, within Asia, *Polygonum Multiflorum* is believed by some to be superior to Ginseng as a longevity herb—and also as a sexual tonic. Part of *Polygonum Multiflorum's* youth-promoting and potency-enhancing properties probably rely on the fact that it has a cleansing effect on the liver and kidneys, which strengthens these vital organs. Recent research has also shown the root of this herb to be helpful in reducing elevated cholesterol levels.

The legend associated with *Polygonum Multiflorum* is the story of Ho Shou Wu, who had been impotent, and never been able to father the children he desired. After discovering *Polygonum Multiflorum* growing in the forest and partaking in a medicine made from the roots for several days his potency was restored. Ho Shou Wu reputedly went on to father four children—and live for 132 years.

LYCII BERRIES *(Gou Qi Zi)*

Lycii berries are in the nightshade family, and are another herb which has a great reputation for promoting longevity. In Chinese herbalism, the berries are used as a blood and liver tonic, as well as to "nourish the vital essence." Like many Chinese herbal medicines, *Lycii* berries are associated with one person for whom using the berries promoted a long life—in this case Li Ch'ing Yuen—who is reputed to have lived for more than a quarter of a millennium.

SCHIZANDRA CHINENSIS *(Wu Wei Zi)*

Along with *Eucommia Ulmoides, Ginseng, Ho Shou Wu* and *Astragalus, Schizandra Chinensis* makes up part of the ancient formula which apparently allowed Moo San Do Sha to live for 142 years. In terms of the Chinese theory of medicine, Schizandra is a very balanced tonic, being sour, sweet, bitter, pungent and salty at the same time! It is also considered to be able to tone both the yin and yang energies of the body.

The overall effect of *Schizandra Chinensis* is that it assists in balancing the functions of the organs, hence increasing both physical and mental energy. In fact, this is one of the herbs known to improve both short and long term memory. The tincture form of *Schizandra Chinensis* has sedative properties.

Like many of the other herbs which have been traditionally used for longevity, *Schizandra Chinenesis* also reputedly has a positive effect on sexual function and enjoyment. According to one herbal researcher, taking 5 ml of *Schizandra Chinensis* in a glass of wine has aphrodisiac effects by stimulating the nerves of the genital area.

SIBERIAN GINSENG *(Eleutherococcus Senticosus)*

Eleutherococcus Senticosus or Siberian Ginseng, an adaptogenic herb, has been the focus of intensive research in recent years. In Russia, this herb is used by athletes to boost performance—a use which is backed up by research undertaken in Japan which showed that (male) athletes who used the herb improved their exercise capacity by an average of 23 percent. By contrast, athletes who received a placebo improved by only seven percent.

Studies in Europe have found that taking *Eleutherococcus* boosts the immune system, increasing the production of Natural Killer Cells and T helper cells in the healthy volunteers who took the herb. That this can result in less sickness was demonstrated in a double blind study of factory workers in Siberia, which found that absence from work due to sickness dropped by 40% in the group taking Siberian Ginseng.

The use of Siberian Ginseng is indicated for people who need a supplement to boost mental and physical performance as well as tolerance to stressful situations. It may also be used to treat people suffering from exhaustion, insomnia or irritability caused by overwork. Finally, this herb can also be of assistance to mitigate the side effects of radiation or chemotherapy, and hasten recovery from surgery.

Caution: Although Siberian Ginseng is excellent for helping to prevent infections, it should not be used during the acute phase of infection. Some researchers consider that Siberian Ginseng should also be avoided by people suffering from elevated blood pressure. Other studies have shown that Siberian Ginseng can improve cardiovascular function and lower blood pressure. However, to be on the safe side, do not take Siberian Ginseng except under supervision if you have these problems.

ASTRAGALUS MEMBRANACEUS *(Huang Qi)*

The herb *Astragalus* is used to promote vitality and promote healing within the Chinese system of medicine. It has been shown to have a diuretic effect, and has been used to treat edema and kidney problems. It has also been shown to increase immune function and levels of antibodies. *Astragalus* was also part of the longevity formula used by Moo San Do Sha. Like other adaptogens, taking *Astragalus* can help to prevent viral infections. It may also be used to treat chronic viral conditions, particularly those characterized by spontaneous sweating. *However, it should not be used during the acute phase of an infection.*

CHAPTER 6

BREATHING, EXERCISE AND RELAXATION

There is an old proverb "Life is in the breath. He who half breathes, half lives." Breathing supplies us with much of our essential nourishment. We make our energy by metabolizing food and the air we breathe. Breathing is the gift that sustains life. It has the power to revitalize us, clear our minds, calm our emotions, cleanse our bodies, aid our circulation and ensure our well-being. But in the haste and humdrum of modern civilization people learn to take breathing for granted, or distort it, robbing themselves of their rightful nourishment.

There are many books written about how poor breathing contributes to illness. One of those is *"The Oxygen Breakthrough—30 Days to an Illness-Free Life"* by Dr Saul Hendler. He claims that poor breathing can contribute to respiratory and cardiac symptoms, angina, chronic fatigue, anxiety, depression, headaches, seizures, dizziness and immune disfunction including susceptibility to colds. Also bear in mind the cumulative effects on health of a combination of poor nutritional intake, a sedentary lifestyle, the ingestion of toxins from our food and environment and lazy or stressed breathing patterns.

Breathing engages the abdominal, thoracic and clavicular (chest) muscles in a powerful rhythmic cycle. But habitually people lapse into breathing patterns that under-utilize one or more of these muscle groups. This can result in patterns of rapid, shallow upper chest breathing, usually punctuated by a pause between the exhale and the inhale, or breathing mainly through a distended abdomen. Both of these can be destructive to health and well-being.

Shallow upper chest breathing is in fact a primal response to being threatened. When the abdomen is tightened and breathing confined to the upper chest, the blood pressure and heart rate increase, providing impetus for a primate to fight or flee. In our modern existence stress can provoke this response. Inasmuch as breathing is regulated by the sympathetic nervous system, any breathing pattern that impacts upon the nervous system continues the stress. Therefore anxiety disorders, sleep disorders and depression can result. In addition rapid upper chest breathing accompanied by frequent sighs is a mild form of hyperventilation which may be experienced by people under stress. Habitual shallow breathing can manifest itself in round shoulders, collapsed chests and respiratory infections and disorders.

Breathing mainly in the abdomen can result in a permanently distended stomach and congested liver and inhibit drainage of lymph fluids because the abdominal muscles do not provide enough pressure to disgorge the organs of excess and stale blood.

Incorrect breathing patterns can in many cases be attributed to poor posture. Thought patterns, emotions, injury, trauma, back problems, prolonged pain and stress are all embodied in the body and can be reflected in our posture. If postural problems develop, often so does poor breathing. Posture can often be the reason why people develop shallow breathing patterns and the problems associated with it. The well known Alexander Technique is successful in correcting postural problems. There are now many teachers qualified in this technique. If there are spinal problems due to injuries an osteopath or qualified remedial body therapist could be sought who specializes in muscular-skeletal problems. This can include therapeutic massage. A booklet listing available therapists can usually be obtained from a health store or consult the therapeutic massage section in the telephone directory.

Correct breathing is essential for cardiovascular patients. A report in the *British Medical Journal* stated that improper breathing can result in "progressive damage to the heart" due to repeated coronary artery spasms. This is because poor breathing may trigger neurological and biochemical changes resulting in sensitization and constriction of the coronary artery and damage to nerves that help regulate the electrical activity and rhythm of the heart. For example heart attacks are more likely to occur in individuals where there is a consistent pause after the exhale and before the inhale. The longer the pause, the more the risk.

Fortunately our breathing apparatus is equipped to work like a well-oiled machine, even under pressure. In a compression pump-like action the dome shaped diaphragmatic muscle moves up and down the thoracic cavity supported by the clavicular and abdominal muscles. On the in breath the diaphragm descends pushing the internal organs (liver, spleen, intestines) back creating a vacuum in the chest which allows air to be sucked in. Firm stomach muscles will provide counter pressure and the resulting confined abdominal cavity has a massaging effect on organs. When breathing out, the diaphragm moves upwards supported by contracted abdominal muscles and forces stale air from the lungs. This action pushes organs back and upwards where they disgorge stale blood and receive a renewed supply as the breathing cycle continues.

When full breathing is practised it sends a huge energy wave up and down the whole being and a renewed oxygen supply to the brain. This affects the body, mind, emotions and spirit. As breathing is regulated by the nervous system, a message of calm and well-being is sent throughout, counteracting the effects of stress. It promotes clearer thoughts and perceptions. In some cases, breathing fully may stir up repressed trauma. Repression of trauma requires a great deal of energy and some people compromise their breathing to do this. Free breathing is the basis of many therapeutic practices, and although this can be used at home (below are some ideas on how to do this), dealing with really serious trauma may require the assistance of someone qualified in the field. Suitable therapists include qualified rebirthers, psychotherapists or counsellors. After all, breathing freely sometimes means facing our worst fears, feeling them fully and moving on. It means we accept that life is a learning process.

The following is an exercise for full breath based on the yoga pranayama technique. If you do not already breathe fully, practising this 10–20 minutes a day will guide your own breath into becoming fuller and more relaxed. In fact when you inhale fully into the bottom of your lungs, a better exchange of gases occurs. It is then that we have the capacity to inhale the seven liters of air per breath that we are designed to do rather than the one to two liters normally inhaled. But first access your breath and decide whether you do or do not breathe properly. For example, is your breath shallow or short and fast? Does your chest only slightly rise? Is there any other movement? Do you distend your abdomen?

Is your posture preventing you from drawing a full breath? Do you suppress your breath? If you breathe fully and fill your abdomen, diaphragm and chest with a strong relaxed motion, congratulations. Your body thanks you for your good habits.

Inhale to a count of 5, hold to a count of 2–5 (depending on the strength of your lungs), and exhale to a count of 5. For this exercise a pause may also be taken after the exhale and before the inhale to a count to 5. This can allow a better exchange of gases in the lungs. You can imagine a four sided square with colored lights which light up to each count.

- Get into a comfortable position. Initially it is best to perform this exercise lying down or reclining, because the weakened respiratory muscles do not have to work against gravity. (However the yogis perform pranayama in the lotus or yoga kneeling position.) If you are serious about developing your breathing and have circulatory or other problems, a small inexpensive yoga stool which supports the body in the correct posture can be purchased from a yoga or meditation school.

- Place your hands on your abdomen with fingers of each hand pointed towards each other but not quite touching.

- Inhale slowly (through the nose if possible) and let your abdomen expand like a balloon. Feel your hands rising and being pushed apart slightly.

- Move your hands up to your diaphragm, continue inhaling and again feel your hands rising and expanding. (Initially some of your breathing muscles will be weak and you may not get much expansion, but keep at it and it will improve.)

- Move your hands to the top of the chest and gradually fill the upper part of the lungs, feel your hands rise. Again breathing muscles may be weak but you will learn to expand this part as well.

- Begin to exhale with your hands still on the top of the chest. Exhale from the top of the chest, move your hands to your diaphragm, exhale, move hands to abdomen, exhale. Feel each part flatten as you exhale.

With practice this becomes a continuous fluid movement. The hands are only used as a guide. Once this is accomplished you can leave the hands out of the movement. If you take in a fraction of air before exhaling, this stops the breath from gushing out. When your lungs are strong enough, hold the full breath for a count of 3 to 5.

THERAPEUTIC USE OF BREATH TO DEAL WITH FEELINGS OR TRAUMA

If you are troubled by thoughts or feelings that your deep breathing stirs up, lie or sit comfortably; breathe your own essential breath, but deeply. As you exhale release the negative or troubling emotion or your reaction to memories, people etc., through the top of your head—which is known as the crown chakra in natural therapies. Say "I accept that this happened and I cannot change it but I wish to free myself from it and move on. I therefore release my anger, hate, sorrow" etc. With your inward eye see it float out of the top of your being. When you inhale say to yourself whatever you need to say, i.e. "I am angry and sad now but I will move on and I breathe from the universe, peace, serenity, well-being, strength," or whatever it is you need.

Louise Hay's book *"You Can Heal Your Life"* has a step-by-step section on resistance to change, and coping with change. There are many other self therapy books in your local bookstore.

Alternatively use this breath every morning or evening, just to breathe out and release anything negative, like anger, frustration, hate, sadness, annoyance, and breathe in positive vibrations from the Universe like peace, strength, love, or colors.

ALTERNATE NOSTRIL BREATHING

This breath is also derived from yoga. It is designed to clear the breathing passages and calm the nervous system. Anyone who has ever used it to cure their sinus problems can attest to its effectiveness. It brings energy as well as a sense of calm and tranquility.

Place the index finger on the gap between your eyebrows at the top of the nose. Place your right thumb against the right nostril (if right handed) and the little finger and fourth finger against the left nostril. Start by pressing the right nostril closed with the thumb and inhale slowly through the left nostril to a count of six. Retain the breath for up to a count of six and close the left nostril with the fourth and little finger, exhaling through the right nostril. Carry on the sequence by inhaling through the right nostril and exhaling through the left. Then inhale through the left and exhale through the right. Try to repeat it up to 7 times every day or few days. A good time is after your morning exercises or yoga or other exercise.

BREATHING FOR PAIN RELIEF

There is a technique in Raja Yoga that creates a rhythm by synchronizing breathing and heartbeat to send pain out of the body. This is based on the belief that pain is a wave of energy.

It can be done as follows:

Breathe in and out through your nose. Sit or lie down, and relax by taking some deep breaths.

Once you have a rhythm imagine the following:

- Breathe in the life energy of Prana from around you, and on the out breath visualize yourself sending the energy to the painful area to aid healing.

- Breathe in again, now imagine that the energy is going to drive the pain away. When you breathe out visualize all the pain flowing out of your body. Do this 7 times before resting.

HOW TO GET RID OF A SINUS HEADACHE

According to Dr. Morton Walker, author of *The Healing Powers of Garlic, Nature's Ancient Medicine in Modern Deodorized Form*, the natural and safe way to get rid of a sinus headache is the following:

- Lie down flat.

- Put three drops of Aged Garlic Extract™ Liquid (plain) in each nostril. (Made by the KYOLIC^r Company.)

- Wait three minutes.

- Return to an upright position.

- Pinch your nostrils together and blow out of your mouth four (4) times. (Just like blowing out the candles on a birthday cake or pretend you are sneezing.)

- That's all there is to it.

- This treatment is to be used ONLY when you have a sinus headache.

According to Dr. Walker, the best way to eliminate a sinus problem in the first place, is to stay away from all sugars (of any kind), eat no dairy products, some people must eliminate citrus, drink 6-8 glasses of pure water daily and take 3-4 capsules of KYOLIC^r Formula 103 a day.

PRANA

In Yoga, which is the oldest known science of breath, Prana is the energy that fills the universe. It is the force that drives life and matter. Everything that moves is a manifestation of prana. Western science substantiates this and says that not only does the atmosphere have an electrical field but it also vibrates with an energy made up of electrically charged particles called negative ions. This is the energy that we breathe in and metabolize. It is important for well-being to absorb it and discharge it. Prana is especially found in forest and sea air, sunlight, living food, and pure spring water. It is negated by chemicals used in growing foods, additives, preservatives, smog, environmental pollution, air-conditioning and synthetic clothing. Metabolized prana is released through our organs and through the skin. This process is activated by sunlight. Going barefoot on a warm day is a good way of getting and releasing prana. Ill or frail people who become confined inside, become disused to absorbing prana. A negative ionizer may be a useful investment.

EXERCISE

How often do you read that as part of the aging process we can expect hardening of the arteries, breakdown of cells and organs, wasted muscles, brittle bones, and memory loss?

Our society has promoted the idea that it's natural to die frail, arthritic, diseased, incontinent, senile, and medicated to the hilt. However, the pain and long drawn out suffering that accompanies degenerative diseases should not be necessary. Aging and chronic degeneration happen only to the degree we let them.

For those people who would prefer to live fully, and hopefully die peacefully when the time has come, exercise is a part of the holistic formula for health and well-being in old age. When exercise is used in balance with correct diet, antioxidants, rest and relaxation, full breathing and even detoxifying the body, it is possible to build health in the advanced years. It is now thought that movement even stimulates the manufacture of new cartilage and releases enzymes to digest old worn out cartilage.

The amount you should exercise is relative. Some people become hooked on fitness and the endorphins—the natural form of morphine that your body manufactures when you engage in vigorous exercise. But it is not necessary to exercise excessively to obtain and maintain fitness.

The body basically needs a program of exercise that includes some aerobic exercise for cardiovascular strength, leisure sports and enjoyable activities like puttering about outdoors or working in the garden and exercises that promote muscular strength and flexibility.

Cardiovascular fitness is basically measured by how well the body can utilize oxygen. When the body is exerted the muscles and cells need more oxygen. Since oxygen is carried in the blood, the heart muscle responds by pumping around more blood. It does that by pumping greater volumes of blood with each stroke. It can only do this efficiently if there is sufficient oxygen available and the lungs have the capacity to take the increased oxygen and transfer it to the heart. How well the increased oxygen is used then depends upon the ability of the muscle cells to take it up. If you live in a city, try to get your exercise where oxygen levels are highest; near water, dense vegetation, or as far as possible away from heavily used main traffic routes where cars pump out noxious fumes.

SOME GOOD REASONS TO EXERCISE

Most people know that they should be getting more exercise, and yet don't make the extra effort to get the exercise their bodies need. Most people know that exercise strengthens the heart, but there are many more good reasons to get into the exercise habit. Here are some of them:

- Exercise helps prevent cancer. The combined effects of exercise in helping to control your weight, alleviate depression, tone your endocrine system, improve cellular nutrition and waste product elimination, and boost your immune system will not only make you feel good, but significantly reduce your chances of becoming a victim of the most feared diseases of our time.

- Exercise normalizes blood pressure. If you have high blood pressure, exercise can help reduce it—but make sure you exercise under medical supervision. Exercise will also help to increase your blood pressure if it is abnormally low.

- Exercise increases the ability of the blood to carry oxygen, and allows a greater volume of oxygen rich blood to circulate around the body.

- Exercise lowers your resting pulse rate. People with a resting pulse rate of 71 beats per minute—or lower—are 50% less likely to die from coronary heart disease than people who have a resting pulse rate of 84 beats a minute or higher.

- Exercise promotes better blood circulation. This not only means that your cells get better nutrition, but waste products are removed more effectively.

- Exercise has a chelating effect on the cardiovascular system due to the production of lactic acid.

- The deep breathing necessary during vigorous exercise can strengthen and expand the lungs. It can also allow the expectoration of phlegm from the lungs.

- Exercise charges your brain and nerve cells with electrical energy.

- Exercise strengthens your bones, muscles and ligaments. It can help prevent the bone mineral loss which is part of osteoporosis.

- It promotes intestinal activity, reducing constipation. It is generally good for your digestion.

- Exercise improves the function of your immune system. Moderate exercise has been shown to increase the production of lymphocytes, interleukin 2 and neutrophils and other specialized cells and chemical helpers of the immune system. Exercise which builds muscle, such as working with weights, also has the advantage of increasing your body's production of the amino acid glutamine. Glutamine is needed for the replication of immune system cells and must be produced by your muscles—your immune system cannot produce glutamine itself.

- Exercise can delay the aging process by releasing damaging stress and tension and developing an efficient cardiovascular system which delivers nourishment to the cells, as well as removing toxins.

- Exercise tones and beautifies your body.

- Exercise helps to balance your endocrine system. As a result, the pituitary gland, pancreas, adrenal and sex glands become more efficient.

- Exercise increases your metabolic rate so that you not only burn fat and calories while you do it, but also while you sleep!

- Exercise, when taken regularly, can help lift spirits and alleviate depression.

- Exercise increases your endurance.

- Exercise adds energy. Amazingly enough, it adds more energy than it uses.

- Exercise improves your brain power and makes you smarter.

- Exercise stimulates the brain to produce endorphins, your body's natural form of morphine. This increases your pain threshold and gives you a nice relaxing 'high'.

WALKING: THE SUPREME AEROBIC EXERCISE

Aerobic exercise is exercise that requires a lot of oxygen. Aerobic exercise should be vigorous, continuous, and involve the large muscles of both arms and legs (preferably simultaneously) in rhythmic contractions. (As you get fitter, you can build more muscle while you walk by carrying weights.) Walking fits all these categories and it is natural and convenient. Firstly pumping increased volumes of blood and oxygen keeps the heart muscle strong and the lungs working to full capacity. Exercise builds muscle strength and flexibility, bone mass, better cellular respiration and body shape. Cardiovascular fitness is most important by older people because it has the ability to lower the heart rate when active and when resting.

Anyone who is not disabled can walk regardless of their age, and it only requires a decent pair of walking shoes. Most experts agree that it is the perfect exercise for building cardiovascular fitness and strength after a heart attack. It's not hard on the joints and there is little risk of straining muscles and tendons. However it is still important to limber up by first doing some stretching exercises and taking some deep breaths, swinging arms and walking on the spot. Check your posture. Experts say the best posture for walking is chin tucked in, eyes ahead, square shoulders (rather than hunched or rounded) arms moving close to torso, stomach in and buttocks tucked in. Step off the toe of the back foot and strike the ground with the heel of the back foot. This allows a rolling action that keeps joints aligned and helps to prevent back problems. Using a wide stride lowers the body's centre of gravity, and rotates the hip joints. It also reduces the likelihood of falling.

For lower back problems alternate between the wide stride and a shorter stride. To get the benefits of a full aerobic workout keep elbows bent and pump arms backwards and forwards. This exercises the upper back and shoulders.

Other aerobic exercises are jogging, steady swimming, aerobic (or similar) classes, rebounding and cycling.

Exercises like tennis, golf, skiing, bowling, dance, tai chi, yoga, or gardening, are important in a fitness program and vital to enjoyment or creative outlets, but are not classified as aerobic because there may be a certain amount of waiting or standing around when the heart can slow down.

AEROBIC EXERCISING AT HOME

Exercising has never been so affordable and so convenient. Modern civilization ensures that you can aerobically exercise without ever leaving your house, with compact stepping machines, rowing machines, stationery bicycles, treadmill machines—all are available for purchase through mail order and department stores. Specialized exercise equipment outlets have them for sale and for hire at very reasonable rates. For as little as a few hundred dollars it is possible to have a mini gym at home or rent some equipment to see if it's going to suit you.

TRAINING

Everyone's heart has a maximum rate at which it can beat per minute, during maximum effort like aerobic exercise. This rate is largely determined by age. Calculate your maximum heart rate by subtracting your age from 220. (For example, if you are 70 years old, 220 minus 70 = 150). When exercising you should work your heart within 60 to 80 percent of this figure. But your absolute maximum heart rate during exercise should be 80 percent of that figure. Calculate this by multiplying your maximum heart rate by 0.80. (For example, if you are 70 years old, multiply your maximum heart rate of 150 x 0.80, which equals 120).

You can check your heart rate when exercising by taking your pulse for 10 seconds and multiplying the number of beats by 6. You can calculate your resting heart rate too. Most people's heart rate is between 60 and 90 beats per minute when resting. Through your exercise program, you are aiming to keep your heart rate in the lower margin.

Start with five or ten minutes of aerobic exercise a day for a week and build up to 10 minutes per day for a week, 15 minutes, 20 minutes, to whatever is comfortable providing your physician supports it. Gradually increase the speed of your walk and keep your stride wide and strong. Most health experts agree that maintaining cardiovascular fitness only requires exercising within your maximum heart range for 20 to 30 minutes per day, 3 times a week. That's a brisk two mile walk.

EXERCISE COUNTERACTS EFFECTS OF GRAVITY

As we go about our daily activity our internal organs are subjected to the downwards pull of gravity. We stand and move upright and spend hours sitting on comfortable chairs where our lower body muscles, which support our viscera, slacken and weaken.

Hardly surprising that the combination of gravity and weak lower body muscles contribute to degenerative illnesses of the lower body—prolapse of the bowel, bladder or uterus, hemorrhoids, hernias, ulcers, varicose veins and prostate problems. Many young people suffer from a sagging transverse colon which causes a build up of impactions along the wall of the descending colon and prevents food residue from passing freely through the colon to excretion. The resulting fermentation of food causes colitis, constipation and gas.

Most exercise should aim to keep our outer body toned and our hearts strong as well as strengthen the muscles that support our viscera. The following exercises are designed to tone the abdominals and to help reverse any lower body conditions.

Abdominal lift: standing: Place hands on thighs, hands facing inwards. Fully exhale. Draw in the abdominal muscles strongly and hold for 5 to 10 seconds. Inhale and release snapping the stomach out. Repeat 5 to 15 times daily.

Abdominal lift: kneeling: This position may not be comfortable for arthritis sufferers. Kneel, put elbows and forearms on the ground and rest your head on them. Exhale fully and then tighten the abdominal muscles. Release slowly, breathing in. Repeat 5 to 15 times daily.

Buttock raise - lying on back: Hands clasped at back of head. Exhale fully. Keeping soles of feet flat on floor, draw heels close to buttocks. Raise buttocks off floor as high as possible. Hold 15 seconds. Inhale slowly and lower buttocks. Repeat 5 times.

If health allows, lie on a slant board supported by a strong surface for 5–10 minutes a day. You can vary the degree of slant a little, as long as the head is lower than the feet. This is very helpful in reducing the effects of gravity. Alternately, if you are strong enough, incorporate into your yoga routine, the plough or half shoulder stand, which is a reverse position. Performed carefully (and to help the neck) most of the body weight can be taken across the top of the shoulders. This is also an ideal exercise for toning the viscera.

The easy version of a shoulder stand is as follows:

• Lie on your back and place outstretched legs against a wall. Pop a small cushion under bottom to slightly raise pelvis. (Elevating legs encourages the return of blood and the elimination of wastes through the lymph system.)

There is a yoga breathing technique which helps to reduce the effects of gravity. Sit comfortably. Take a deep breath. Let your chin fall to your chest closing off your glottis (which is the top of the trachea in the throat). Lock the muscles of your anus (and if a woman the pelvic floor) and tighten and pull everything upwards. Release the lower body lock and the glottis lock and breathe out. Practice 4 to 5 times daily. This will add energy to the body *but should not be practised by anyone with very high blood pressure or heart problems without their health advisor's consent.*

THE RISKS OF OVERDOING EXERCISE

Exercise is generally beneficial, but pushing yourself beyond your capacity even if you are extremely fit, can be detrimental.

Firstly a new exercise program, or any change in an exercise program, should be discussed with your health advisor who will probably test your heart and lung capacity and advise the type of exercise you should be doing.

With **coronary artery disease** (atherosclerosis) blood is forced through restricted arteries. If exertion is severe enough it can result in a temporary oxygen debt in the heart. This may cause breathlessness, an angina attack or, if heart cells die, the permanent damage of a heart attack. Unfortunately you can be extremely fit and an imminent fatality. In the United States coronary artery disease is one of the leading causes of exercise related deaths.

The following are signs that your body may be overstressed. If they occur you should decrease your activity and rest. If they are severe, or persist, consult your doctor.

- Lingering fatigue and tiredness, inability to complete a normal exercise program and heavy feeling in legs

- Lowered general resistance (swollen glands, persistent sore throats, colds, headaches, stomach upsets, diarrhoea)

- Loss of appetite or a significant change in elimination habits

- Weakness, dizziness (especially when getting up), nausea

- A significant decrease or increase in blood pressure during normal exercise

- Insomnia

- Breathlessness, difficulty in catching breath

- Feeling of pressure in the chest

- Pain of any kind, particularly chest pain, however slight

FREE RADICAL DAMAGE

Research in America has concluded that during exhaustive exercise free radicals are formed in muscle tissue (including cardiac tissue) beyond the body's capacity to neutralize them. Free radicals are a by-product of large quantities of oxygen being pumped around muscles. They occur also when blood that has been diverted to working muscles floods back into organs that were blood and oxygen deprived. There are a number of supplements which are useful to protect your cells against exercise induced damage.

SUPPLEMENTS

HERBAL

Both the herbs **ginkgo biloba** and **garlic** reduce the likelihood of clots and are a natural help if your condition requires blood to be kept thin. **Hawthorne** is also a natural heart stimulant and is thought to dilate coronary arteries. In Germany, where herbal medicine is more mainstream, Hawthorne is prescribed for abnormal heart rhythms and to alleviate cardiac complications, and angina attacks. Use heart herbs in quantities as prescribed by a naturopath and in conjunction with your doctor.

OTHER

- Potassium
- Vitamin B Complex
- Balanced multi-minerals
- Antioxidants *(prevent free radical damage of strenuous exercise for those exercising regularly within the upper level of their maximum heart rate.)*
- Vitamin E *(d-alpha tocopherol)*
- Vitamin C *(mixed ascorbates)*
- Vitamin A *(Beta Carotene)*
- Selenium

ALL IMPORTANT FLEXIBILITY

Flexibility is about keeping the muscles stretched and strengthened to allow a full range of movement. It allows you the freedom to make the daily transition from inactivity to vigorous activity without strain or injury.

As we age we expect the decline of our mobility, strength and coordination, the onset of stiffness, aches, pains and often the degeneration of arthritis.

Part of the problem is that, for many elderly people—as well as middle-aged and young people—the desire for activity and movement declines. Staying put in your favorite armchair with a little bit of activity here and there sets up a vicious cycle. Unused muscles shorten and atrophy, creating poor posture which sets up mechanical imbalances in the hips, back and neck. These imbalances put body segments out of line causing further problems. Muscle tension and moving about with tightly held muscles can result in joint strain, damage to ligaments and cartilage and the deformity often associated with old age.

The ball and socket joints in the hips and shoulders, hinge joints in the knees and elbows, condyloid joints in wrists, pivot joints in the spinal column and gliding joints in the metatarsals of the feet are designed to allow movement while also providing support. Genetics predetermine much of our natural range of movement. But due to the erosion of the microscopic spaces that separate connective tissue fibres caused by inactivity and toxic build up, even those blessed with flexibility may stiffen. Stretching can prevent this and anyone that regularly stretches three times a week can considerably improve their range of movement.

To maintain flexibility a balanced daily program of static stretching is advised. The jerky motions of ballistic stretching and exercise, although useful for building strength, trigger a protective mechanism called the stretch reflex which causes muscles to contract in order to prevent injury.

STATIC STRETCHING

Static stretching is the slow pull of a muscle (or muscle groups) just beyond its normal length (about 10 percent) until you feel tension and mild discomfort but not pain. Hold the stretch for between 10 to 60 seconds. The gentleness of static stretching reduces the muscle spindle reflex action and allows full lengthening of the muscle. It is an ideal form of stretching for those with arthritis.

Static stretching is also mental. It teaches you to listen to your body and understand how it moves. As you stretch, your mind automatically focuses on the part of the body being stretched. This in itself is a valuable form of relaxation as it clears the mind of idle chatter and is one of the main principles of yoga. Sometimes due to tension, inactivity, activity and our conditioning, our muscles shorten with age, and we form mental limits and blocks. Try to make an effort to mentally elongate each muscle as you stretch it physically.

There is a grace and ease about people who stretch regularly. Fortunately even advanced cases of inflexibility like sunken chests and curvature of the spine can be reversed. The body is forgiving.

For those who are really stiff and suffering from arthritis it is advisable to start your stretching program before you get out of bed. Full length body stretches that elongate hands, arms, shoulders, torso, legs and feet may be helpful. You need to move, stretch and flex all of the muscles and joints you will need during the day, i.e. fingers, wrists, elbows, shoulders, upper back, neck, hip joints, knees and ankles. For lower back, pull knees up to the chest and rock from side to side.

YOGA

What we commonly refer to as yoga is only the physical aspect of yoga— Hatha Yoga, handed down from the wisdom of ancient Indian medicine. It translates into the physical, the control and harmony necessary for unity of self. It gives us certain exercises and breathing to benefit and treat individual parts of the body. Today it remains unchanged and in fact many modern stretching exercises are adapted from it. Its balanced system of static stretching is a form of relaxation and, because it impacts on the mind and parasympathetic nervous system, it is useful for controlling hypertension. It creates flexibility, and some people claim to control and even reverse arthritis with it.

The beauty of yoga is that it can be started off very simply. It is of little importance how old, stiff, tense or cramped you are. You only need to stretch as much as your body allows. But yoga activates the life force within, builds strength, brings renewed energy and naturally becomes easier. It is best to get a good teacher to learn. Once learned you can work away at it in your leisure time using books or videos. Most public libraries have information about local classes or of people interested in taking classes. People in retirement homes are in an ideal situation to pool some money and invite someone in for teaching.

RELAXATION

Stress is a result of our response to changes and demands that occur in our lives. Everyday changes in our thoughts and emotions, pleasant or unpleasant, can provoke stress—bad news, worry, annoyances, emotional conflicts and hostilities, the excitement of a new grandchild or going for a holiday. A typical stress response is increased activity in the nervous system and faster breathing, the result of adrenaline and other hormones into the bloodstream which increases the heart rate. Kept in balance, the stress response is a necessary part of life as it provides the stimulus to survive and the power to cope in difficult situations.

But the pace of twentieth century living means that people have to adjust to more demands and changes—noise, haste, activity, environmental pollution, time restraints, and so on. If the stress response is prolonged it throws the body/mind out of balance. People may find that their coping systems fail and they begin to feel overburdened and anxious. Chronic stress and anxiety are now common causes of physical illnesses. Symptoms of stress can range from physical and muscular tensions causing headaches, spinal and back problems, sweating, inability to relax, being easily moved to tears, nervousness, restlessness, fatigue, insomnia and heart, respiratory and intestinal illness symptoms. In its extreme form it is accompanied by anticipating the worst, fearfulness and thoughts of impending doom. Stress is stored in the body and over a period of time is proven to induce some serious illnesses.

With a holistic approach it is possible to control stress and its effects. It is a modern disease of the mind, body and soul. For many people, the natural state of relaxation has become unfamiliar and must be learned. The most important act of relaxation is making the time to be alone, to think, unclutter the mind, to become aware of your stress indicators. Think, dream, or watch the grass grow. The holistic approach combines simple relaxation techniques (including aromatherapy, music therapy, massage), meditation, exercise, breathing, proper nutrition, supplements, herbs, and self expression through creative outlets.

Actively practising relaxation can prevent everyday stress from accumulating and tipping you over the edge into a breakdown or depression.

Once you have internalized the ability to relax and the techniques of relaxing, they become part of you, easily called upon when needed. It is a way of mastering life and not being a slave to mental and emotional ups and downs. It also helps you to keep the balance between your parasympathetic and sympathetic nervous systems. When you are stressed your sympathetic nervous system is dominant. Balance means you have the drive necessary for life's challenges as well as the ability to slow down when necessary.

MAKING TIME FOR RELAXATION

Poor management of time will mean that you may never get time to relax. You may need to evaluate and identify your time robbers so that you can slot in your periods of relaxation. Knowing that you fritter away time, yet never get the benefits of being relaxed, can be quite stressful.

Time Robbers

- Telephone interruptions
- Crisis
- Lack of self discipline
- Procrastination
- Unrealistic time estimates
- Poor communication
- Fatigue
- Inability to say 'no'
- Attempting too much at once
- Demands from others
- Perfectionism to the extreme
- Lack of preparation
- Not listening properly

Decide which of the above stem from your personal nature and which are caused by others. Decide which can be controlled or eliminated, allowing time to slot in periods of relaxation.

OTHER TIPS FOR TIME MANAGEMENT

Spend a few minutes at the start of each day planning and prioritizing. Do not over schedule your day because you may have to accommodate forces beyond your control. Time spent in effective planning is time saved in execution. Putting unrealistic deadlines on yourself leads to indecision and procrastination. Divide large tasks into smaller blocks and allocate regular time to it. A 'do it now' attitude of getting distasteful tasks completed will give you a sense of relief. Every problem is not a crisis. Over-responding leads to anxiety, impaired judgement, hasty decisions and wasted time.

Below are simple relaxation and meditation techniques. However meditation does not make your problems disappear—only somewhat easier to deal with. Take time to explore what comes up during relaxation and after meditation.

SIMPLE RELAXATION

When simple relaxation is done methodically through the entire body on a daily basis it can bring a great sense of relief from tension—and prevent tension from accruing in the body.

Lie down or sit comfortably. Direct your attention to and physically tense, and then relax, each of the following muscle groups: Left foot, calf, thigh, right foot, calf, knee, thigh, buttocks, stretch out the hips, pelvis, waist, upper back, tense and stretch the shoulder and give them a good shake, gently rotate the neck with shoulders raised, tense the muscles in your scalp and screw up your face, stretch our your arms and bend your elbow, wriggle your fingers and shake our your wrists.

Take some full deep breaths, feel the heaviness of your limbs and body and allow yourself to sink further into the comfort of what is supporting you. Feel the coolness of the air going into your nostrils and its warmth coming out. If you drift off or fall asleep, all the better. When you are finished stretch luxuriously and slowly get up and go about your business. This relaxation can precede meditation or visualization.

SYMPTOMS OF RELAXATION

Heaviness, lightness, warmth, yawning, deeply sighing, softened muscles, breathing slower and easier and into abdomen, feeling open and calm, peaceful, letting your feelings flow and being able to cry if healing is needed, indicating emotional release.

MEDITATION

Once learned, meditation can be practised at any time. It can be used as a pick-me-up when you are tired, drained and busy instead of reaching for caffeine.

There are many different schools of meditation. The best advice is to select the type that suits you and develop your own unique way of meditating. Choose a quiet place where you are unlikely to be disturbed and take up a comfortable position with a straight back. This can be sitting in a chair, on the floor on a cushion, propped up on your bed with cushions, on a yoga stool, or if you are supple—in the yoga kneeling or lotus position. Try not to meditate within an hour after eating as you may feel sleepy. Meditation is best learned in a relaxed state so begin with simple relaxation or stretching. Equip yourself with music especially designed for meditation which goes beyond the emotional responses that can be provoked by even quiet classical music. Using meditation music and the ritual burning of incense or use of aromatic oils can induce more of a meditative feeling.

The basic technique for learning meditation is to find a point of focus either with eyes open (on a candle, flower or picture) or with eyes closed (the space between your eyebrows, your breathing, a mantra, a part of your body, an image of something pleasant). Begin by focusing on your breath. Feel the air cool as it comes into your nostrils and warm as it leaves. Count your breath one to ten (one-inhale, two-exhale) two or three times or gently direct your attention to your focus point. The heart chakra—the energy centre of your chest—is the spiritual centre in meditation. Feel yourself centered there also. If thoughts occur, detach and passively witness them floating by. If you become caught up in the anxieties of your body or psyche simply generate the desire to be free, breathe through the anxiety and let it go. Then gently bring your attention back to your focus point. The aim of meditation is to achieve release from the relentless churning of the mind. As we age we may accumulate data and fears and insecurities and become used to living in the intellect that has been subjected to years of stimuli. Initially it is hard to detach but well-being is beyond the mind and inside our own inner stillness. Everyone has experienced moments of pure stillness, peace and happiness. That's a glimpse into your own deeper self and into the world that meditation can open up. It can allow you to experience pure states of joy and bliss through your higher awareness.

The effects of meditation, if practised twice daily for between 10 to 20 minutes—are dynamic. The enforced stillness of the mind gives you back mental clarity, a better memory, energy, peacefulness and the contentment to experience the present moment and live in the 'Now.' The benefits to health are lower blood pressure and pulse rate, more relaxed breathing and less demand for oxygen, increase in alpha brain waves and decreased activity in the sympathetic nervous system. It can help you control anxiety, stress and even some physical conditions.

CHOOSING A MANTRA

Mantra meditation was originally taught by Indian sages to their students. Some suggestions for mantras are Shalom, Om, Ahmam, Rama, One, Shanti or Peace. Choose a sound that pleases you and experience it by saying it out loud a few times and then mentally say it each time you exhale. Feel it reverberating upwards from your heart chakra, out of your body and allow it to change, grow louder, feel closer, far away. It will become very important to you.

MUSIC AND WELL-BEING

Music has evolved into a healing therapy. Music therapy produces certain physiological changes in people. This includes decreased blood pressure and pulse rate, deeper more relaxed breathing, the activation of beta-endorphins (an immune response), and changes in brain waves and emotions. Hospital patients treated with music therapy are bothered less by pain, recover faster, relax more, breathe deeper, cope with anxiety on reduced medication, and experience peaceful mental images. In the 1960s Helen Bonny pioneered a form of music therapy called Guided Imagery and Music (GIM) which combines music with relaxation techniques to alter the state of awareness of a client. Then, to especially chosen music, the client is guided through a verbalized self revealing journey of mental imagery, spontaneous movement, emotions and other insights which open the door to healing and change. Simply focusing on pleasant or familiar music is an effective relaxation tool, great for reducing anxiety, a form of self expression and conducive to discharging tensions and emotions such as grief, fear, joy, etc.

Playing a musical instrument or singing for your own pleasure can be a marvellous way to relax, especially if you can improvise or learn a repertoire of pieces which are beautiful, but not too technically demanding. If you play music which you have created yourself, or something that you know so well that it has become a part of you, you can often experience a feeling of great relaxation. If you haven't yet learned to play a musical instrument, a recorder is a good first choice. It is easy to play and makes an attractive sound—as well as being cheap to buy. We are also now blessed with the recorded sounds of nature, flowing water, the sea, bird songs, and the sophisticated sounds of new age music. A new world of relaxation awaits you.

AROMATHERAPY

Essential oils which have been extracted from plants have been used as relaxants since ancient times. Aromatherapy is now also very much a modern relaxation therapy. When blended with massage oils and massaged into the body, used in the bath, or vaporized, they have a distinct effect on the mind, calming and relaxing it. Essential oils are readily available at health stores, body shops, or craft markets. Choose water-distilled, not solvent extracted, essential oils. *However, they should not be used during pregnancy except under professional advice.*

Suggested oils for treating stress are:

- Camomile   useful for insomnia—or just to relax
- Clary sage   useful for nervous tension and insomnia
- Hyssop   sedative and general nerve tonic
- Jasmine   antidepressant and pain reliever
- Lavender   eases headaches—it is also a relaxant
- Marjoram   useful for anxiety
- Orange flower useful for anxiety and depression
- Patchouli   useful for anxiety and depression
- Rose   calms anger and soothes the nerves
- Sandalwood   useful for anxiety and nervous tension
- Verbena   a nerve tonic
- Ylang Ylang   useful for anxiety and tension

Full body massage is one of the most relaxing things in the world and an effective way of dealing with tension in the body. Either learning massage with a partner, or having a massage with a fully trained massage therapist once a week or fortnight, is very effective in managing stress.

PERSONAL AND SOCIAL SUPPORT SYSTEMS

Having people that you can relate to well on a social and personal level is an important way of reducing your stress. It is great to have people to lean and cry on, laugh with and enjoy hobbies with. People with close personal friends to confide in have lower stress levels. Perhaps it is true that a trouble shared is a trouble halved.

Support systems can include family, friends and neighbors, religious groups, sports or hobby groups, self-help groups, 'retired' people's social networks, and travel groups. It can also be valuable to foster good relationships with your doctor, naturopath or herbalist.

Evaluate your situation and if necessary seek new areas of social support and foster new relationships.

SUPPLEMENTS FOR STRESS

- Vitamin B complex
- Balanced multi minerals
- Vitamin C

HERBAL HELP

- **Whole oat groats** (not rolled oats) cooked, as cereal or mixed in food, are a tonic for nerves.
- **Garlic** Kyolic Liquid with vitamin B1 and B12
- **Ginseng** reduces the damage caused by stress.
- **Siberian ginseng** is can also help your body cope with stress.
- **Skullcap, camomile** and **yarrow** are relaxing teas. (Use one teaspoon of dried skullcap leaves per cup of water or two teaspoons of camomile or yarrow in a cup of water).

CREATIVE OUTLETS

Self expression and hobbies are an important part of relaxation. When you become absorbed in something that is enjoyable and time passes without your realizing, it becomes a kind of meditation, **because you are enjoying the present moment**—experiencing the 'Now'. However if your creative outlets are also your income, be careful that they do not put burdensome time demands on you. Take a break when it becomes tedious and you become caught up in the anxieties of yesterday and the future.

Endorphins are part of a family of naturally occurring opiates made by our bodies. Activities that give you that 'thrill' (like listening to some sorts of music) or produce a 'high' are accompanied by secretions of endorphins in brain chemicals. Endorphins are also produced by exercise and many people become hooked on these safe endorphins. All the better, because research now proves that endorphins stimulate the immune system especially in the fight against cancer.

CASE STUDY 1

Vern and Marge are very healthy for their ages, 78 and 81 respectively, and they are both confidently looking forward to living into their 90s. Their recipe for health is a positive attitude, a sense of humor, a healthy diet and regular exercise. Seven years ago, when Vern was very depressed he was encouraged to take up exercise by one of his sons and he began 'staggering' around the block. Those early efforts snowballed to a fitness level that has enabled him to fast walk several half-marathons over the years, boasting a fastest time of 2 hours 37 minutes. Marge comfortably walks 5 kilometers or so with the Y's walking club once a week. She also accompanies Vern on his walks.

As they have grown older they have recognized that energy becomes more precious and they have put in place other good habits to preserve their well-being. Their morning exercise regime is an important part of this. They rise early and complete individual exercise routines—for Vern this can include up to 100 sit-ups. This is followed by breakfast, meditation and Yoga together. They clearly enjoy practising these healthy pursuits together and have recently taken up Tai Chi twice a week which they find both relaxing and invigorating. An active and enjoyable sex life is also important to them, and was enhanced when birth control no longer became an issue.

Their diet is both nutritious and simple comprising "a lot of vegetables," many of which they grow in their pesticide and commercial fertilizer–free garden. The rest of their diet is made up of fruits and grains like oatmeal and brown rice and a little bit of meat. They eat few refined foods and sugar, opting instead for a healthful acidophilus and bifidis yogurt and sometimes a have bit of ice cream as a treat.

Although they have a yearly check up with their doctor, their lifestyle has thus far resulted in their having little need for medical treatment. Over the past year with Marge's support Vern has become an author with a book entitled *A Darker Shade of Pale* which is a 100 year saga about romance and racism in New Zealand.

CASE STUDY 2

Frank is another fine example of an exceptionally healthy older person. At 81 he is active and remarkably free of arthritis and other diseases, which he claims has much to do with having had the right parents. A combination of good genes and healthy living habits has meant that over the years it has only been necessary for him to visit his doctor once a year—to renew his driver's license.

Twice a week before breakfast he power walks 10 to 12 kilometers which he follows with a hot shower (obviously an excellent combination to rid the body of toxins). He follows this up with a half a litre of water and later his usual impressively healthy breakfast of prunes, stewed apple and a small glass of orange juice, wheat bran, oatbran, and wheat germ with warm milk, porridge (no sugar), a cup of tea and a slice of toast and marmalade. Both he and his wife usually eat a lunch of mainly fruit and wholemeal sandwiches and a well balanced evening meal which includes meat four times a week. With an acquired taste for Greek yogurt, they now make their own. Frank's healthy diet—for which he praises his wife—and level of exercise (he also walks with the Y's walking club) allow him a daily treat of a light portion of dessert and a glass of wine without ill effect.

His fitness is evidenced by the fact that his average time for power walking a half marathon of 21 kilometers, which he regularly takes part in, is 2 hours

40 minutes. Power walking is the fashionable speed walking that is non-jarring to joints and ligaments and doesn't produce stress fractures that running can.

CHAPTER 7

A FEW WORDS ON DETOXIFICATION

The first victim in any war, as they say, is the truth. The fact that the idea of detoxification has not yet permeated through to a mass audience is stark testimony to that fact. People are encouraged to drink, smoke, eat to excess and essentially poison themselves with the effluent and accruances of an industrial machine that has tried to turn everything into a commodity.

It is profoundly significant that people are encouraged to think of themselves as 'consumers,' for at the same time that they busy themselves consuming the planet, they are in fact consuming themselves. Interesting, too, that we still think of cannibals as being 'primitive.'

After all these years it seems incredible that we still haven't got the hang of it. It's almost as though the 'death urge' is getting in the way of our ability to assimilate useful information, and instead is promoting through mass indoctrination its various addictions. To be perfectly honest, these addictions are basically different forms of suicide. In fact there are people of influence who make no apology for it and ardently promulgate the idea that "everyone has to die sometime" so you may as well smoke cigarettes, drink and eat to excess, drive recklessly and do other dangerous things, because it really doesn't matter. One radio commentator was heard recently disparaging the

idea that cellular phones may cause brain tumors with the above 'argument.'
"After all," he said, "you could get killed crossing the street."

If you are still among those fortunate few who believe in the power of love,
light, and forgiveness and who are interested in assimilating good
information into your daily routine, there is no substitute for detoxification,
whether it be fasting, yoga, saunas, hot pools, pure water, enemas or juices.

Many serious students of the aging process believe that aging has partly to do
with the buildup of toxins in the cells, toxins that the body struggles gamely
to eliminate, but, over time, the body is gradually overwhelmed. The often
repeated observation that these toxins can trigger various illnesses from
arthritis to cancer is borne out by various studies. "Every day a little older and
a little slower," sang The Beatles many years ago, and living on a typical
Western diet of the 20th century one can see the relevance of the song.

The truly insidious aspect of this slow poisoning is that it often helps to
prevent people from taking any constructive remedial action on their own.
The systemic toxic buildup promotes sluggishness, neurotic thinking,
unsupportable adaptations to the status quo, mental laziness, addictive
behavior, conformity and mental illness. Heavy metal poisoning such as from
lead, can alone lead to nearly all of these symptoms.

Unfortunately, most people have to wait until the onset of a devastating
illness before they are spurred into actually helping themselves to heal. The
trouble with waiting until sudden illness develops is that the doctors who are
usually called in to help the troubled patient themselves are steeped in the
philosophy of symptom abatement rather than immune building or the
regeneration of cellular vitality. In addition, by the time the symptoms
manifest, much damage has already been done to various organs. While the
body can regenerate most of the time given appropriate care and nurturing,
the person affected is usually content with merely having symptoms subside.

The modification of symptoms is often confused in Western countries with
"good health" and this confusion is encouraged by Western medical
practices, most of which have nothing whatever to do with strengthening the
immune system.

This is largely because orthodox medicine has over the past 100 years or so become dependent—addicted—to the pharmaceutical establishment, a gigantic web of conglomerates whose primary interest is in making money from disease. "Doctor, heal thyself" becomes a plea and a demand from the vast majority of people who have been exploited and discarded by a profession whose vow used to be "Above all, do no harm."

In fact the entire culture seems to conspire to denigrate those for whom good health is a priority. 'Health nuts' and 'health food faddists' are but two expressions of denigration hurled by those for whom our poisoned crops, water and air are "not a problem." It is only when some disaster strikes them or their family that they begin to question their assumptions and their support of a system that values property accumulation over the well-being of the planet. It is not until their own children begin to succumb to leukemia from living and playing near high tension power lines that they begin to ask serious questions of the system.

Perhaps, then, we should think of detoxification as beginning when we start to detoxify our thinking. To what extent are we trying to live by precepts that are untrue and which cannot stand the rigor of critical analysis? To what extent would we "rather not talk about it" or do we try to seal our thoughts off from self criticism. In an age of rapid breakdown or rapid change we often find ourselves seeking the salvation of instantaneous gratification or comfortable thoughts—or no thought at all. Are we merely managing a bad situation because we believe those who would persuade us of the power of the negative? Or are we still willing to set our house in order, starting with our own thoughts and attitudes.

FASTING

Long venerated as a practical way of detoxifying the body, fasting is often mentioned in the Bible as an appropriate technique for the maintenance of good health. Fasting was associated with holidays like "The Day of Atonement" on which Jews would fast and pray for forgiveness for the sins they committed over the past year. Fasting is extolled in the Moslem religion as well, and Jesus' time in the desert was also a time of fasting.

The idea that we need to give our bodies a rest from food is an interesting one, but one that makes sense when you try it. At first you feel just awful and may get headaches and nausea. Don't fast for more than a day or two when you're getting started, since you will be eliminating toxins (pesticides, additives, heavy metals, caffeine, etc.) that are stored in the liver, fatty tissue, the bowel and elsewhere. When you get serious about fasting you'll notice a marked improvement in your general energy level, your vitality and even your sexuality, as your body begins to thank you for caring for it in such a loving way.

Various experts on fasting recommend that you increase your fluid intake, especially carrot juice, pure water, other juices or potassium broth (potato soup, for example, as recommended by Dr Max Gerson). You will want to give your system as much help as it can get to detoxify itself, and there is no substitute for pure water. The juices supply sugars for energy, but water helps to flush the system.

Note: It is vitally important only to drink pure juices and pure water. Reconstituted juices are often made with water contaminated by chlorine and fluoride, alum, pesticides, etc. Do your body a favor. If you cannot obtain pure juices or water, join a group in your area promoting the removal of these harmful substances from your drinking water. Then go out and buy some spring water in a bottle.

SAUNA AND HOT POOLS

For untold thousands of years people have been using the power of dry heat to detoxify themselves. Sweating profusely is a great idea! It gets the heart rate up, it purifies the lymphatic system (emphatically!), it feels great, and it reinvigorates the 'third kidney'—your epidermis. Sweat lodges in North America, sweat huts in Scandinavia, even your local health club, are all places where you can find a half an hour of pure bliss, and if it feels good, chances are you should try it. Combining sauna (and a plunge pool) with exercise and massage are probably some of the most salubrious things to which you can treat yourself.

Can't find a sauna? A hot bath with mineral salts is one substitute, but try to end the bath with a cold shower or at least a lie down afterwards. Hot baths can sap your energy, so late night baths may not be a great idea, if your energy is already depleted from a hard day's work. If you must, try to limit the time you spend in the bath to under fifteen minutes.

Mineral pools are an excellent healing medium and can be found in virtually every country on earth. Having a holiday? Find a place with mineral pools. While the medical profession still doesn't understand why the pools are so good for you and therefore attributes your sense of well being to some 'psychosomatic' phenomenon, there are ample elements in mineral water that have well known healing properties. Sulphur, for example, is found in many hot mineral spas around the world. Sulphur is known for its healing properties, not the least of which is its anti–cancer activities. Just ask your local broccoli.

The skin is a permeable membrane and can and does absorb some of the minerals your body needs from the pools, however 'trace' the amounts. This is why it is so important to keep toxic materials away from the skin such as solvents, gasoline, glue and virtually all artificial (and many naturally occurring) chemicals.

Caution: If you have problems with your heart, you should use saunas or soak in hot mineral pools only with the permission of your health practitioner.

CHAPTER 8

SEX AND SENSUALITY

Contrary to the images fed to us in the media, an active love life is not just reserved for the young. Many older couples enjoy happy and healthy sex lives. Age, *per se*, is no barrier to sexual happiness.

At any age it is the quality of the relationship in which sex takes place which determines how satisfying a sexual relationship is for both partners. Therefore nurturing a loving relationship with your partner is the most important thing you can do to enjoy your sex life.

Communicating your needs to your partner about matters both sexual and nonsexual is the keystone to creating an honest and loving relationship. Unfortunately, many couples who have been together for a long time tend to take each other for granted and make less of an effort to communicate. As a result they may find that their sex life becomes a routine or stale. Fortunately if sexual relations have become less than satisfying, there are ways to revitalize your sex life.

One of the best ways to rejuvenate a sexual relationship is to make an **effort to make love into a sensual as well as sexual experience**. Try massaging your partner's body with a fragrant oil. This can be both nurturing for your partner as well as a physical 'turn on.' Other simple tricks which can add a new sensual dimension to your sex life include: creating a romantic candle–lit atmosphere in your bedroom; burning incense to create your own fragrant boudoir; or indulging in a purchase of sexy lingerie. Vitamin E or oysters can also enhance male sexual appetite.

The problem of boredom can be tackled by recreating the elements which made sex exciting earlier in the relationship. Pretending to be lovers or a courting couple can re-ignite the excitement. Instead of taking regular—if less than passionate—love making for granted because you have been together for so long, plan dates which will bring you closer together in a more exciting setting than your usual domesticity. Make an effort to dress to please your partner and share a morning, afternoon or evening in a way you will both enjoy whether it is a movie, candle-lit dinner, or walk along the beach.

You could even try driving to the top of a quiet hill, by the seashore, or anywhere else that's reasonably secluded and 'make out' in the car the way you might once have when you were teenagers before you went 'all the way.' The idea is to expand your social and sexual relationship into new and stimulating spaces.

If you are a single person in the 1990s and beyond, sex becomes a slightly different proposition. Perhaps one of the best things about sex as you age, for women at least, has been that you no longer have to worry about unwanted pregnancy, and are free to enjoy your sexuality, without taking contraceptive precautions. Unfortunately, single men and women of all ages and sexual preferences in the 1990s and conceivable *(forgive the pun)* future, have to consider the threat of HIV and AIDS when considering making love. Condom use is recommended for intercourse and also fellatio, since body fluids such as semen and vaginal fluids can contain the HIV virus. Condoms, preferably lubricated with the spermicide nonoxynol–9, which kills the HIV virus, help to prevent transmission of the virus although they do not offer total protection. Totally safe sex includes massage and mutual masturbation, bathing together and other activities which do not allow for the exchange of bodily fluids. Your local Planned Parenthood Association Clinic, Sexual Health Clinic or MD can give you up to date information about safer sex practices. If you are not in a long term monogamous relationship, it is also a good idea to have regular checks for other sexually transmitted diseases. Even if you have passed the stage in your life where a sexually transmitted infection could result in the loss of your fertility, other diseases such as syphilis require prompt treatment.

SEXUAL HEALTH ISSUES FOR MEN

Other sexual health issues for men include inflammation of the prostate gland, as well as prostate cancer. These topics are discussed in the chapter "Prostate Disorders." Some men who have seldom or never had any trouble with achieving an erection earlier in life may begin to experience problems with gaining an erection later in life. Men in this situation are more likely to be suffering from a physical problem, rather than emotionally caused impotence.

IMPOTENCE

As they grow older, many men experience difficulties in maintaining erections. This is due in some part to declining levels of the sex hormone testosterone, but impotence is not necessarily a part of the aging process. Healthy men can maintain an active sex life into their 80s and older and many do.

Testosterone is manufactured in the testicles, and in smaller amounts in the adrenals. The pituitary gland regulates blood levels. The sexual response requires the testicles to manufacture more testosterone. The message is sent via pituitary gland and travels through the brain, spinal column and nervous system. The problem occurs when the body is not maintained in a healthy state and either the testicles cannot manufacture enough testosterone or they simply do not get the message. Also one of the prime physical culprits in preventing a happy and eager older male from being able to have an erection is hardening of the arteries that lead to the penis, with the result that there is insufficient blood flow to produce and maintain an erection.

Psychological factors and fear can also play a role in impotence. Obviously once a pattern of impotence develops, it can be hard to overcome because of anxiety.

CAUSES

Probably the most common cause of declining sexual function is a declining state of health brought about by a high fat diet and sedentary lifestyle. It follows that coronary artery disease, lung problems, diabetes, arthritis and other diseases contribute to it. So do stress, depression and a damaged nervous system from accidents or strokes.

Alcohol decreases the body's ability to make testosterone. Alcohol and all substances toxic to the body will affect performance in the long term because residues accumulate in the vital organs. Cigarettes are responsible for the build up of deposits in the arteries, including those supplying the penis.

Some prescription drugs (tranquillizers, ulcer drugs, and beta-blockers) may affect sexual potency.

Blood levels of testosterone may decline when there is reduced demand for sex from a partner.

TREATMENT

- Enjoy a healthy diet. *(See chapter on Nutrition and Health)*

- Improve your fitness with a progressive exercise program.

- During sexual activity the heart rate may peak at 120 beats per minute. That's the equivalent to briskly walking up three flights of stairs.

Daily supplements that may assist:

- Vitamin E – 400 I.U. (Check with doctor if you have high blood pressure as vitamin E may increase it.)

- Vitamin C – 1 to 5 grams.

- B complex preparation plus vitamin B6.

- Zinc – 80 mg (Do not take more than this amount).

- Jason Winters 'Golden Lion' formula – 3 tablets daily.

- Kyolic Aged Garlic Extract.

Other herbal, orthomolecular therapies and manipulation may be helpful. Consult a registered natural therapist.

Talk to your doctor about the possibility of reducing medication that affects sexual function.

Taking a course of Chelation therapy is often an excellent remedy for this problem. (See *the chapter on Chelation Therapy about this eminently useful therapy.)*

After ejaculation, it may take longer for an older man to develop another erection. None of these age-related changes, of course mean that a man's ability to satisfy his partner diminishes with time. Love making is not, or should not be, a race to achieve orgasm after orgasm, rather an expression of mutual enjoyment. A holiday together away from stress may help.

If necessary, seek professional help and counselling to address anxiety or any other psychological factors involved.

Practice meditation and relaxation faithfully. Stress and tension interferes with hormone function and circulation.

SEXUAL HEALTH ISSUES FOR WOMEN

After menopause, sexual health issues for women change, since the prospect of unplanned pregnancy is no longer a problem. Some of the sexual problems which women may experience during or after menopause such as reduced vaginal lubrication, and gradual thinning of the lining of the vagina are discussed in the chapter The Natural Approach to Menopause. If these problems are treated appropriately, and a woman has the support of a sensitive and loving partner they are unlikely to cause any long term disruption in her sexual life.

Older women do need to pay attention to other areas of their health, however, especially since the risk of developing cancer generally increases with age as toxins accumulate and the immune system becomes overloaded.

Women need to continue having regular cervical (pap) smears which can detect early changes in the cells of the cervix which may develop into cancer. If you have had a hysterectomy you may need to check with your doctor to find out whether you still need to have smears. Cervical smears are recommended to be taken every two years, unless you have had past abnormal smears, or cancer. If this is the case it is recommended that you have a smear annually.

Cervical smears can be performed by your MD, or in some cases, by a specially trained nurse or midwife. If your MD is a man, and you would rather your smear was taken by a woman, your local Planned Parenthood Clinic may be a good place to have a smear taken, since the female doctors and nurses at these clinics take a lot of smears and are well practised and at ease with this part of their job.

Participating in a cervical smear screening program, however, does not give you a guarantee that any precancerous or cancerous changes in your cervix will be detected. Depending on the circumstances the false negative rate on a cervical smear can vary from 20–30%. This means that up to 25% of smears taken will fail to diagnose an existing abnormality. There is also a 10% chance of a cervical smears returning a false positive result and diagnosing an abnormality where none really exists.

You can maximize your chances of the cells on your cervix being as easy as possible for the laboratory technician to read by not having intercourse 24 hours before your cervical smear appointment, and not using vaginal products such as thrush treatments, douches or spermicide for 48 hours prior to your smear being taken. However, if you find it impossible to fulfil these conditions, don't cancel your appointment. A less than optimal smear test is better than none at all.

Regardless of whether you have smear tests regularly or not, if you experience any suspicious symptoms such as otherwise inexplicable abdominal pain, bleeding between menstrual periods or bleeding after intercourse after you have completed the menopause, you should see your doctor promptly.

(See Suggested Reading, Appendix B for more useful information about cervical smears.)

CHAPTER 9

MEDICAL TESTS

HOW ACCURATE AND HOW SAFE ARE THEY?

If you are one of the many people who has assumed that medical tests are universally accurate and safe, think again.

Take the case of the stress electrocardiograph test, used to diagnose heart disease. The equipment used to perform this test is impressive, but the information gained from it is as often misleading as it is helpful. The stress electrocardiograph involves the patient walking on a treadmill, pedaling a bicycle, or performing some other vigorous form of exercise, while his or her heart's activity is recorded.

The stress electrocardiograph will only aid diagnosis of unsuspected heart disease of those people who suffer from it less than 50% of a time. So, people who wrongly believe that having "passed" the ECG (electrocardiograph) test, that they don't have to worry about heart disease, may not follow an appropriate treatment plan for heart disease, and may suffer as a result. Moreover, the test also has a very high false positive rate. It can indicate that heart disease exists—when it actually does not exist—almost 70% of the time. This not only means great stress for those people who are wrongly diagnosed as having heart disease, it may also mean that their doctor recommends unnecessary drug therapy, or surgery, to cure a nonexistent disease!

A study (published in the New England Journal of Medicine) of 2,000 people who had an ECG test concluded that this test was "useless" for predicting heart disease.

There are also dangers inherent in taking an exercise ECG test in itself.

At least four people out of every 10,000 people who take an ECG stress test will have a heart attack during the test, and one of these people will die while the test is performed.

So, what can you do to protect yourself against the danger posed by some medical tests?

Your best protection is information about the risks and benefits offered by a particular test. To find out what you need to know you should question your doctor carefully.

The first question you should ask is: "Why do I need this test?" If your doctor can't give a satisfactory answer to this question, don't take the test.

If you are satisfied with the reason why you need a test, then question your doctor more closely about the test. Ask: "What is the accuracy of this test?" A poor test is one which is able to correctly diagnose the presence of a disease 80% of the time. In medical language such a test is said to have 80% sensitivity. A test is considered to be "good" if it is correct 95% of the time. There are very few tests which are 100% accurate.

As a general rule, avoid any test which offers you less than 80% sensitivity. Even a test which offers 80% sensitivity will be wrong (that means failure to diagnose a disease) in 20 out of 100 people who take the test.

The other factor you need to know in order to judge a test's accuracy and significance is called its specificity. A test with a relatively low specificity, say 80% will wrongly show the presence of a disease, when no disease actually exists, in 20% of the people who take the test. A test with a 93% specificity, for example, will give a false positive result in only 7% of people tested.

Once you know how often a medical test you are advised to take is right or wrong, question your doctor further: "Are there any other factors which can affect the accuracy of this test?"

For example, a blood test for syphilis may return a false positive result for a number of diverse reasons. These include: the person has, or is recovering from, pneumonia; glandular fever; some kinds of anaemia; lupus and other diseases. The same test can also give a false positive result if the person uses narcotics.

Other tests, such as some enzyme evaluation tests can show a false positive result in a healthy person who takes moderate exercise.

Once you have established how accurate a test is likely to be, you need to establish if there are any likely side effects of the test, such as an adverse reaction to a dye, injury by a medical instrument, or death. It is wise to consider that in every procedure which requires general anesthesia, there is a risk, albeit a small one, that you will never wake up and die on the table. It may be possible to use acupuncture instead of injected or inhalant anesthesia if you have liver disease, or any other condition which makes chemical anesthetics particularly risky for you.

Your doctor should be able to supply you with information about any possible risks associated with a test which you may choose to submit to, and he or she should also give you a good idea of how often each sort of problem is likely to occur (i.e. in 5% of people who take the test).

If your doctor recommends any sort of test which is invasive or carries a high rate of risk, ask if there is another way that the test can be performed. For example, one way to test for the presence of gallstones involves the following procedures: swallowing tablets containing a special chemical dye which are supposed to concentrate inside the gallbladder, and then being X-rayed over the gallbladder area. If you're lucky, this test will reveal the presence of gallstones in your gallbladder. I write "if you're lucky", since the accuracy rating of this test averages between 13 and 30%. For this dismal rate of diagnostic success, you expose yourself to a large amount of harmful radiation. What's more 1 out of every 20 people who take the test, i.e. 5%, experience a dangerous side effect, such as a severe breathing problem or kidney failure. Moreover, there are a significant number of people who have such a severe allergic reaction to the dye that they die as a result of this test.

The good news is that there is a much more effective and safer test to diagnose gallstones. It's called cholecystosonography and it uses ultrasound to visualize gallstones. This test has an accuracy rate of 97%. However, the less effective X-ray technique is still used in some hospitals.

A word of caution: most medical tests are inaccurate to some degree.

This short chapter is obviously not the final word about medical tests, but perhaps it will raise your awareness of some of the possible negative consequences of common medical tests, so that you will be vigilant in questioning your doctor in order to avoid the most ineffective and hazardous.

(See Suggested Reading, Appendix B for recommended books on the subject of medical testing.)

"Your first time in a theater—hey, that's a coincidence!"

CHAPTER 10

PRESCRIPTION DRUGS

Prescription drug use has grown tremendously within the last forty years. While this is great for drug companies' profits, the overconsumption of prescription medicines can be hazardous.

Older people tend to use more prescription medicines than younger people. In fact, people fifty years and over make up only a quarter of the U.S. population, yet consume one half of all prescription drugs. Even more significantly, people sixty-five years and older use, on average, three times as many prescription medicines than people younger than sixty-five.

Unfortunately, the same older people who consume the greatest amount of medicines are also most vulnerable to side effects. One large study of older people admitted to hospital, showed that drug-induced problems were responsible for ten percent of admissions.

Adverse drug reactions are believed to be more common in older people for a number of reasons. These include gradual shrinking of the liver, and often (not always!) a decline in its ability to metabolize drugs. Poor kidney function can also be a factor. Kidneys which are less efficient take longer to excrete drug by-products. This may mean smaller doses of drugs are advisable. Kidney function can be tested and this information used to prescribe an appropriate dosage.

Another problem faced by older people who use prescription drugs is that their organs and other body systems become sensitized to the effects of drugs. Sedative drugs such as Valium (diazepam) or Dalmane (fluazepam) have a greater effect as the brain becomes sensitized to them. This can lead to older people who are taking a normal dose of these drugs being over-sedated. This can be dangerous for several reason—people who are over-sedated tend to become more sedentary, and lose fitness. A lack of fitness can reduce physical confidence and mobility. A person who falls under these conditions may not be able to break the fall in time to avoid a hip fracture.

Apart from physical problems caused by over-sedation, there are of course mental ones.

People who are over-sedated are less likely to exercise their mental faculties and may suffer a decline in intellectual function through not using their brain. Even worse, drug-induced confusion or stupor may be mistaken for senility and result in unnecessary hospitalization.

A further problem with the use of tranquilizers is that age-related differences in drug distribution in the body may mean that it takes longer for adverse effects to show up from a 'normal' dose of the drug which didn't cause problems at first. Thus problems such as confusion may occur several weeks after taking a daily dose of a tranquilizer.

Many doctors prescribe drugs without taking enough time to talk to their patients about their dosage rate, or any potential problems.

Therefore if you want to be better informed about your prescription medicines, it will probably be up to you to take the initiative and question your doctor. Or even better, your local library has a copy of a good prescription manual or the PDR (Physician's Desk Reference) which will tell you many of the 'side effects' of various drugs.

Most of the following questions are those suggested by the National Council on Patient Information and Education, an American nonprofit organization which aims to improve communication between patients and health professionals. We have added some additional questions to their list:

Question 1: What is the name of this drug? What is it supposed to do?

Question 2: How and when do I take it—and for how long?

Question 3: What foods, drinks, other medications, or activities should I avoid while taking this drug? This question could literally save your life, since some drugs interact with other drugs causing fatal reactions. People who are seeing more than one medical professional, such as an MD and a specialist, should ensure that each practitioner is aware of the other's prescriptions. Many cases of medical misadventure have been caused through a lack of communication between doctors. For example, if you are taking Seldane for an allergy and you also take Nizoral for candida, you could have a fatal heart spasm.

The combination of Tylenol and the anticoagulant Coumadin can also be fatal. Tylenol blocks the necessary destruction of Coumadin by the liver, which can result in a possibly fatal hemorrhage.

A report by Alfredo A. Sadun, professor of neurosurgery at the University of California, has warned that taking Tagamet "can make a person 100-1000 times more sensitive to organophosphate poisoning."

The list of dangerous drug combinations is almost endless. Always question your doctor if you are prescribed more than one drug. Remember to tell your doctor if you are using any over–the–counter or nonprescription drugs, no matter how innocuous they may seem.

Also ask: Do you know how this medication might interact with my vitamin/mineral supplement, or herbal medicine? Some nutrients can act against drugs, making them ineffective. e.g. taking vitamin B6 will prevent L–Dopa (a drug used to treat Parkinson's Disease) from working.

And: How will the drug affect my nutritional status? (Some drugs such as the Pill and HRT can cause multiple nutritional deficiencies. Some anti-epileptic drugs can produce folate deficiency, for example). Commonly used nonprescription drugs can also have an adverse effect on your nutrition—aspirin, for example depletes your body of vitamin C.

Question 4: Does this drug have any side effects? What are they? What should I do if they occur?

Question 5: Are the risks really justified with this disease? Would you take this medication if you were suffering from the same illness that I am? (If your doctor is honest with you, the answer may surprise you. For example, a number of surveys have shown that the majority of doctors would refuse chemotherapy if they had cancer.)

Question 6: Is there a natural tendency for the body to overcome or correct this disease if I choose not to take this prescription?

Question 7: Is there any written information available about the drug?

Written information about a drug is important, since unless you're good at taking notes, or have a great memory, it will be difficult to remember all of the information you need to know about a particular prescription drug. If you are taking more than one drug, it may quickly become impossible to keep up with all the details.

There are usually two different types of information about drugs. Some manufacturers produce pamphlets about their products intended for patients. These tend to be written in simple (or very simple) English and contain only very basic information about the drug. They may also be misleading, since they are designed to sell the drug to the patient, by soothing any health and safety concerns he or she might have. Hence they could tend to play down potential side effects and risks.

More objective information can be found in *The New Ethical,* a book which both your doctor and pharmacist will have on hand. Photocopy the relevant pages and take it home for your records.

Some prescription drugs are over-prescribed or misused. One of these is the antibiotic class of drugs. In American Congressional hearings related to the misuse of prescription drugs, it was determined that 40-60% of all antibiotics were improperly prescribed. This figure is probably similar in most western countries using drug therapies of this type. In fact, the World Health Organization has suggested their use should be reduced urgently.

It has also been reported in the USA that 50% of antibiotics produced actually enter the human body via the food chain, because they are used to treat sick animals, as well as being routinely added to many animal food stuffs.

Antibiotic overuse has encouraged bacteria to develop resistance to many commonly used antibiotics. This necessitates the development of new, more powerful drugs to combat these 'superbugs'.

One of the most dangerous medical abuses of antibiotics is in the treatment of viral diseases. Antibiotics have no effect on viruses, and in fact, antibiotic drugs are toxic and destroy the natural bacteria living in harmony with your body. This can aggravate the situation to the degree that when the disease abates, the patient is left with post viral syndrome.

The side effects of antibiotics can include: inflammation of the digestive system—which can lead to diarrhoea; liver and kidney damage and allergies. In fact, some antibiotics can be taken for a number of times without apparent side effects, and then, without warning, cause a reaction that can kill.

In fact, in a Congressional Hearing which took place in 1994, Mitchell Zeller of the FDA revealed that **the 'normal use' of prescription drugs was responsible for 150,000 deaths each year.**

In addition to this shocking number of drug-induced deaths, many nonfatal drug side effects can be surprisingly severe. In a recent report by the health research group of the consumer organization Public Citizen, some startling reports of FDA-certified 'safe' drugs were reported.

- Each year, 61,000 older Americans develop drug induced Parkinsonism.

- 32,000 hip fractures are caused by drug related falls.

- 163,000 Americans develop drug-induced memory loss, or impaired thinking.

- More than 243,000 people over the age of 55 are hospitalized each year because of adverse drug reactions.

- More than two million elderly Americans are addicted to minor tranquilizers and/or sleeping pills.

With statistics like these perhaps the best strategy of all is to avoid the use of prescription drugs as much as possible. Older people tend to use drugs to treat or relieve the symptoms of arthritis, high blood pressure, heart failure and diabetes.

If you suffer from any of these conditions, you may well be able to use some of the non-drug therapies described in this book. For serious problems, seek professional advice from a registered naturopath or other practitioner of natural medicine. Improving your nutritional intake and lifestyle is, in the long run, a better way to stay in good health than taking drugs to suppress or moderate the symptoms of disease.

There should be a number of books available through your public library system about prescription drugs and their effects if you feel you need more information about a specific drug.

"Is there a Naturopath in the house?"

CHAPTER 11

VACCINES

PROTECTION OR PROTECTION RACKET?

Every autumn, advertisements are placed in local newspapers and in the windows of some medical clinics urging people to protect themselves against influenza by submitting themselves for vaccination. Elderly people and those with chronic illnesses such as heart disease and diabetes are particularly targeted in the drive to vaccinate.

If the scientific evidence proved that vaccination against influenza was safe and effectively protected the people threatened by influenza, offering immunization to people with compromised immune systems would be wise. However, the effectiveness of the vaccines used to combat influenza can vary widely. Even more worrying is that people with medical problems such as diabetes, who are also the most likely to be offered the vaccine, may also be the most likely to suffer side effects.

WILL HAVING A FLU SHOT PREVENT YOU FROM CATCHING THE FLU?

One of the first things to consider if you are offered a vaccination against influenza is that while it may (or may not) protect you against various strains of the influenza virus, it has no effect against other viruses. Both the rhino virus and adeno virus can produce the classic 'flu' symptoms of fever, headache, runny nose, stomach ache, diarrhoea and aching muscles. Having a flu shot will not necessarily protect you against a flu-like illness. To protect yourself against these viral infections, it is wise to support your immune system.

Avoid getting chilled, stressed or malnourished since these are factors which can predispose to viral infections.

A NEW 'SUPERFLU'—IT COULD BE COMING TO YOUR TOWN SOON

A further point to consider when thinking about being vaccinated is that the influenza vaccine, even if it is effective against the influenza strains it is designed to combat, may not protect you against newer or mutant strains of the influenza virus.

In 1992, Dr Adrian Gibbs, Australia's National University Microbiologist spoke out publicly about the danger of a new 'superflu' evolving. Dr Gibbs explained to reporter Simon Troeth of the *Sunday Herald-Sun* that as the human population grew larger, so did the microbial population, increasing the "chances of parasites throwing up more deadly mutants." Dr Gibbs cited the example of a mutant virus which almost destroyed the Australian State of Victoria's poultry industry earlier in the year. That particular flu virus was stopped only with the destruction of 17,000 chickens from a farm near Bendigo, Victoria. A 'superflu' which affected humans would obviously be more difficult to control.

Current flu strains cause only mild to moderate illness in people who are normally healthy. However in people with impaired immune systems, the influenza virus may weaken the body enough to leave it vulnerable to complications like pneumonia which can be life threatening.

A new 'superflu' epidemic, should it occur, could endanger the lives of many more people than those who are already in poor health.

According to Dr Gibbs, it is the nature of the influenza virus which creates the risk of a 'superflu' developing. A strain of the virus which infects birds' digestive systems (ducks are a major carrier of influenza viruses) could infect a pig which is also carrying a human flu. Since the influenza virus has separate genes—something which makes it unusual among viruses which tend to have their genes all in one piece—it would be possible for a virus to evolve which has the genes to affect humans, but an outer sheath derived from the bird virus. Such a flu virus would be unrecognizable to the human immune system and could kill by causing massive internal bleeding.

Dr Adrian Gibbs is not alone in warning about a potential 'superflu'. His colleague, Professor John Laver, who, in 1992 worked at the John Curtis School of Medical Research in Australia said that should a 'superflu' evolve, it would "make AIDS look like a picnic." He added that vaccinations would be almost useless as a weapon against such a virus.

EFFICACY OF CURRENT INFLUENZA VACCINES

So, being vaccinated against the flu is most unlikely to offer you any protection against any 'superflu' which may develop. How effective have influenza vaccines been against the strains of influenza they are designed to protect you against?

The Morbidity and Mortality Report from the US Center for Disease Control discusses a study of the population of a nursing home in the winter of 1989–1990. Some of the residents were vaccinated against influenza A, the predominant viral strain at the time, in the month of November and the first two weeks of December 1989. Fifty-six percent of the residents were vaccinated. The residents who were vaccinated and those who were not were roughly matched for age and gender as well as for underlying problems such as congestive heart failure.

As expected, an influenza epidemic hit the hospital after the first half of December and continued until the end of January. Twenty-one of the 114 (19% of the residents) who had been vaccinated, experienced an influenza-like illness during this time. Of the 88 residents who had not been vaccinated, 14 suffered from an influenza-like illness—a total of 16%. (Swabs taken from residents confirmed that the organism responsible for the illness was an influenza A virus similar to the killed influenza virus contained in the vaccine.)

So, on a percentage basis, more of the people who had been vaccinated suffered from the influenza strain than those who had not been vaccinated. Nursing home figures showed that the efficacy of the vaccine in preventing illness was just 20%, with a 95% confidence level.

The only benefit that those people who had been 'immunized' against the influenza virus seem to have received was a shortening of their illness. The 'average' vaccinated resident was sick for six days. The average non-vaccinated resident, on the other hand was ill for eight and a half days.

After January 12, 1990, the Washington Department of Health ordered nursing home staff give the drug amantadine as a prophylactic against the flu. Ninety three percent of the residents received the drug in a 100 mg dosage every day. The dosage was not adjusted according to the individuals' kidney function. The medication was given to vaccinated and non-vaccinated residents alike. It seemed effective as a flu preventative, since the number of new cases dropped from an average of 1.6 per day, to 0.3 per day after residents began taking it.

However, some people who took the drug did suffer an adverse reaction to it. Three percent of residents who took the drug suffered from unpleasant symptoms such as anorexia, dizziness, insomnia, agitation and hallucinations. It is possible these side effects may have been avoided had the residents' kidney function been tested prior to the administration of the drug and the dose adjusted downwards if necessary. However despite the potential adverse effects of this drug, The Centre For Disease Control in the USA recommends the use of this drug for every member of nursing homes during an influenza outbreak, regardless of whether the individual has been vaccinated or not—indicating a rather strong lack of confidence in the efficacy of the influenza vaccine.

Failure of influenza vaccination to protect against illness is not limited to older people, or those who are chronically ill. A study of a boarding school population in the January 1990 *British Journal of General Practice* reported that 39% of children who had been vaccinated twice caught the influenza strain they were supposedly protected against, while only 31% of the children who had never received an influenza vaccination became ill.

SIDE EFFECTS OF INFLUENZA VACCINATION
IN PEOPLE WITH UNDERLYING ILLNESS

A letter by Dr. Peter Daggart of Great Britain published in *The Lancet* (February 8, 1992) expressed his concern at the adverse reactions suffered by patients under his care following the administration of an influenza shot. He wrote: "I have so far this winter admitted six patients (to the Staffordshire General Infirmary) with diabetes, all who have become acutely ill within 24 hours of influenza vaccination. Every winter I hear complaints from diabetics that they have been made ill by the influenza vaccination. Their symptoms have included generalized myalgia (aches and pains), a frozen shoulder at the site of the injection and instability in their diabetes." Dr. Daggart concludes his letter by stating he no longer routinely recommends influenza vaccination to people with diabetes.

The same issue of *The Lancet* includes two other letters by doctors concerned about the lack of protection—if not actual harm—the influenza vaccination offers to people with asthma. Doctors Wajahat Hassan, Allan Henderson and Niall Keanney of Great Britain's Royal Infirmary reported cases where an asthmatic who received an influenza vaccination needed assisted ventilation in the intensive care ward after the inoculation. The same writers warn that the commonly used vaccines have "many side effects," and that should they consider vaccination necessary for a person who has unstable asthma, and a history of experiencing an exacerbation of that asthma during viral upper respiratory tract infections, they would recommend a more highly refined sub-unit vaccine. These doctors also stated that "We do not recommend an annual influenza vaccine in stable asthmatics because of side effects."

NUTRITION AND IMMUNE RESPONSE

It is well known that adequate nutrition gives an individual a better chance of fighting off an infection. On the other hand, people who are poorly nourished are more likely to succumb to an infection.

Human (and animal) response to the immune threat posed by the influenza vaccination appears to be also influenced by nutrition. Pioneering nutritionist Adele Davis reports in her book *Let's Have Healthy Children* that volunteers who were known to be deficient in vitamin B6 and pantothenic acid (vitamin B5) who were given diphtheria toxin were not able to produce any antibodies. Rats given the same toxin when they were deprived of adequate protein, vitamin A or any one of the B complex vitamins became much sicker than those who received a nutritionally complete diet.

It is quite possible that the failure of vaccines, at least in some cases, may be attributable to the poor nutritional status of the recipients. This would seem particularly likely in the case of people living in nursing homes and boarding schools, since both of these institutions are notorious for serving overcooked, vitamin-depleted food. It would also seem plausible that those people with poor nutritional status would be most likely to suffer adverse reactions as a result of being vaccinated. Quite simply, a body which is not properly nourished is less able to meet any sort of immunological challenge.

CONCLUSION

Your best defence against any of the influenza viruses is good nutrition, enough sleep, adequate exercise to oxygenate your body—and avoiding getting chilled. With the known effectiveness of the influenza vaccines ranging from as low as 20% to a maximum of 80%, you cannot rely upon them to protect your body from the common strains of influenza, let alone any 'superflu' which may occur at any time.

'Immunization' with killed viruses injected subcutaneously poses a significant challenge to the immune system, since this route of virus particle transmission bypasses the body's normal defense in the mucous membranes and goes straight into the bloodstream. It is perhaps not surprising that people whose immune systems are already compromised—such as those with suboptimal nutrition or with chronic illnesses like asthma or diabetes—can react badly to this novel way of introducing viruses into their bodies.

For these reasons, it seems most wise to concentrate upon healthy living strategies as a protection against viral—and other illnesses.

SELF CARE FOR INFLUENZA

If you suspect that you are coming down with the flu, take as much vitamin C as you can until you notice your bowel movements beginning to loosen.

At this stage, reduce the dosage, so that diarrhoea doesn't result. Continue taking enough vitamin C to keep your bowels loose until all symptoms of the flu have disappeared. This strategy is frequently all it takes to detoxify a viral illness. For details of suggested dosages, see the section on 'Taking Vitamin C' in the chapter Nutrition and Health. Zinc and vitamin A have also been known to help. Stay within recommended dosages.

Secondly, increase your intake of Spirulina, Kyo-Green and fresh fruit and vegetable juices, as well as pure (unchlorinated, unfluoridated) water. Take adequate amounts of garlic and aged garlic.

Thirdly, go straight to bed without waiting for the flu to manifest. Often you will either moderate the severity of the illness or bypass it altogether.

"Actually, yes. I am a doctor!"

CHAPTER 12

CHELATION THERAPY

AN OVERVIEW

Chelation Therapy consists of a series of intravenous transfusions with a synthetic amino acid called EDTA (Ethylene Diamine Tetra-acetic Acid). Oral chelation therapy is discussed elsewhere.

EDTA has the ability to bond to metals such as cadmium, aluminium, mercury and lead which are toxic to the body. Once the harmful metals have been neutralized by the EDTA, they pass harmlessly through the kidneys and are excreted in the urine. Since the kidneys play an important excretory function, it is necessary to let your doctor know if you suffer from kidney problems—or ask that a test be done to determine their function. If your kidney function is impaired, it may be necessary to begin chelation therapy with a lower amount of EDTA. Chelation therapy can benefit kidney function in the case of people whose kidney disease has been caused by atherosclerotic buildup, or heavy metal poisoning.

Chelation Therapy is the standard treatment for lead poisoning in most western hospitals. It is also an excellent treatment for arteriosclerosis and atherosclerosis (hardening and blocking of the arteries). This is because the EDTA can remove the calcium which acts as a 'glue' binding cholesterol and other fats to the artery walls. As the calcium 'glue' is removed by the EDTA, the fatty deposits or plaques which block the arteries dissolve, resulting in improved circulation.

As well as removing heavy metals from the body and reversing atherosclerosis, chelation therapy has been reported to have good results in the following conditions:

- Stroke—chelation therapy has improved blood flow inside the brain in people who have suffered strokes.
- High blood pressure.
- High cholesterol.
- Poor circulation (cold hands and feet).
- Leg ulceration and gangrene.
- Intermittent claudication (leg cramp pain when walking).
- Irregular heartbeat.
- Diabetic retinopathy (damage to the retina of the eye suffered by people with diabetes). Using chelation therapy to treat this condition is more successful than laser treatments. Untreated, the condition of the eye generally deteriorates, leading to blindness.
- Macular degeneration of the eye.
- Rheumatoid and Osteoarthritis.
- Kidney Stones.
- Symptoms of Senility/early Alzheimer's.
- Tinnitus (ringing in the ears). Chelation therapy will only help this condition if it is caused by poor circulation, since tinnitus can be caused by other problems than reduced circulation.

In addition to the benefits of chelation therapy noted in medical literature, the following improvements have been reported by people who have used chelation therapy:

- Improved exercise ability.
- Improved heart function.
- Improved hearing and eyesight.
- Disappearance of small cataracts.
- Improved memory and mental perception.
- Symptoms of Parkinson's disease reduced. Parkinson's sufferers who have chosen chelation therapy report clearheadedness early on in their treatment program.

- Improved skin tone and texture. Other people report a reduction in brown spots (sometimes called age or liver spots) on their hands and face.
- Improved sexual function—the decline or inability to achieve an erection experienced by some men of 'middle age' and older, is often caused by a reduced blood supply to the penis, the result of atherosclerotic plaque gradually building up inside the artery which supplies blood to the penis until the penis receives insufficient blood to become erect.

Other benefits of chelation therapy include:

- Reduced blood viscosity and platelet stickiness.
- Improved prostaglandin metabolism.
- Removal of free iron which acts as a catalyst in free radical proliferation.

A study in Switzerland showed that people who took a course of chelation therapy because they suffered from lead poisoning had a much lower cancer rate than other people (with similar life-styles, etc) who had <u>not</u> had the lead removed from their bodies. Thus, it makes sense to think of chelation therapy as a possible cancer preventative, as well as to remove atherosclerotic plaque from the arteries.

If you decide to consult a physician who practises chelation therapy, choose a practitioner who is affiliated with the American College of Advancement in Medicine which lays down a strict protocol for its members, and routinely prescribes a multivitamins/mineral preparation to those undergoing chelation therapy.

ORAL CHELATION

Oral chelation is a viable and successful alternative to EDTA, and in some circumstances may be the preferred choice. Unlike chelation therapy with intravenous EDTA, which is relatively expensive, and requires regular clinic visits, oral chelation can be conveniently incorporated into your daily health routine.

Oral chelation can complement positive dietary and lifestyle to maintain—or improve—the health of your cardiovascular system, reversing degenerative changes caused by poor diet and bad habits.

Degenerative changes in the cardiovascular system are not normal, but are signs of premature aging. Studies of people living in more natural environments—and eating a natural diet—show that cardiovascular disease in these populations is a rare occurrence. The Hunza population, who eat a mostly vegetarian diet and get plenty of exercise routinely live to be more than 100 years. Likewise, the Polynesian people of the Pacific showed no signs of cardiovascular degeneration until they were introduced to a European diet and lifestyle, whereupon their health rapidly declined.

A properly nourished human body has the potential to both build healthy tissue, and breakdown unhealthy tissue, as well as detoxify waste and toxins. Chelation is a normal part of human physiology. This process has been recognized in plant and animal biology for over 30 years, and is an essential part of the biochemical processes involved in the digestion, assimilation and production of enzymes, hormones, the utilization of vitamins and enzymes, and the detoxification of chemicals, metals and toxins.

Chelation is a binding process, where one substance is chemically bound to another. An example of this is the utilization of iron, which is chelated in the form of hemoglobin to carry oxygen. If iron were not chelated in this way, it would be very toxic to the tissues. All of the minerals we ingest are powerful nutrients when complexed with amino acids.

The following nutrients can accelerate the natural chelation processes in the body. For maximum benefit, an oral chelation program should be supervised by a qualified health practitioner. However, the following recommendations can be safely incorporated into your daily schedule.

Exercise: Moving your muscles creates a powerful natural chelating substance in the form of lactic acid. This, combined with the increase in circulation created by vigorous exercise helps to remove toxic heavy metals from the tissues.

Vitamin C and Bioflavonoids: Vitamin C assists in transforming cholesterol into bile acids. It also assists in the detoxification processes of the body and the elimination of heavy metals. Vitamin C is essential to the formation of collagen and connective tissue, including blood vessels. It is important for iron absorption, and the production of folic acid. Since people—unlike most other biological beings—cannot produce vitamin C for themselves, it is important to take vitamin C daily. The daily requirements for vitamin C vary with the amount of stress, chemical ingestion and metabolic functions.

Aged Garlic Extract has been shown to assist in the removal of heavy metals from the blood. Various heavy metals (copper, mercury, aluminum and lead) were added to two sets of blood samples. These heavy metals ruptured the red blood cells in each of the samples. In the samples in which Kyolic Aged Garlic Extract was also added, no rupturing occurred demonstrating a protective effect from the Aged Garlic Extract.

Dosage: In order to achieve maximum benefits start with 500 mg daily. For higher dosages consult your naturopath or health professional. *Caution: If you take the oral contraceptive pill or Hormone Replacement Therapy do not take more than 500 mg of vitamin C daily.*

Vitamin B6 *(Pyrodoxine HCI)*: The conversion of the amino acid methionine to l-cysteine occurs in the presence of B6. The amino acid l-cysteine is a powerful detoxifier of heavy metals, protecting cells and mucous membranes. L-Cysteine is also a precursor to l-glutathionine which is one of the body's best free radical destroyers. It also plays an important role in oxygen utilization and insulin function.

When there is a deficiency of vitamin B6, methionine breaks down to homocysteine which is thought to contribute to the hardening and damage to the arterial walls and heart muscle and the deposition of cholesterol. Vitamin B6 is involved in more bodily functions than any other nutrient. It is vital for the production of hydrochloric acid, fat and protein absorption, and helps to maintain a healthy sodium-potassium balance.

Women taking the contraceptive pill or Hormone Replacement Therapy should ensure that they take this vitamin as these hormonal medications depletes bodily reserves of B6.

Dosage: 250 mg daily.

Niacin *(Vitamin B3)*: This vitamin is an important chelating nutrient. It improves circulation, as it is a vasodilator and also thins the blood. It contributes to the production of coenzymes necessary for carbohydrate metabolism. It also reduces cholesterol deposits within the circulatory system.

Dosage: 100 mg daily.

Vitamin E *(D-alpha tocopherol):* This fat soluble vitamin is a powerful antioxidant. It prevents cell damage by inhibiting lipid peroxidation and quenches free radicals. It is essential for healthy circulation and promotes normal clotting processes while improving oxygenation of the blood and tissues. Vitamin E also reduces platelet stickiness and thus improves circulation in the capillaries, important for effective chelation.

Dosage: Take only natural Vitamin E in the form of D-alpha tocopherol— 200–800 mg daily. *Caution: If you have high blood pressure or rheumatic heart disease, take Vitamin E only under professional supervision.*

Selenium: This trace element is a powerful antioxidant which boosts the immune system and protects against free radical damage. When selenium is combined with vitamin E, it aids the production of antibodies as well as helping to maintain healthy heart muscle. An adequate intake of selenium helps to ensure body proteins are synthesized correctly. Many soils are deficient in selenium.

Dosage: 100–200 mcg daily.

Magnesium: Magnesium is capable of displacing calcium in the cells of the body; therefore it is an excellent chelator for hardening of the arteries. This calcium buildup contributes to the loss of flexibility in body tissues. Magnesium has a relaxing effect on tissue, and also prevents spasms. In this respect its action is somewhat similar to the cardiac drugs known as calcium channel blockers. Magnesium is also vital for the activity of enzymes needed to digest or break down food or tissues. Vitamin B6 combined with magnesium dissolves calcium phosphate stones.

Dosage: 1000 mg daily.

Manganese: In minute amounts, this mineral is needed for protein and fat metabolism. It is also required for vitamin E and B1 metabolism. Like magnesium, manganese helps to reduce the build up of calcium in body tissues.

Dosage: 5–10 mg daily.

DMG *(dimethylglycine)*: DMG, also known as B15, is a metabolic enhancer which can aid the utilization of oxygen at the cellular level. It also enhances the energy output of cells and can be used to improve athletic performance.

Dosage: 150 mg daily or 2–5 ml liquid form daily.

These supplements, combined with an increase of high fiber foods, raw fruit and vegetables, ginger, garlic and onion, along with fish (which contain omega oils) will, over time, rejuvenate a tired and blocked cardiovascular system. This system may be used alone—however, in serious and urgent cases, EDTA therapy should be used first, with this oral chelation therapy acting as a backup.

"Hey! Who stuck that needle up his nose?"

CHAPTER 13

OVERCOMING THE DISEASES OF DETERIORATION

CAUSES, PREVENTION, AND CURES

This section on diseases is designed to inform you about some of the natural approaches to preventing and treating some of the illnesses which become more common as people become older. Obviously, if you are suffering from a serious health condition, the advice in this section is not intended to be a replacement for a consultation with a doctor, or natural health practitioner.

If you, or someone you love, have any of the health problems in this section, we hope that you will gain encouragement that healing (or at least improvement) is possible from the stories of the people featured in the case studies. It appears as though nothing is incurable, given enough love, energy and wisdom.

This section begins with one disease that is commonly thought of as incurable —Alzheimer's Disease. However, it, too, can apparently be cured as Tom Warren has demonstrated to the world.

ALZHEIMER'S

The symptoms of Alzheimer's disease include severe memory loss, disorientation, and sometimes aggression.

Autopsies of people who have died of this disease reveal tangled nerve fibres in the brain, as well as an excess of toxic minerals in brain tissue.

CAUSES

- Genetic susceptibility—an extra 21st chromosome has been found in Down's Syndrome sufferers. However this chromosome is found only in 10% of Alzheimer's victims.

- Excess amounts of aluminum, mercury and silicon, bromides, calcium and sulphur in memory centre and cerebral cortex. Autopsies have revealed four times the normal level of aluminum levels in Alzheimer's victims and the presence of an unidentified protein not found in normal brain tissue.

- Vitamin B12 and zinc deficiency—this may occur because of poor absorption of nutrients from food, rather than a dietary deficiency.

- Free radical damage.

- Insufficient oxygen and blood flow to the brain due to arteriosclerosis (hardening of the arteries), the loss of brain tissue from minor strokes, toxic reactions to drugs, (many antacids used for indigestion contain aluminum hydroxide), advanced syphilis, brain tumors and underactive thyroid can also create the same symptoms as Alzheimer's.

TREATMENTS

- Correcting diet and nutrition to ensure an adequate intake of vitamin B12, zinc, selenium and the antioxidant vitamins A, C, E, and bioflavonoids. Lecithin supplementation may be helpful, as may be other orthomolecular formulas.

- Avoid tap water—drink distilled or filtered water.

- Detoxification and removal of heavy metals is essential. Mercury amalgam (also known as silver amalgam) fillings should be removed and replaced with non-allergenic alternatives. Chelation therapy and homeopathic remedies can also help reduce the toxic burden on both body and brain.

- Avoiding aluminum and silicon found in most processed foods, antacids, underarm deodorants, bentonite clay, aluminum cookware, and 'painkillers,' such as aspirin.

- Herbal supplements of Gingko biloba (120 mg a day).

- Progressive exercise and massage.

- Reduction in prescription drugs.

- Music therapy is shown to help with attention span, focus and existing cognitive capabilities.

PREVENTION

- Ensure proper nutrition to maximize absorption of nutrients from foods. Supplements of digestive enzymes may be advisable.

- Take adequate exercise.

- Minimize exposure to aluminum and other toxic metals.

- Undertake regular detoxifying programs under the care of a registered health practitioner.

- Avoid coffee, tea, sugar, cigarettes, over-the-counter or prescription drugs. (Increased health from better diet will result in less need for drugs, and less desire for stimulants such as caffeine.)

- Avoid fluoridated water. Use a Reverse Osmosis or Ion Exchange water filtration system if your water is fluoridated. Drinking distilled water is another option.

- Learn new strategies to become empowered and cope with stress and change, inevitable in this life.

Like the victims of many degenerative diseases such as multiple sclerosis, people who are diagnosed as suffering from Alzheimer's disease have to contend with the emotional blow of being told that they have a disease which gradually reduces the quality of their life until they die. Conventional medicine has yet to develop a successful treatment for Alzheimer's disease, and still disputes the quite substantial evidence that a buildup of toxic metals in the brain may be a contributing factor, if not the major cause of this disease.

People who receive a diagnosis of Alzheimer's disease from their doctor, therefore, may expect to die a lingering death of misery and confusion. Fortunately, this expectation has now been challenged, and may soon be recognized as a myth.

The first known case of a complete recovery from Alzheimer's disease was that of Tom Warren, an American who was diagnosed as suffering from Alzheimer's at the age of 50 years. His case is particularly important, since he not only presented the clinical symptoms of Alzheimer's disease, but **a CAT scan of his brain proved that the frontal lobe of his brain had atrophied**.

With the support of his wife and the help of a team of clinical ecologists— doctors who specialize in identifying and treating allergies to foods as well as environmental contaminants—Mr. Warren made a full recovery from the dreaded disease which he had feared would claim his life. Mr. Warren wrote a book about his experiences *Beating Alzheimer's: A Step Towards Unlocking the Mysteries of Brain Diseases* (Avery Publishing Group, New York, 1991.)

*"Look on the bright side of Alzheimer's—
you get to hide your own Easter eggs!"*

Mr. Warren demonstrated the positive connections between heavy metal poisoning, especially from mercury in tooth fillings, and an allergic reaction in the brain. This reaction resulted in swelling and progressive deterioration of his brain tissue—both of which he was able to stop and reverse.

Tom Warren was diagnosed as suffering from Alzheimer's disease after experiencing personality changes, such as irritability and memory loss. Recalling the time around his diagnosis, he reports that he felt as if he had "been beaten up by Joe Louis." He suffered from a burning sensation inside his head, as well as a near constant headache. His handwriting deteriorated and he found himself unable to remember names. He even forgot his own telephone number, and when he went to look it up, he became confused part of the way through this simple task, and was unable to complete it. During conversations, he would ask people the same question several times, since he would forget that he had asked it previously.

As if these awful symptoms of mental dysfunction weren't enough in themselves, in his lucid moments Tom Warren also grieved for the fact that if his disease continued to progress, his wife and family would have the unenviable task of powerlessly watching him die a miserable death. He also felt regret at the fact that his premature death would prevent him from making a positive contribution to society. It was a miserable existence, and conventional medicine offered him no hope of a reprieve. So one day, Mr. Warren found himself asking for help from a higher power. He writes in his book: "One morning when I was feeling particularly miserable, I asked the Lord that if I had to die this death, to help me be the means through which the cure for Alzheimer's disease would be found. And in his infinite grace and mercy, God answered both of my prayers."

Gradually, through sheer persistence, together with flashes of intuition and a willingness to seek help from health practitioners who practised a brand of medicine which differed from the conventional allopathic approach to most diseases, Mr. Warren and his wife Louise developed a program which gradually reduced and finally eliminated his distressing symptoms. In his book, Tom Warren describes his program as being similar to a three-legged milking stool. Just as the milking stool needs all of its three legs to stand up, Mr. Warren's program needs three crucial elements for it to be successful.

These elements are: The removal of mercury amalgam fillings and detoxification of the body of mercury and other heavy metals; the diagnosis and elimination from the diet and environment of foods or pollutants to which you are allergic; and a comprehensive program of nutrition to rebuild the brain and body.

The other fundamental tenet of the program which Tom Warren developed to heal his Alzheimer's disease was a commitment to take responsibility for his own health and healing.

A critical part of Mr. Warren's recovery plan was testing for and avoiding foods and other substances to which he was allergic. Mr. Warren believes that allergies are a little known causative factor in the development of Alzheimer's disease. When a person eats something to which he or she is allergic, a measurable swelling occurs in the brain. When the brain swells in response to an antigen, the nerve endings, or synapses, swell the most. This swelling can cause the information travelling between the synapses to become garbled. Over time, residue from brain tissue leaks out through the broken nerve endings which have been weakened by frequent swelling of the brain. This residue hardens into plaque. Support for this theory of plaque formation also comes from researchers from the University of British Columbia who found microglia, a substance formed in the body where it is trying to fight off a foreign substance, present in the brains of Alzheimer's victims. The conclusion of the researchers was that Alzheimer's disease involved "an active chronic inflammatory process." This theory of Alzheimer's disease does not discount the theory that the accumulation of aluminum and other toxic metals in the brain causes the formation of plaques, since these toxic metals could well provoke an allergic response.

For all the reasons outlined above, finding a reliable way of testing to find out whether a person with Alzheimer's is allergic to different foods or environmental pollutants is very important. Tom Warren recommends provocative testing as the best way to diagnose allergies which can cause inflammation and swelling of the brain. Provocative testing for allergies involves fasting, and then introducing a suspect food or other substance to see if you have a reaction to it.

Provocative testing must be done under medical supervision, since the allergic reaction may be extreme. This sort of testing should not be undertaken by anyone with heart problems. In Mr. Warren's experience, other methods of allergy diagnosis, such as scratch testing are not helpful for people with what he calls cerebral allergies. Substances to which Tom Warren reacted badly which may also be a factor in the development of Alzheimer's disease in other people include: mercury; petroleum fumes; chlorine, as well as scented soaps and laundry powders.

Mr. Warren's nutritional program included a protein-rich diet, since people who have brain diseases often suffer from protein deficiency. He also limited his intake of carbohydrate rich foods, eschewing all junk carbohydrates such as white flour and sugar. Specifically prescribed orthomolecular vitamin and mineral supplements also aided Mr. Warren's recovery from what is becoming Western civilization's most feared disease.

Mr. Warren also reports in his book the obvious, but often overlooked, fact that even the best quality nutrition will not be an aid to restoring health if there is a significant problem in the digestive system resulting in the malabsorption of nutrients.

One of the first clues that Tom Warren picked up which gave him his first real hope for a recovery came when he asked one of his doctors to give him a Heidelberg Stomach Acid Test. The test showed that the pH (level of acidity) of his stomach was close to that of water. Since neutral water cannot dissolve food in the same way that strong acid can, the whole of the digestive system is severely compromised in its ability to extract nourishment from food. Mr. Warren concluded that one of the reasons that his brain was atrophied and malfunctioning was that his brain was deprived of food, and was "to put it bluntly...starving to death."

Later, Mr. Warren was able to hypothesize a possible reason why his body was failing to produce enough stomach acid to digest the food he ate. He believed that his body had shut down its production of stomach acid as a protective measure. At the time that he was diagnosed as having Alzheimer's disease, Mr. Warren had cavities in his teeth filled with mercury amalgam fillings which were constantly leaching mercury into his mouth. The result was that every time he swallowed food, drink, or just cleared his mouth of saliva, Mr. Warren was also ingesting tiny amounts of a highly toxic metal which went into his stomach every time he swallowed. Mr. Warren believes that his stomach stopped its secretion of acid in an effort to limit the amount of mercury that he would absorb.

Once Mr. Warren became aware of the connection between mercury and brain disease, and was diagnosed as suffering from mercury poisoning as a result of years of exposure to mercury leaching from his dental fillings, he signed on for a course of chelation therapy. Chelation Therapy, when administered according to a strict protocol *(see chapter on Chelation Therapy)* is the most effective way to remove toxic metals such as mercury, lead and aluminum from the body. Mr. Warren also reports that he found homeopathy useful for removing mercury from the body. According to his book, taking a homeopathic remedy for mercury poisoning caused the metal which had accumulated in his body to migrate to his skin. In Mr. Warren's case, after taking the homeopathic remedy, tiny particles of black metal became visible in a "shotgun pattern, with a circumference about the size of a coffee can lid" on the skin above his heart. However, Mr. Warren warns from his experience that neither chelation therapy, nor homeopathy will result in the long term disappearance of your symptoms if you are continually exposed to the mercury which caused your health problems in the first place.

This makes the removal of any amalgam fillings you may have in your mouth essential. However, Mr. Warren warns that this must be done according to a strict protocol. Do not start a program of amalgam filling removal or replacement until you have read and understood the book *It's All in Your Head* by American dentist, Hal Huggins. If you have fillings removed in an incorrect order, permanent damage to your brain may result. For more information about mercury poisoning, please read the chapter on Metal Toxicity.

It is also possible that you may have mercury fragments lodged in your jaw, and these may continue to leach mercury into your body even once your amalgam fillings have been removed. It is worthwhile checking your dental X-rays extremely carefully to see if there are any tiny dark specks which may be amalgam fragments. If these are present, and you continue to experience ill health, oral surgery to remove the offending amalgam may be advisable.

There are also other ways in which you may be exposed to mercury, such as in some latex paints which contain mercury.

Tom Warren concludes his book by saying "The hard fact is no one but you can save you." Once you have embarked on a comprehensive program of dental amalgam removal, and the elimination of heavy metals from your body, allergy diagnosis and avoidance, and nutritional support that is working successfully you must continue to follow the program. If you become lax about any area of your health care program, you risk the reappearance of your symptoms, and once again face the gradual and pitiful decline which characterizes Alzheimer's disease.

The good news, however, is that Alzheimer's Disease has been cured once— and can be cured again—so take heart. To conclude with the words of the first man to beat Alzheimer's: "Never mind what diagnosis your physician blessed you with. Your mental health and memory can improve. Mine did."

ARTHRITIS

DEFINITION

Arthritis is a term used to describe inflammation, pain and/or swelling and deposits in the joints. There are two major types of the arthritis: osteoarthritis and rheumatoid arthritis.

Osteoarthritis is sometimes known as the 'wear and tear' form of arthritis. In osteoarthritis the cartilage surrounding the joints deteriorates, leading to damage to the bones of the joints. Osteoarthritis tends to affect older people, particularly women.

Rheumatoid arthritis involves not only joint pain, but also swelling, stiffness, and sometimes heat in the affected area. In severe cases of rheumatoid arthritis, other parts of the body in addition to the joints, may be damaged by the rheumatoid process, including the skin, heart, lungs, liver and kidneys.

CAUSES

Arthritis is thought to have a number of causes. The primary cause of arthritis is thought to be *acidosis*—the over-acidification of body tissues due to the consumption of dead and highly refined foods creating residues which build up in the body. *Allergy* to specific foods has also been implicated in arthritis, particularly rheumatoid arthritis. *Vitamin C deficiency*—which is common because of the high consumption of cooked foods and raw foods which have lost vitamins while in storage—also contributes to the establishment of an arthritic condition, since vitamin C is essential for the maintenance of the connective tissues which deteriorate in the arthritic process. Rheumatoid arthritis is also thought to be caused by a virus or bacteria in some cases.

PREVENTION

Arthritis can be prevented by eating a diet high in easily digestible raw foods which help to keep the body's acid/alkaline level in natural balance. Daily supplementation with non-acidic vitamin C can also be helpful, particularly for people who live in polluted cities, since vitamin C helps to detoxify the body. Avoid foods to which you are allergic. Regular massage, Hatha Yoga, and aerobic exercise like walking or hiking keeps the body limber and oxygenated, bringing *prana* (life energy force) to all your cells and organs. Here again regular detoxification is very helpful and a vegetarian (or semi vegetarian) diet, is a wise choice.

REMEDIES

Nutritional changes combined with supplementation with specific nutrients have alleviated many cases of arthritis. Many people have been helped by supplementing their diet with aloe vera juice. Aloe vera is detoxifying. It helps to purify the system and is well known as a healing agent for burns and cuts. Less well known is its ability to reduce inflammation of joints. Others have been helped by fasting and then removing meat and bread from their diets, going on a raw food diet, and drinking an ample amounts of fresh vegetable juices. The traditional Vermont cure *cum* preventative is apple cider vinegar in a glass of water, taken two or three times a day. It seems to work for many Vermonters, one of the coldest states in the US. Grapefruit and grapefruit juice is reputed to work 'wonders' for some arthritis sufferers, along with antioxidants like Pycnogenol. Sea cucumber extract is a marvellous natural antiinflammatory and has no appreciable side effects. Exercise and massage are also helpful. Numerous studies indicate that EPA (Kyolic EPA, Fish Oil with Garlic) is an essential nutrient for alleviating pain in arthritic patients as it has very powerful anti-inflammatory compounds.

NUTRITIONAL THERAPY

Eliminate processed, salty foods and white flour and sugar from the diet. Also eat little or no meat. Losing excess weight is beneficial for many sufferers of osteoarthritis. Avoiding animal fats and refined carbohydrates is the easiest way to do this.

Identify food allergies: Unless you are underweight or frail, an elimination diet is worthwhile to determine any food allergies. Foods particularly suspected of provoking osteoarthritis include potatoes, tomatoes, peppers and aubergines (eggplant)—all members of the nightshade family.

Foods implicated in cases of rheumatoid arthritis include: dairy products, wheat, oats, chicken, pork and yeast-containing foods.

FOLK MEDICINE

Apple Cider Vinegar: For more than a century Vermonters have used a simple and effective remedy for their ailments. In the 1960s, Dr. Jarvis wrote a book called *Folk Medicine* in which he detailed the many uses of cider vinegar and honey and Lugols Solution of Iodine.

One of the things he discovered was that when chickens were fed this mixture, they stayed healthier, and their meat was more tender. People used Lugols, honey and cider vinegar to treat colds, as well as stomach and digestive problems. Another ailment that many people find responds well to this remedy is arthritis. Taking Lugols, cider vinegar and honey can ease the pain, remove the inflammation and reverse the progression of the disease.

The Procedure: With every meal take one teaspoonful of unpasteurized apple cider vinegar and one teaspoon of raw honey in a glass of water. Apply one drop of Lugols solution of Iodine to the internal side of the wrist (take care, since it can stain clothing). When applied to the skin, this iodine compound is absorbed through the skin and into the bloodstream. If you do not want to apply the Lugols solution to the wrist, it may be applied to the sole of the foot.

Do this daily. If the skin becomes irritated, stop for a few days before resuming applications of Lugols solution. It is usually absorbed rapidly for a while, and then when the body is no longer seriously deficient in iodine, absorption slows down. This is a safer method than the one suggested by Dr. Jarvis, who suggested adding one drop of Lugols solution to the cider vinegar once daily.

Case History: Mrs. A.W., a lady with acute arthritis of the neck and upper spine was prescribed the cider vinegar and honey drink and external applications of Lugols solution after x-ray diagnosis confirmed the presence of serious disease. In the case of this lady, her problems with arthritis were probably caused by an earlier injury. Within a few weeks, the inflammation had subsided, and within 2 months, her symptoms had disappeared.

Over the next twenty years, every time she became aware of any pain, she would return to the apple cider vinegar and the condition would return to normal within a short time.

Now, some thirty years later, this lady is 75 years old, and is seldom bothered by arthritis, despite a serious deterioration of the spine. She still takes the cider vinegar treatment when she feels it is necessary. No medical drug therapy has been necessary over all these years for her condition.

SUPPLEMENTS

Caution: Before taking supplements, always consult with your health professional.

Supplements useful for people with arthritis include the antioxidant nutrients A and C. Vitamin C should be taken according to bowel tolerance, see the section on taking vitamin C in the chapter on Nutrition and Health. People with arthritis need to take a non-acidic form of vitamin C such as calcium ascorbate or a mixture of ascorbates. Occasionally people suffering from rheumatoid arthritis experience a worsening of their symptoms after taking vitamin C. If this happens, stop taking the supplement and consult a natural health practitioner.

Other useful supplements are Beta carotene and Vitamin E. Vitamin E has been tested for its effectiveness against osteoarthritis and was found to give better results than a placebo. A daily supplement of 600 I.U. is worth a try. However seek professional.

In addition, supplementation should be given to remedy trace mineral deficiencies. Useful minerals include: iron and selenium—the latter is essential for immune function. Copper, manganese and zinc should also be taken (under supervision) since these three minerals are needed for the proper functioning of an enzyme called superoxide dismutase which can inhibit the inflammation found in rheumatoid arthritis. Zinc also has antiviral properties. Copper bracelets have been found to be of value by sufferers of both osteo and rheumatoid arthritis.

Green-lipped mussel extract may also be helpful for both forms of arthritis. Supplementation with 1–4 g of niacinamide (under medical supervision) may also be helpful. The amino acids tryptophan and histidine have helped some people with rheumatoid arthritis.

Cold pressed flax seed oil supplies the essential fatty acids which enhance immune function. Two tablespoons of flax seed oil daily can be helpful, and will not lead to weight gain if fat from other areas in the diet is restricted.

Kyolic Formula EPA has powerful anti-inflammatory substances which have been proven beneficial for the arthritic patient.

MASSAGE

Massage is useful for arthritis because it can ease pain, and also increase blood flow to the affected joints. Wintergreen Oil may be used as a massage oil to provide pain relief. *(This should not be used by pregnant women however, since it promotes menstruation and may cause miscarriage.)* Also, a liniment of cayenne pepper and cider vinegar, boiled together in water for 10 minutes, can be helpful. Strain the mixture and then soak a cloth in the mixture, and apply it warm to the affected area. Do not use on broken skin. Wrap a dry cloth over the wet cloth and leave on for 20 minutes.

EXERCISE

Most people with arthritis benefit from a program of gentle exercise. However, exercise is not appropriate when your arthritis is in a period of acute inflammation. This should be allowed to subside before any exercise program is begun or resumed. Some stretching exercises may cause discomfort. If exercise provokes severe, prolonged pain, discontinue the exercise. Yoga and other stretching exercises are valuable for people with arthritis. For more information, read the chapter on Breathing Exercise and Relaxation. Walking is a good form of aerobic exercise for people with arthritis. You may find it easier if you go for two shorter walks rather than one long one.

IS ARTHRITIS REVERSIBLE?

In recent years there have been some very interesting reports of people actually reversing their arthritis, something which if true could be of tremendous importance to millions of people.

It is currently estimated that more than 40 million people suffer from some form of arthritis in the US alone. They usually 'manage' their pain with a variety of techniques ranging from the traditional 'pain killers' to wearing copper bracelets. In most cases, the pain killers require ever-increasing dosages to accomplish the same amount of pain relief; diet, supplements and exercise usually work better.

GLUCOSAMINE SULFATE

Sherry A. Rogers, MD., reports in the *Townsend Letter for Doctors and Patients* (April 1996) that there is an experimental treatment that seems to be getting results in not only eliminating pain altogether but in reversing the pathology of osteoarthritis, rebuilding and healing osteoarthritic cartilage.

That treatment consists of measured doses of Glucosamine Sulfate.

According to Dr. Rogers, there are at least two studies of this compound that attest to its rather marvellous healing potential.

Glucosamine Sulfate in one controlled study (*Pharmatherapeutica* 2:8. 259. 1981) improved the patients' well being with no side effects. In another, Glucosamine Sulfate was compared for pain relief with Ibuprofen for 8 weeks and won. After several weeks the Ibuprofen was weakening in its effectiveness, while the Glucosamine Sulfate was actually gaining (*Curr Med Res Opin* 8, 3:145, 1982).

The average dosage was 500 mg three times a day. Glucosamine Sulfate is actually one of the "building blocks of the substance that cartilage is made out of; it is one of the preferred constituents and actually stimulates the biosynthesis of more cartilage. And, as it is rebuilding it also inhibits the degradation that is part of the normal physiology of osteoarthritis and which is accelerated by nonsteroidal anti-inflammatory drugs."

The article goes on to recommend that arthritis patients consult with their health professional about Glucosamine Sulfate. Dr. Rogers recommends, as well, a good multiple vitamin and mineral preparation to help the body with its task of "biosynthesis that it is called upon to do."

The authors of this book make no recommendation as to the efficacy of Glucosamine Sulfate; we merely draw the reader's attention to the article by Dr.Rogers and her citations. Dr.Rogers is available for correspondence at Box 2716, Syracuse NY 13220 USA.

CANCER

In discussing the definition and causes of cancer one should be aware of the multi-factored nature of this disease.

Research pioneers like Raymond Royal Rife, Wilhelm Reich and Gaston Naessens isolated microscopic life forms that seem to evolve into cancer agents in the bodies of people with compromised immune systems.

Dr. Tilden, a medical doctor, in the early part of this century stated that all disease is caused by toxemia. That is a state whereby the toxins produced and ingested into the body are in excess of the body's natural detoxification processes. As these toxins increase they damage cell function causing free radical damage. As the cells deteriorate, organ systems fail and become prone to disease. It is possible that some cancer may be partly due to the premature aging of the cell itself due to free radical damage.

Natural medicine acknowledges that cancer is, by the nature of it, a chronic breakdown of the nutritional/elimination process, a complex and challenging disorder to treat.

However, it can be treated holistically—spirit, mind and body. It is seen as a disease of the whole metabolism rather than in body parts.

Metaphysically, cancer is viewed as the result of unexpressed emotion or energy. Quantum Physics demonstrates the ability of mind to affect matter. Repressing emotions places a severe stress upon the body and mind, and diminishes the energy which would otherwise be used for healing and renewal.

Spiritual and mental attitude in the treatment of cancer is vitally important to the restoration of health.

Fear, anger and other negative emotions shut down the life force and inhibit healing. For many people the diagnosis of cancer is equivalent to the aboriginal technique of 'pointing the bone'. Death is certain to the believer. That is why in natural medicine, and metaphysics, no diseases are acknowledged to be incurable.

The emotions we choose to suppress are generally the 'negative' ones—those we feel least comfortable about or able to express. The source of such emotions may vary from violence, job loss, negative relationships, bereavement or any other long term stress. It is important both to acknowledge the true cause of and express feelings of sadness, loss, anger, frustration and betrayal. Clearing 'emotional baggage' is often painful—but once you are free of the hurts of the past, you will find you have more energy to deal with the problems of the present.

OTHER FACTORS THAT CAN ACTIVATE CANCERS ARE

Radiation, one of the few factors that may be totally primary in cause.

Chemicals now found throughout our environment, such as pesticides, herbicides, and fungicides with residues found in fruits, vegetables, milk, grains, legumes and meats—unless organically grown. Other chemicals are used in food preservation, tap water, pharmaceutical drugs, cigarettes, food coloring or artificial sweeteners, cleaners and solvents. There are over 60,000 chemicals used in our society now, with more being produced weekly.

It is now generally recognized that plants also synthesize toxic chemicals as a defence against predators. If our body is low in antioxidant nutrition, these chemicals may induce cell damage.

For example: Nitrates, nitrites and nitrosamines are present in beets, celery, radishes, lettuce, spinach, rhubarb. High levels of nitrates are also added to preserved meats such as bacon.

Carcinogenic moulds such as sterigmaticystin and aflatoxins are present in mold-contaminated foods such as corn, grain, nuts, peanut butter, bread, cheese and apple juice.

Glycoalkaloids such as Solanine and Chaconine are present in potatoes.

Pyrrolizidine alkaloids are found in many herbs and herbal teas.

This list of cell-damaging chemicals which occur naturally in foods may seem alarming. However, it is important to remember that vegetables and herbs which contain these compounds are almost always good sources of antioxidants which protect against cancer and other illnesses. In fact, numerous studies have shown that a diet high in fresh fruit and vegetables protects against cancer. It is, however, important to avoid green potatoes, and mold-contaminated foods. Aflatoxin is a potent carcinogen.

One of the dietary factors known to be most important in determining your cancer risk is the type and amount of fats you consume. A high intake of saturated fats from animal products and tropical oils has been linked to cancer. However, even polyunsaturated vegetable oils can also be toxic to the body if they are heated. Cooking unsaturated fatty acids creates fatty acid peroxidase, fatty acid epoxides and hydroperoxy radicals, all of which are bad news for your cells. Likewise, the polyunsaturated oils which are used to make margarine become toxic after they undergo artificial hydrogenation. The trans fatty acids which are created in the hydrogenation process cannot be utilized properly by the body, and, when incorporated into the membranes of your cells, result in abnormal cell function.

PREVENTION

A study of the prevalence of the different types of cancer worldwide reveals a wide difference in the rates of this disease. New Zealand has a high rate of colon cancer and Japan has a high rate of stomach cancer. In China women get lung cancer from cooking with oil in unventilated kitchens. In the West the lung cancer rate is high, and the current view is that cigarette smoking is the major factor. However, the Japanese smoke heavily and do not exhibit the same lung cancer problem.

Macrobiotic theory suggests that our high intake of milk is the precipitating factor in the effects of smoking upon the lungs. Certainly homogenized milk contains xanthine oxidase, an enzyme that damages arterial walls.

Antioxidants that have a protective role as nutrients for cell function and health include: Vitamin A, C, and E and aged garlic. Folic Acid, Niacin, and vitamin D are also important. Essential Minerals include: Selenium and Iodine (which are both deficient in many soils), Zinc, Iron, Copper, Molybdenum, and Silica. Germanium, Gallium, Silica and Selenium influence the process of genetic expression at the nuclear level.

In some forms of cancer, hereditary factors are apparent. Homeopathic medicine has always seen cancer as one of the chronic expressions of miasmas, or genetic weakness.

The prevention of cancer must therefore be multifaceted. Firstly we need to remove from our environment many factors implicated above.

- Eat organic foods, and avoid foods contaminated with pesticides, etc.
- Do not use heated oils, or oils which have been artificially hydrogenated such as margarine.
- Avoid foods with added carcinogens, e.g. nitrates, nitrites, saccharin.
- Avoid meats treated with hormones.
- Do not eat irradiated food.
- Reduce yeast intake and avoid mold-contaminated food.
- Reduce occupational risks.
- Avoid radiation and reduce time spent in the sun, as the ozone depletion is allowing high levels of ultra violet light to reach ground level. This damages the immune system.
- Avoid fluoride toothpaste and fluoridated water.
- Consider a daily intake of antioxidant vitamins and minerals.
- Eat a balanced diet with plenty of raw organic vegetables.
- Animal protein intake should be carefully monitored.
- Eat garlic, for its anticancer activity.
- Take a tablespoon of flax seed oil daily to supply essential fatty acids.
- Begin an enjoyable exercise program. Numerous studies have shown that people who exercise regularly have a much lower cancer risk than people who lead a sedentary lifestyle.
- Develop a relaxed lifestyle. Learn skills necessary to cope with changes that

will happen in your life.

- Drink organic fruit and vegetable juices fortified with Spirulina, or any of the other green super foods.

AN ALTERNATIVE PERSPECTIVE ON CONVENTIONAL CANCER TREATMENT

Not generally recognized among the population as a whole—or even medical practitioners themselves—is the fact that people who refuse medical intervention for their medically diagnosed cancer, actually, on average, may live longer than people who undertake conventional medical treatment.

According to Dr. Hardin Jones, Professor of Medical Physics and Physiology, reporting to the American Cancer Society's Science Writers Seminar in 1969, amplifying his paper published in *Transaction of the NY Academy of Sciences* in 1955, "Evidence for benefit from cancer therapy has depended on biometric errors. People who refused treatment lived for an average of 12.5 years (after diagnosis). Those who accepted surgery and other kinds of (orthodox) treatment lived an average of only three years. Beyond the shadow of a doubt, radical surgery on cancer patients does more harm than good."

This should hardly come as a surprise to those who know that many drugs used for cancer chemotherapy are themselves carcinogenic; that radiation suppresses the body's immune system and is also carcinogenic; and that surgery can spread cancer cells throughout the body, cells which are, until surgery, usually confined to the tumor site. According to Dr. Michael Feldman of the Weizmann Institute in Israel, cancerous metastases are actually inhibited by the primary tumor.

Any impact these studies might have had on orthodox medicine, aside from instilling an even more rigorous cover-up, has not come to the attention of the authors.

NATURAL TREATMENT OF CANCER

The principle of all natural cancer therapy is to enhance the body's own tendency towards normal function. Even when surgery may be required, it is this function that must repair damage to tissues caused by the surgery.

There are a number of natural cancer therapies, some of which have a good success rate. Many of these therapies may be used synergistically. However, different herbal therapies should not be combined except under the supervision of a competent naturopath or herbalist, since inappropriate herbal combinations may cause toxic reactions.

1. Relaxation, meditation and visualization
2. Paw Paw (Papaya) tea—a traditional remedy
3. Essiac Tea—another traditional remedy
4. Wheatgrass
5. Laetrile (Vitamin B17)
6. Gerson Therapy
7. Orthomolecular Medicine
8. Jason Winters
9. Oxygen Therapy
10. Hoxsey Therapy
11. Intravenous Vitamin C

1. RELAXATION, MEDITATION AND VISUALIZATION

It is important to see cancer as a disease of the whole being rather than just one part of the body being affected. In many cases cancer has occurred because all is not well in your being. The first part of healing is to overcome the fear and make a total commitment to healing. People do recover from cancer by natural means and many books have been written about their recovery. The first step is to take control of the disease. Your attitude can often determine survival.

Dr. Simonton, an Oncologist/Radiologist, and his wife Stephanie, a Psychotherapist, pioneered treating cancer patients with a program of radiation/chemotherapy, meditation and visualization. Their first student of the program was a 61 year old man with throat cancer. They taught him to practice visualization several times a day. He survived cancer and went on to treat his arthritis and impotence with visualization. Their book *"Getting Well Again"* was published in 1978.

The Simonton's found that the healing process was enhanced when the brain's normal operating frequency of rapid Beta waves changed slowed to Alpha waves which are associated with relaxation. Immune system studies confirm the correlation between mental state and immune response.

With practise you can learn to relax fully and enhance your body's natural healing powers using the method outlined below.

1. Get comfortable sitting or lying down on the floor or bed. Let your feet fall apart naturally and rest arms away from body at a natural angle. Try to ensure you will not be interrupted.

2. Take a couple of deep breaths and then breathe normally, becoming aware of the rise and fall of the chest and stomach, the cool flow of air into the nose and throat and the warm air flowing out, and any other aspects of your breathing you are aware of. As you focus on it, your breathing will settle into a comfortable, steady rhythm.

3. Take your awareness to your back. Feel it against the floor or bed. Then take your awareness to the front of your body and feel the light touch of the cool air on your skin or clothing.

4. Begin to direct your attention to each part of your body. This allows the brain and the body parts to relax. Do not stretch them or picture them in your mind. Just focus your awareness for a moment or two and move on to the next one. If there is anything there it will be felt - perhaps just a warm feeling. This is a yoga sleep which automatically relaxes the mind because the attention is directed elsewhere. Start with the left side and work up to the shoulders, and then go back to the right side starting at the foot.

    - Toes and feet
    - Calves
    - Thighs
    - Hips and buttocks
    - Waist and lower back
    - Ribcage
    - Chest
    - Shoulders and shoulder blades
    - Fingers
    - Hand
    - Forearm

* Upperarm

Then do the following in whole parts:

* Throat
* Back of neck
* Head and scalp
* Forehead
* Cheeks
* Nose
* Mouth and inside of mouth

Focusing on that part of the body that is beset by cancer can elicit anxiety and fear. Accept this and don't force it. But remember putting energy into that part and reclaiming it as a well part of the body is desired for healing.

5. When this is complete, focus again on the breath. Feel the heaviness and total relaxation of the body.

6. This is the meditational stage. Your heart and pulse have slowed, less oxygen is required. The body is being recharged. The mind is free of external stimuli. If thoughts come, let them drift in and out; focus on your breathing and experience pure primordial sound for a moment or two…the body and mind are connected with high consciousness…If you have time you can meditate before visualizing. *(See Relaxation, chapter 6)*

7. Now visualize the cancer and the strengthening immune system (if using natural therapies) or the radiation/chemotherapy (if using orthodox treatment), seeking out and destroying those imperfect and confused cancer cells. See them being taken out of the body. Allow creativity and intuition to make this your individual experience. Others have visualized the cancer as snowflakes to be melted by love; or shoals of beautiful fish that come and gobble up the cancer; or white polar bears, or huskies, which hunt down the cancer. A tree surgeon saw cancer as a diseased tree and systematically chopped off its limbs and dug out its roots. The immune system or the orthodox treatment must be all-powerful to destroy the cancer and remove it from the body.

8. At the end of your visualization count back from five to one and open your eyes. Slowly stretch and get up and go about your business, relaxed and happy, experiencing and remembering what you have achieved.

Practice this for 15 minutes, at least three times a day, until your condition improves. Then you could reduce it to twice a day. Relaxation, meditation and visualization, all become easier with practice. Use your meditation to discover why you might have contracted the disease in the first place. See into your repressed emotions and hostilities and release them.

For additional relaxation use relaxation tapes with sounds of nature, or other meditational tapes. Music has long been associated with healing.

Do not attempt meditation or visualization if you are in a hurry, or have just eaten, or it is late in the evening. If you are drowsy you may fall asleep, but you need to be conscious to do this exercise and master your condition. If you think you are going to fall asleep, open your eyes, stretch, or take some deep breaths. If you are interrupted, go back to the previous part of the exercise and continue, or slowly stretch and get up.

Affirmations: Writing out affirmations and placing them where they will be seen regularly is another positive step, such as: "I am in health," or "My body is intelligent, it knows how to care for itself," or "I cooperate with my body."

2. PAW PAW TEA

Paw Paw (Papaya) Tea is a traditional Australian aboriginal medicine which has recently been hailed as a promising cancer therapy. Stan Sheldon of the Gold Coast in Australia, who completely cured himself of cancer in 3 months in 1962, after learning of this ancient Aboriginal remedy. He had advanced cancer in both lungs. He regularly boiled up paw paw tea on his kitchen stove and drank it in plentiful amounts. He reputedly saved the lives of thirty other people using this recipe.

According to an article in *New Scientist*, a chemical discovered in one variety of paw paw is one billion times more toxic to cancer cells than anti-cancer drugs.

Recipe: Take a quantity of chopped paw paw leaves and fill a pot (not aluminum) to the top. Cover with purified water and bring to a boil. Simmer for two hours. Cool, then filter and bottle liquid in sterile glass bottles with cap. Take 200 ml, 3 times a day.

3. ESSIAC TEA

Essiac Tea was developed from a traditional Ojibway Indian Remedy by Canadian Nurse Renée Caisse. Its four-herb combination in the correct amounts form a powerful synergistic compound which can be effective against metabolic diseases like cancer and diabetes.

Some people with cancer have made complete recoveries using Essiac tea together with diet and vitamin therapies. Others experienced improved well-being and tumor regression.

Its healing qualities seem to be in its ability to detoxify the liver and regulate the bowel. It improves digestion and thereby improves absorption of vital nutrients. It is available from many health stores.

In 1937 The Royal Cancer Commission found that Essiac was effective against cancer. Essiac came three votes short of being declared a legalized remedy for terminal cancer in Canada.

Recipe:
- 6.5 cups of cut burdock *(Arctium lappa)* root. Grown wild, or from health store.
- 16 oz powdered sheep's sorrel *(Rumex acetosella)*. Grown wild, or from health store.
- 4 oz powdered slippery elm bark. Available from health store.
- 1 oz of Turkish rhubarb root. Available from health store.

  Put 2 liters purified water in pot (not aluminum), and bring to a boil. Weigh 45 grams of above herbal mixture (thoroughly mixed) and add to boiling water; stir.

  Cover pot, boil for 10–12 minutes (rolling boil).

  Scrape any herbs from side of pot back into mixture.

  Let stand at room temperature for 10-12 hours.

  Stir; heat solution to 85°C (185°F), but do not boil.

  Remove from heat and add 180 ml of purified boiled water to compensate for evaporation.

  Cover for 20 minutes.

Strain liquid into closeable sterile jars, discard the sediment.

Store in cool dark place or refrigerator.

Shake the tea well before pouring a dose. Take 4 tablespoons, 3 times daily on empty stomach, diluted with 4–8 tablespoons of pure water.

The tea should keep for at least a year in sterile closed jars, but discard if any mold appears. Essiac Tea can be purchased from many health stores.

4. WHEATGRASS

Ann Wigmore, who pioneered wheatgrass therapy, selected wheatgrass after studying 4,700 species of grasses. It was chosen because it grows quickly, can be grown inside, requires little soil, is laden with chlorophyll and is high in carotene. She first used it on sickly elderly neighbors and then, encouraged by its healing potential used it to treat people suffering from degenerative diseases.

The Hippocrates Institutes in Boston and San Diego use wheatgrass juice, Rejuvelac (the liquid from wheat grains soaked overnight), and a diet of raw food, seeds, nuts, sprouts, grains and legumes, to treat degenerative diseases including cancer.

In her book *How I Conquered Cancer Naturally* Eydie Mae Hunsberger tells how she reversed malignant breast cancer (several lumps in breasts and under arms) with a cleansing program, wheatgrass juice, Rejuvelac, wheatgrass enemas, and a living foods diet.

While wheatgrass is not in itself a cure for cancer, it has been scientifically proven that it is a whole food and supplies the body with the vital nourishment it needs to heal itself. Its capacity to do that may be because wheatgrass is rich in chlorophyll.

Chlorophyll is similar to hemoglobin, the blood's own oxygen-carrying molecule. Hemoglobin is made up of a group of carbon, hydrogen, oxygen and nitrogen, centered around a single atom of iron. In chlorophyll the group is the same except the single atom is magnesium.

Animal studies have also shown that animals which were allowed chlorophyll in their diet have a greater resistance to the deadly effects of radiation. It seems likely that wheatgrass therapy could therefore assist people with cancer undergoing radiation treatment by protecting healthy cells against some damage which would otherwise be inflicted on them by the radiation.

5. LAETRILE THERAPY

Laetrile (also known as Vitamin B17) is a naturally occurring compound in foods which contain nitrilosides. These include bitter almonds, macadamia nuts, broad beans, all sprouts, sesame and flax seeds, barley, brown rice, oats and buckwheat groats, millet, rye, wheat berries, most wild berries, the seeds of apples, apricot seed kernels, and other fruit stones.

B17 molecules contain cyanide and benzaldehyde components, chemically locked together and inert. However, an enzyme called beta-glucodisase, which the body uses to surround cancerous material, can divide the B17 molecule. When these two components are released at a cancer site, they synergistically break down cancer cells. Elsewhere in the body, if all nutritional needs have been met, large amounts of rhodanese (another enzyme) neutralizes the excess cyanide component.

Although it is not considered to be a complete cancer cure, in clinical studies vitamin B17 has been shown to dramatically reduce pain in terminal sufferers. It has also been effective in inhibiting some tumor growths, improving appetites, stimulating weight gain and inducing well-being in cancer patients. Where it is used in natural medicine clinics, it is called Amygdalin which is a more effective derivative ensuring that cyanide will only be released at a cancer site. An important part of the therapy is a diet high raw vegetables and low in protein. Coffee enemas, pancreatic enzymes and supplementary vitamins also make up part of the program. Amygdalin is available in The Del Mar Clinic in Mexico, The Fairfield Clinic in Jamaica, The Silbersee Clinic in Hanover, The Ringberg Clinic in Bavaria, The Mooerman Clinic in the Netherlands, and the Bristol Cancer Help Centre in Britain.

The Hunzas who live in the Himalayas have a nitriloside intake 200 times higher than Westerners, usually live to be over 100, and have no cancer. Their prized food is the apricot which they grow without pesticides. From the time they are children they eat the apricot, cracking open the stone and eating the kernel with it. Their pure mountain water is full of calcium carbonate which activates apricot nitriloside enzymes.

If you wish to use apricot kernels as part of plan for cancer treatment—or prevention—make sure you have the guidance of a qualified health practitioner. Used incorrectly, apricot kernels can be toxic.

6. GERSON THERAPY

Dr. Max Gerson's therapy is based on his belief that cancer is a disease of the whole metabolism and that it is preceded by an impaired liver. His program is aimed at detoxifying and rebuilding the liver.

His therapy includes coffee enemas which flush the liver and stimulate bile production and flow, eliminating from the body the poisons which would otherwise cause life threatening toxemia. In addition his patients are given castor oil orally or by enema every other day.

The program also aims to rebalance sodium/potassium levels. (Cancer sufferers retain a high level of sodium in cells yet lose potassium). His patients received a potassium compound and thyroid and iodine in half strength lugols solution which inhibits cancer cells' fermentation process.

To help the liver further and improve digestive function, patients receive liver extract injections, Vitamin B12, niacin, betaine hydrochloride and pancreatic enzymes.

The diet consists of fruit and oatmeal for breakfast, with salad, vegetable soup, cooked vegetables and baked potatoes for lunch and dinner. Raw fruit and vegetables are allowed for snacks. Animal protein is limited, since this leaves enzymes free for breaking up cancerous tissue. Juices are taken every hour - 8 oz glass of carrot juice, green leaf juice or other freshly prepared juices. Calve's liver juice used to be part of the program but was discontinued due to the difficulty in obtaining liver uncontaminated by pesticides, hormones and antibiotics. Carrot juice with Spirulina and desiccated liver tablets may be used instead. A natural health practitioner could also assist with a good orthomolecular herbal liver regenerator. Two tablespoons of cold pressed flax seed oil is the only fat or oil allowed.

Gerson's book *A Cancer Therapy: Results of Fifty Cases* is still available widely, and is highly recommended. Alternatively, you may contact The Gerson Institute, PO Box 430, Bonita, California 91908, USA.

7. ORTHOMOLECULAR THERAPY

This therapy is based upon the nutritional and eliminatory pathways of the cell. It requires a good knowledge of biochemistry and physiology.

Many of the products used have been formulated to act synergistically with the natural physiological function of the cell. Vitamins, minerals, trace elements and amino-acids are the ingredients for the formulas used.

Nutrients are an essential part of the human environment and health is only as strong as its weakest link. One missing link in the nutritional requirements of the cell may leave it vulnerable to disease, such as cancer, induced by a toxin excess.

Restoration of normal cell physiology can occur by strengthening the weak link, through the replacement of the necessary nutrients. This therapy requires professional expertise as the specific needs of nutrition vary from one individual to another. For advice consult a qualified therapist.

8. JASON WINTERS

Jason Winters was a terminal cancer patient who was given three months to live. He refused surgery and travelled the world for a herbal remedy. He located three herbs which when mixed together and taken as a tea reduced the size of his tumor and eradicated cancer from his body.

His herbal remedy containing Red Clover, Indian Sage and 'Special Spice' is marketed under his own name and is available from health stores in tea and tablet form.

He has written numerous books on alternative health. *The Jason Winters Story* is a compilation of four of his books. *Killing Cancer; In Search of the Perfect Cleanse; Breakthrough: An Australian Legend;* and *The Ultimate Collection.*

9. OXYGEN THERAPY

Cancer cells are less virulent in a high oxygen environment.

A study carried out at Tottori University of Medicine determined that the effect of radiation and chemotherapy on cancer cells was enhanced by increasing the oxygen tension in a cell. In the study hydrogen peroxide was infused prior to radiation and chemotherapy over 10 days. Out of 15 cases with maxillary cancer, 8 showed an almost complete tumor disappearance, 6 a partial reduction, and 1 had little change.

The most natural way of getting oxygen into the body is by full correct breathing (see Breathing section). Unfortunately in industrialized cities the oxygen levels are decreasing and the carbon monoxide levels are increasing.

The treatment of cancer by natural therapies should be supervised by a registered naturopath. In some cases, 6–30 drops of 35% food grade hydrogen peroxide may be given by infusion or taken orally in a glass of purified water.

Cell oxygen is a product available in some health shops. It is a culture of special young yeast cells very high in oxidizing enzymes. Dr. Seeger of Germany discovered that it was useful in starting normal cell oxidation in cancer cells. It is best used with royal jelly.

10. HOXSEY HERBAL THERAPY

The herbal remedy for cancer used by Harry Hoxsey in the United States to cure cancer is basically a combination of herbs taken internally which act synergistically to detoxify and strengthen the body. For cancers on the skin, there is also an external powder paste, and also a liquid formula. The herbal formula was first discovered in the 1840s by Harry Hoxsey's great grandfather, John Hoxsey.

John Hoxsey used the herbs to treat animals suffering from cancer and before his death passed the herbal remedy down to his son. Harry Hoxsey, the most well known of the Hoxsey family cancer therapists, received the formula from his father around 1920.

The internal form of the herbal medicine developed by the Hoxsey family included: licorice, red clover, burdock root, stillingia root, berberis root, poke root, cascara, aromatic USP 14, prickly ash bark and buckthorn bark in a base of potassium iodide. Depending on the individual, some of these herbs might be excluded.

The powder contains arsenic sulphide, yellow precipitate of sulphur and talc. The paste contains antimony trisulphide, zinc chloride and bloodroot. The liquid used is Tri-Chloro-Acetic Acid. Since many of these ingredients are toxic, Hoxsey used zinc oxide ointment or Vaseline around the affected area to protect healthy skin.

A medical herbalist should be consulted if you wish to try this therapy—since some of the herbs have contra-indications prohibiting their use by certain people. Licorice for example may raise blood pressure, and should not be used by people who have a problem with fluid retention.

More information about Harry Hoxsey and his therapy is available in *Suppressed Inventions and Other Discoveries,* edited by Jonathan Eisen (Avery Publishing Group, 1997). Also, Hoxsey's autobiography *You Don't Have to Die* is still in print and is available from the Hoxsey Clinic in Tijuana, Mexico. Both books are well worth reading.

11. VITAMIN C AND CANCER

Although there has been some controversy surrounding the role of vitamin C in the treatment of cancer—it does seem to be an important nutrient for people suffering from this illness—as well as in cancer prevention. It has several properties which make it useful. The first of these is that an adequate intake of vitamin C is needed to boost the function of the immune system which is generally depressed in cancer patients. The second important property of vitamin C is to maintain the strength of the connective tissue—collagen—in the body. In a state of vitamin C deficiency, collagen is known to break down. Cancer can spread much more easily in a body in which the connective tissue is weak.

In addition to these immune boosting and tissue strengthening properties, an ascorbate—non acid—form of vitamin C has also been shown to be toxic to Ehrlich ascites-carcinoma cells.

Some physicians recommend that people who have cancer should take vitamin C daily to bowel tolerance. (See section on "Taking Vitamin C" in the chapter on Nutrition and Health.) Intravenous vitamin C is also available from physicians who practice Chelation Therapy.

Research suggests that people with cancer who take vitamin C can expect some therapeutic benefits. Ewan Cameron, one of the doctors who pioneered the use of vitamin C in cancer therapy, studied the response of 100 people suffering from advanced cancer taking 10 g of vitamin C, as sodium ascorbate daily. The people with cancer who took the vitamin C enjoyed an improved appetite, improved energy levels and feelings of well-being. Some experienced a reduction in pain. Some also experienced a reduction in the size of their tumor, and in a fortunate small number of people, the tumors disappeared. Also encouraging was that the people taking vitamin C had an increased survival time of an average 293 days. The average survival time of people who also had advanced cancer—but who did not take the vitamin C —was just 38 days. The definitive book on the benefits taking vitamin C can have for people with cancer is *Cancer and Vitamin C: A discussion* by Ewan Cameron and Linus Pauling.

Case Study: Mrs. MJG, a 59 year old woman, had been suffering from a fluid buildup in the lungs for some time, accompanied by a cough, nausea and loose bowels. Medical tests discovered a tumor in the lung, which was considered terminal. Her doctors considered that conventional therapies would be of no use, so she was sent home to die.

The first consultation with a Natural Health Practitioner was on October 29, 1994. At this appointment, the woman explained that she had felt breathless for the past 3-4 years. She also had high blood pressure. In addition, she had a history of lumps in her breasts, as well as feeling she had a lump in her throat. She also reported that between the ages of 9 and 13 years, she had suffered from pleurisy. As an adult she had worked for about four years in a glasshouse where chemical sprays were used for pest control.

Using the Vega test system, severe pancreatic disfunction in addition to liver and gall bladder problems were diagnosed. The testing also revealed she had problems with both nutrient absorption, and toxicity from pesticides.

Her therapy began with an antioxidant and lipotropic nutritional supplement. Homeobotanical herbs were prescribed to encourage detoxification via the kidneys.

At the next consultation, mushroom extract and multi digestive enzymes were added to the supplements and homeobotanical remedy she was already taking. The patient was advised to restrict her diet to fresh organic vegetables and fruit, with small amounts of fish, meat, rice and pure water. All processed foods, and those containing yeast or preservatives were eliminated from the diet. In addition, 300-400 ml of carrot and cabbage juice, and 100 ml beet root juice were added to the diet. Gentle exercise such as walking on the beach, rests and plenty of sleep were added to the daily prescription.

In addition, this lady was given counselling and affirmations to help her stay positive and focused on healing.

By December, she was showing signs of improvement. The function of both her liver and pancreas had improved, and her feeling of well-being was returning. She was prescribed further antioxidant formulas, as well as a formula for her circulatory system and additional vitamin C. She was also referred to the Hoxsey Clinic in Mexico.

By February, marked improvement was obvious. At this stage, 90,000 IU of vitamin A and 800 units of vitamin E were added to her program. She was also given a formula containing essential fatty acids.

Late in March, a healing crisis occurred, with the expulsion of great quantities of smelly green mucous from the lungs. This continued for a couple of weeks with a marked improvement in breathing quality. *No* antibiotics were used, and the crisis was allowed to take its course.

This was the turning point, and by May 1995, a medical examination showed the cancer to have disappeared. Treatment continued with the addition of Coenzyme Q10, and Jason Winters tea.

As of April 1996, the patient was fit and well, with no evidence of cancer. She will need to continue taking her regime of supplements for perhaps five years. However, more important to her continued good health is that she continues to follow her holistic lifestyle and nutrition program.

Note: The little understood phenomenon known as the *healing crisis* is a vital part of natural therapy. The body **must** be allowed to clear itself of the toxins which have accumulated over the years. It has the intelligence to do this.

GARLIC AND CANCER

Case control epidemiological studies in northeast China and Italy showed that there were strong reverse trends in stomach cancer risk with dietary intake of garlic. A number of animal studies have reported inhibitory effects of garlic and its constituents on the development and growth of cancer.

- Aged Garlic Extract significantly inhibited the growth of bladder tumors in mice.

- Aged Garlic Extract and S-allyl cysteine (SAC) significantly inhibited the growth of melanoma cells.

- Aged Garlic Extract and its constituents inhibited the development of skin cancer and showed an inhibitory effect on mammary (breast) cancer in numerous studies. Constituents in Aged Garlic Extract may have anti-cancer properties toward colon cancer and prostate cancer.

- Aged Garlic Extract, S-allyl cysteine (SAC) and diallyl disulfide (DADS) inhibited the initiation of DMBA mammary carcinogenesis. Selenium appeared to enhance the activity of these compounds.

- Researchers found that oil-soluble sulfur compounds found in Aged Garlic Extract (diallyl sulfide, diallyl disulfide, diallyl trisulfide) markedly inhibited canine mammary tumor cell growth.

- Studies show that Aged Garlic Extract and its constituents inhibited aflatoxin (a most powerful toxic fungi) from binding to DNA and prevented it from being converted into active cancer-causing compounds in the body.

- Research has found that Aged Garlic Extract inhibited the mutagenesis induced by benzopyrene which is found in cigarette smoke, charcoal broiled meat and automobile exhaust. Benzopyrene is a potent procarcinogen causing a number of animal tumors.

- In humans, an Aged Garlic Extract preparation was found to reduce the side effects associated with head and neck tumors suggesting that it may be an excellent adjuvant to cancer therapy.

CONCLUSION

Remember cancer is not a death sentence. In fact cancer cells must overcome a number of hurdles to express their life threatening potential. It is not just a matter of uncontrolled growth. Supportive nutritional therapy provides an environment that puts increasing obstacles in the way of continued mutation of cell function.

Many people have recovered from so-called 'terminal' cancerous conditions. Read Doctor Max Gerson's book mentioned earlier. Another inspiring book is *The Cancer Survivors and How They Did It* by Judith Glassman, published by Dial Press of New York.

You should immediately be checked by a physician or health professional if any of the following signs occur:

Type of Cancer	Signs
Colon	Rectal bleeding, blood in stool, change of bowel habits.
Breast	Lumps, thickening, or any physical changes.
Cervical/Uterine	Bleeding between periods. Unusual discharges. Heavy or painful periods.
Bladder/Kidney	Blood in urine and increased frequency.
Lung	Any persistent cough. Sputum with blood, or chest pain.
Mouth/Throat	Chronic ulceration of mouth, tongue or throat that does not heal.
Prostate	Difficult urination. Pain in lower back or pelvis.
Stomach	Constant indigestion after eating.
Testicular	Lumps or enlargement of the testicles. Pain or discomfort in a testicle or scrotum.
Skin	Tumor or lump under the skin. Wart or ulceration that will not heal. Any change in moles

CANDIDIASIS

Candidiasis (Thrush) is caused by the overgrowth of *candida albicans*, a fungus type yeast that lives in the body. It usually lives on the skin, mouth, bowel, vagina and vulva. Many yeasts and bacteria, friendly and unfriendly, normally live in balance within the body and *candida albicans* is one of those.

SYMPTOMS

When your immune system is strong, different organisms in your body are kept in balance. However, if your immune system is weakened, an over-proliferation of candida albicans may cause the following symptoms.

- White sores on gums, tongue, inside of cheeks (thrush)
- Recurring sore throats.
- Stomach cramps, rectal itching, mucous in stools,
- Women—vaginal/vulva itching and a white cheesy discharge. (thrush)

Once candida albicans and the bacterial flora become out of balance, the candida can multiply rapidly and travel through the bloodstream releasing toxins into the system. Sometimes the immune system is hard pressed to keep up with the illness and it can also affect the nervous system and the emotions creating a multitude of symptoms. In addition the liver may become overburdened from filtering the toxins from the bloodstream.

Symptoms of Systemic Candidiasis may include:

Skin problems, eczema, psoriasis, excessive mucous secretions and congestion, diarrhea, constipation, colitis, bloating, gas, irritability, hyperactivity, anxiety, fatigue, lethargy, depression, inability to concentrate and memory problems, headaches, urinary tract, reproductive tract and respiratory infections, joint pain, hypoglycemia and sensitivity to chemicals.

Candidiasis can become part of an illness syndrome. Any immune system dysfunction or other health factors can contribute to the symptoms. For example it can occur as the result of, or following, ME (Myalgic Encephalomyelitis) or Chronic Fatigue Syndrome which are thought to be post-viral conditions which a weakened immune system is unable to recover from.

CAUSES

There are nutritional causes. Eating a rich, predominantly cooked diet reduces the levels of hydrochloric acid and enzymes in the stomach. This acid and enzymes, necessary for breaking down foods, also keep excess yeasts in check. A diet high in sugar and refined carbohydrates also gives *candida albicans* the perfect environment to thrive in.

Yeasts, bacteria, moulds and fungi we come into contact with in the environment or through our water and food can be ingested into our bodies. A weakened immune system, impaired liver, or both, may not be able to deal with this. Note that many AIDS sufferers, whose immune systems no longer function properly, develop candidiasis. Other illnesses, like diabetes predispose to *candidiasis*, so, too, does cancer.

Antibiotics are known to kill off the bacteria that control candida numbers. Excessive use of antibiotics would cause *candida albicans* to flourish. Oral contraceptives, some stomach ulcer drugs, sulpha drugs and steroids contribute to an imbalance.

TREATMENT

The remedy for this illness centres mainly around diet. Start with an good intake of raw vegetables and salads for their enzyme and vitamin content. Lightly steamed vegetables can be combined with raw until the system becomes used to all raw. Digestion of raw foods may be difficult in the beginning if the natural digestive enzyme level is low which is common in the elderly. But persevere. A natural supplement such as papain could be obtained to supply natural digestive enzymes. It is necessary to eliminate all yeasts from the diet—see below for foods to avoid. Yoghurt (unsweetened) containing the cultures lactobacillus and acidophilus provides the friendly bacteria that naturally occur in the digestive tract. These bacteria help keep yeast growth under control. However, if yoghurt is made from cows' milk which has not been organically produced, it can contain traces of antibiotics. So if possible use organic acidophilus cows' or goats' yoghurt. Other foods which can be eaten are fish, poultry (other meat in moderation), crispbread and rice crisps that are yeast free, legumes, brown rice, lentils, whole grains (millet has no gluten), fresh nuts, seeds. Onions and garlic have a natural antifungal action—Kyolic aged garlic is the most beneficial form of supplemental garlic.

Particularly avoid:

- All sugars, refined sugars and fruit sugars. (Gradually add a few fruits back later when condition has improved.)

- Refined carbohydrates white flour, cakes, biscuits, pies etc.

- Foods made with yeast, such as bread. (A concession to this might be finding a yeast free bread from a health store.) However, check carefully, with the staff if necessary, that the bread you wish to buy really is yeast free. Some breads, which are labelled 'No Added Yeast' do in fact contain yeast. A good example is sourdough bread which contains natural yeasts formed during the fermentation process.

- Foods that have a fermentation process (soya sauce, vinegars, alcohol)

- Tea, coffee and chocolate drinks

- Milk and milk products except acidophilus yogurt

- Peanuts (have a high mold content), also nut butters

- Mushrooms

- Pickles, sauces

- Cured meats

- Nutritional yeast, and beer

- Unless they are absolutely essential, eliminate antibiotics or any other drugs that may contribute to candidiasis. If antibiotics are taken, take three or four garlic capsules daily as well. (Kyolic has good anti fungal activity.)

- Eat only organic food. Toxins in the food chain such as pesticide, herbicide and fungicide residues stress the liver.

Daily supplements may include:
- Lactobacillus Acidophilus tablets or capsules

Other suggested supplements include:
- Kyo-Dophilus

- Probiata

- Garlic tablets (Kyolic)

- Vitamin A

- Vitamin B complex (not yeast based) plus extra
- Vitamin B6
- Vitamin C
- Selenium
- Magnesium
- Zinc
- Folic acid
- Essential Fatty Acids (can be taken in oil form).
- Two teaspoons of cold pressed wheat germ, flax seed, olive or safflower oil daily.

In chronic cases of candidiasis, capricin (caprylic acid, made from coconuts) may be of assistance as it inhibits the growth of *candida*. The amino acid l-cysteine, folic acid, biotin and Homeobotanical candi formula can assist with treating systemic candidiasis. A registered natural therapist could prescribe and monitor other treatments that may be necessary. Many herbs have strong antifungal properties. Homeopathy and acupuncture are also helpful in treating candidiasis.

In severe cases, ask your medical doctor about prescribing ketoconazole (sold as Nizoral). It is one strong systemic fungicide that can get into the bloodstream to fight systemic candidiasis.

OTHER TREATMENTS

Natural treatments for vaginal thrush that help restore friendly bacteria are:

- Lactobacillus acidophilus yoghurt: soak natural cotton tampons in this and insert into the vagina or alternatively use applied to a sanitary pad, or use as a douche.
- Salt sitz baths can be used for itch, whenever required, one quarter cup of salt per sitz bath.
- Also lower stress which changes the pH in the vagina.
- Keep air circulating around genitals. Avoid nylon pants, pantyhose, strong detergents in laundry, vaginal sprays and feminine hygiene preparations.

PREVENTION

- A healthy lifestyle—good nutrition and sufficient exercise.

- Reduce stress.

- Reduce alcohol, cigarettes, chemicals and heavy metal intake.

CASE STUDY

Mrs. Y was 40 years old when she sought naturopathic help. She was a busy business person plagued with low energy, allergies, wheezing and candidiasis symptoms.

She had taken antibiotics often during her life. Her symptoms got worse after a bout of the flu. She had difficulty in getting out of bed, and couldn't work properly.

Diagnosis showed candidiasis, and very poor assimilation of nutrients due to the malfunction of her digestive system—especially the small intestines.

Treatment began with an orthomolecular formula with L–Cysteine, an important amino acid for healthy mucosa in the body, as well as a digestive enzyme supplement. This was also supported by a homeopathic formula.

A 'no yeast' regime was introduced and sugar was restricted. Within 3 months she had improved considerably and was able to cope with life's chores.

Treatment continued and liver support, vitamins A, C, E, and bioflavonoids were introduced.

By the sixth month, all of the problems that she sought assistance for had gone and she is now following a healthy lifestyle, and is again an active and successful business person.

CARDIOVASCULAR DISEASE

Cardiovascular disease is the name given to disorders of the heart and circulatory system. The major disorders of this group include:

- Coronary heart or artery disease—the hardening and blocking of arteries supplying blood to the heart muscle.

- Stroke—bleeding from or blockage inside an artery or other blood vessel in the brain. This can lead to death or damage to the affected area of the brain.

- High blood pressure (hypertension)—blood pressure which is elevated above a normal, safe limit relative to your age is considered to be high blood pressure. High blood pressure, along with smoking and increased blood stickiness can lead to strokes.

- Peripheral vascular disease—the narrowing of the arteries in the legs, resulting in reduced circulation.

- High blood fats—elevated cholesterol levels and especially a high IDL cholesterol relative to the HDL cholesterol predisposes to fatty, atherosclerotic plaque being deposited inside the artery walls.

CAUSES

Smoking is the major cause of damage to the heart and cardiovascular disease. If you smoke cigarettes, or any other form of tobacco, and you want to avoid these diseases (or heal health problems you already have) STOP SMOKING. For ideas about how to go about this, please read the section "How to Stop Smoking" in the chapter on addictive substances.

The other major cause of cardiovascular disease is poor diet, especially one which is high in fat. The typical Western diet is high in animals fats which block the proper absorption of calcium in the intestines. The fat and calcium which cannot be used properly in the body become gradually deposited inside the arteries as a kind of plaque, leading to hardening and narrowing of the arteries. In order to push blood through narrowed blood vessels, the heart has to work harder. This often results in increased blood pressure. Angina is the name given to pain felt in the chest when poor blood supply results in oxygen starvation to the heart muscle. A heart attack can result if oxygen rich blood cannot reach the heart because the coronary arteries become completely blocked by plaque, or are blocked by a clot of blood. A stroke may result if narrowed arteries inside the brain are blocked by a blood clot, resulting in lack of oxygen to a particular part of the brain.

Heavy metal poisoning can also cause cardiovascular problems. See the section in this book on Mercury Toxicity.

SYMPTOMS OF CARDIOVASCULAR DISEASE

- Persistent increase in blood pressure (not related to kidney problems).
- Feeling of weakness, especially upon exertion.
- Frequent feelings of burning, tingling coldness, or numbness of the hands and feet.
- Memory loss, occasional or frequent.
- Periods of dizziness or light-headedness.
- Ringing in the ears, vertigo or partial deafness.
- Deteriorating vision, occasional or permanent.
- Shortness of breath, especially when walking quickly uphill.
- Clouding of the lens due to a cataract or white arc around the iris of the eye.
- Swelling around the ankles (not related to injury or kidney problems).
- Ulceration of the skin of the foot, ankle or leg.
- Gangrene of the toes, feet or legs, unrelated to injury.

These symptoms are commonly caused by the poor circulation experienced by people suffering from cardiovascular disease, but some may be caused by other factors.

TREATMENT

If you think you have some of the symptoms of cardiovascular disease, seek professional help. The cardiovascular diseases are responsible for at least a quarter of all deaths in most industrialized countries. Two out of five heart attacks result in sudden death—so don't wait until you have a heart attack before you take action to improve your heath.

The most effective therapy for reversing the hardening of the arteries which accompanies cardiovascular disease is chelation therapy. For a full explanation of this therapy, see the chapter on Chelation Therapy.

Dietary modifications and supplements can also be effective by themselves and should be used as an adjunct to chelation therapy, as well as following chelation therapy to maintain good health.

If you smoke, stop smoking. Also, avoid inhaling other people's cigarette smoke.

Exercise is helpful for lowering high blood pressure, but make sure you have your health professional's approval if you have a serious case of cardiovascular disease.

DIETARY RECOMMENDATIONS

Eliminate white flour and sugar from your diet. Consuming white sugar has been shown to raise blood triglyceride levels. White flour has very little nutritional value—consuming it makes you likely to become deficient in B vitamins. Replace with whole grains and wholemeal flour products.

Reduce fat consumption, particularly animal fats, from meat, cheese, ice cream and butter. Avoid vegetable fats which have been artificially hardened, such as margarine, and hydrogenated oils. These contain trans fatty acids which are harmful.

Increase fibre foods. The forms of fibre which form a mucilaginous mass or gel in the intestines bind bile and cholesterol in the intestines and promote the healthy excretion of excess fats. Examples of this sort of dietary fibre include: Pectin (found in apples), oat bran, and psyllium seeds (available at your health food store as an intestinal cleanser). They have a laxative effect.

Season your food with garlic, onions and ginger. These foods increase the good HDL cholesterol, while lowering cholesterol overall. Ginger also reduces the platelet stickiness. (Platelet stickiness means that platelets—one of the clotting factors in the blood—become unusually sticky, and clump together. This poses a danger for people with cardiovascular disease, since a clot of blood platelets loose in the blood may become stuck in an artery of the heart, or a vein, leading to a heart attack or stroke).

Eat as many raw fruits and vegetables (or their fresh juices) as possible. This, in combination with a low salt diet will supply the body with potassium. Most fruits and vegetables also contain salicylates, a form of natural aspirin which has been shown to reduce the clotting factor of platelets. Many people who have high blood pressure have benefited from this approach.

The following supplements help in the metabolism of fats and cholesterol, and improve the health of the cardiovascular system:

Vitamin C: Low vitamin C has been shown to correlate with raised cholesterol levels. Vitamin C is an antioxidant nutrient which helps prevent 'free radical' attack. A supplement of 1 gram taken in smaller doses throughout the day is helpful. Vitamin C is also necessary for the strength of connective tissue, and a lack of it can cause easy bruising and bleeding and perhaps increase the likelihood of a stroke in susceptible people. *(Caution: Vitamin C increases the availability of estrogen in the body. Women on the pill or taking hormone replacement therapy should take a maximum of 500 mg (½ gram) per day.)*

Vitamin E: Another important antioxidant nutrient, vitamin E, has a number of beneficial effects on the cardiovascular system, including inhibiting platelet stickiness. It has been shown to prevent the process of arteriosclerosis (hardening of the arteries) when taken regularly as a supplement. Vitamin E is also needed for the metabolism of polyunsaturated fats and oils. A daily supplement of naturally derived tocopherols of between 400–800 IU (International Units) is recommended for people suffering from cardiovascular disease. However taking large amounts of vitamin E will cause a (temporary) rise in blood pressure in those people who already have elevated blood pressure. Therefore, you should take this vitamin only under the supervision of a health practitioner.

Selenium: Low blood levels of this important antioxidant mineral have been shown to increase the rates of cancer as well as cardiovascular disease. Since much of the soil in the US is very deficient in this essential mineral, a supplement is essential.

Chromium: Many people with cardiovascular disease have low chromium levels. Supplementation with chromium has been shown to lower total cholesterol, while increasing the good HDL cholesterol.

Calcium: Calcium supplementation has been shown to lower cholesterol levels. It is an important mineral, and often deficient in the diet.

Garlic: Human and animal studies have substantiated that garlic lowers serum cholesterol and triglycerides and increases the amount of high-density lipoproteins (HDL). The incidence of major diseases associated with hyperlipemia, such as cancer, diabetes mellitus, and thromboembolic disorders, could be reduced with regular consumption of garlic. Hyperlipemia is the underlying pathophysiology of the number one killer, atherosclerotic coronary artery heart disease.

Anticoagulation—This effect complements the hypolipemic activity of garlic and further solidifies a role for this herb in the prevention and therapy of atherosclerotic coronary artery heart disease. Platelet aggregation superimposed on an atherosclerotic vessel is a major antecedent event causing myocardinal injury, infarction, and thromboembolic diseases. Studies have shown that garlic has great potential in inhibiting platelet aggregation and enhancing fibrinolytic activity.

Antihypertension—Garlic may have the capacity to be used alone or to supplement allopathic medicines used in current therapy that have side effects, such as impotence and tolerance. Studies suggest that garlic may exert its ability to lower blood pressure by acting like prostaglandin E1, which decreases peripheral vascular resistance.

Various research studies have suggested that Kyolic Aged Garlic Extract may afford protection against occlusive cardiovascular malfunction via anti-clotting and other properties.

Magnesium: Heart attack victims have been shown to have low levels of both magnesium and potassium. Magnesium is needed in order for the heart to contract strongly. Supplementation has been shown to increase the good HDL cholesterol levels and reduce platelet clumping. Milk consumption lowers magnesium levels, and has thus been linked to cardiovascular disease. Magnesium should be taken at the same time as Calcium—the two minerals are synergistic. A supplement should offer about 1000 mg calcium for every 400-500 mg magnesium.

Vitamin B6: This vitamin has been shown to prevent chemical damage done to the interior of the arteries. The body uses B6 along with copper to form lysyl oxidase—an enzyme needed for the cross linking of collagen and elastin. Vitamin B6 should not be taken singly for a long period, since it needs to be taken in conjunction with the other vitamins of the B complex, or deficiency in the other B vitamins may result. Ideally, take this vitamin (B6) accompanied by B vitamin complex and under professional supervision. If you decide to supplement your diet with copper, get professional advice to make sure that you balance this with an appropriate amount of zinc.

DIETARY FATS

Although a low fat diet is very useful for people who either already have—or wish to avoid getting—cardiovascular disease, some fats are essential in the daily diet. People suffering from cardiovascular disease have been shown to have low gamma-linolenic acid or GLA levels. This is caused by a deficiency of linoleic acid in the diet. EPA—eicosapentanoic acid—found in the fat of cold water fish is another essential fatty acid. If you do not want to consume fish or fish oil supplements, take flaxseed oil, since the essential fatty acid contains over 50% linoleic acid which can be broken down by the body to form EPA.

Taking two tablespoons of flaxseed oil each day supplies most of the essential fatty acids to the body, and in a two week period has been shown to decrease platelet stickiness.

NZ HERALD (LPS, REUTER, AAP)
WEDNESDAY HORIZONS, MAR 1994:

TRANSFATTY ACIDS found in margarine could contribute to an increased risk of heart disease, according to an American study.

Harvard University researchers' studies have found that women who eat the highest amounts of margarine are far more likely to suffer heart disease than women who eat less.

Transfatty acids occur naturally in dairy products and are also formed during margarine manufacture. The researchers say the acids block arteries in a similar way to animal or saturated fats.

"We now need to rethink our recommendation that we should substitute margarine for butter," says Professor Walter Willett, who headed the Harvard research team.

Some margarine makers in America are considering changing their products to eliminate trans fatty acids.

DEPRESSION

It would be a rare person indeed who did not feel depressed at some time in their lives.

SYMPTOMS OF DEPRESSION

Depression as a mental disorder is diagnosed according to the following problems reported by the person seeking help.

These symptoms are:
- Appetite changes—either reduced appetite accompanied by weight loss, or increased appetite accompanied by weight gain.

- Changes in sleeping pattern—some people who are depressed have problems with sleeplessness (insomnia) others may sleep too much (hypersomnia).

- Apathy or loss of interest in normal activities, sometimes including decrease in sexual drive.

- Change in patterns of physical activity—a depressed person may become hyperactive, always busying him/herself with something, or become inactive.

- Unexplained tiredness and loss of energy.

- Lowered ability to concentrate and think clearly..

- Feelings of inappropriate guilt, self-blame and worthlessness.

- Severely depressed people often have recurrent thoughts of death or suicide.

Psychiatrists would make a diagnosis of clinical depression in someone who complains of five of the above eight symptoms. Someone who has four of the symptoms will be diagnosed as 'probably depressed.'

Almost one out of every four people will be diagnosed as being clinically depressed during the course of their life.

CAUSES OF DEPRESSION

Depression is thought to be caused by a number of factors. The most straightforward explanation is that depression is a response to a loss suffered by an individual. The 'loss' mourned by the depressed person could be the breakup of a marriage or friendship, death of a loved person, a job loss, theft, loss of self image, or even a habit!

Depression may be a covert expression of otherwise unexpressed anger which a person turns inward against him or herself.

There is also a behavioral model of depression which theorizes that some people who are depressed use their depression to manipulate others. According to this theory, some cases of depression can be seen in the same light as such behaviors as sulking or ignoring someone.

A further theory of depression is the biogenic amine hypothesis. This theory emphasizes an imbalance of amino acids—which are needed to form neurotransmitters in the brain—causing biochemical changes which result in depression.

Physical causes of depression can include lead poisoning, an underactive thyroid gland, hypoglycemia, excessive drug use, anemia and hormonal imbalance.

Deficiency in almost any vitamin or mineral can also cause depression.

If you are depressed, it is important to make sure you have no undiagnosed medical problems which need treatment. However, even if you know your depression is not caused by a physical problem, but a reaction to a job loss or bereavement, for example, if your diet is not already optimal, you will probably benefit from nutritional therapy, in addition to counselling, which gives you a safe space to acknowledge and deal with your feelings.

Appropriate nutritional support for someone suffering from depression includes the following supplements:

B Vitamin Complex: B vitamins are needed by the body for the metabolism of various amino acids which help to regulate mood. Thiamin (vitamin B1)—depleted by sugar consumption and Niacin (vitamin B3) and Pyridoxine (vitamin B6)—required by women using oral contraceptives or HRT (hormone replacement therapy) are particularly important. Up to 50 times the recommended daily allowance of the B complex vitamins may be needed to help depression. However, do not take supplements supplying more than 50 mg thiamin (vitamin B1), 50–100 mg niacin (vitamin B3) or 50 mg pyridoxine (vitamin B6), without a nutritionally educated health practitioner's advice. Diabetics should be especially careful about using vitamin B3 since their condition may be worsened by high doses of this vitamin. Ironically, one form of vitamin B3, nicotinamide may cause depression if taken at high doses. People suffering from depression should also have their B12 level checked, and if necessary take additional B12. **Deficiency in B12 is relatively common among older people**.

Kyolic Liquid with vitamin B1 and B12 can be an excellent nutrition support for anyone suffering from depression.

A herbal medicine which can elevate mood is St. Johns Wort. It also has the effect of improving sleep patterns, relieving insomnia, as well as hypersomnia.

Try the following schedule of doses, three times daily: 2–4 g of dried herb, as is or add 8–12 ml of hot water to make a tincture, or 2–4 ml of fluid extract.

EXERCISE

One of the simplest (and cheapest) ways of alleviating depression is exercise. Exercise stimulates the brain to produce endorphins—a natural form of morphine which are responsible for the pleasant post exercise glow people experience after exercising. To gain the best effect, you should exercise for at least 30 minutes three times weekly, and sufficiently vigorously that your heart rate is raised by 50%.

Do seek professional advice before exercising if you have, or suspect you have, heart problems.

LAUGHTER

Having a good guffaw is a great antidote for depression. One of the benefits of owning a television is having access to great comedy. If you are depressed, restrict your TV viewing to program which make you laugh. *Don't watch horror, thrillers or the News.* Other good ways to laugh are to see funny movies, plays or play games such as charades. Children can be hilarious to spend time with.

DIABETES

Diabetes is a disease in which the pancreas fails to function properly and produce sufficient insulin, or, often in adult onset diabetes, the pancreas can produce insulin but the body can not utilize it properly. A lack of insulin can lead to elevated blood sugar, and problems with fat and protein metabolism. Diabetics are at greater than normal risk of developing atherosclerosis, loss of nerve function and kidney disease.

There are two main types of diabetes. These are:

'Type 1' Insulin Dependent Diabetes Mellitus (IDDM)
This type of diabetes usually begins in childhood and involves the complete destruction of the beta cells in the pancreas which manufacture insulin.

'Type 2' Non Insulin Dependent Diabetes Mellitus (NIDDM)
Usually affects adults. There are two subgroups of this sort of diabetes-obese NIDDM and non-obese NIDDM.

CAUSES

Type 1 diabetes is thought to be caused by viral infection, free radicals or auto immune problems which damage the beta cells in the pancreas to such an extent that they can no longer manufacture insulin. Chemical damage by the N–nitroso preservatives in smoked meats may also cause diabetes in some people. A hereditary–linked failure to repair damage done by chemical and viral agents also seems to play a role in the development of diabetes.

Type 2 diabetes is often found in people whose pancreas can still produce insulin, but whose bodies react to insulin in an abnormal way. Excess fat seems to play a role in the development of some cases of Type 2 diabetes, since losing weight may result in a cure. Another factor which can influence the development of diabetes is trace mineral deficiencies. Correction of these deficiencies can result in improvement of diabetic symptoms. Food allergies may also produce problems with blood sugar control.

SYMPTOMS

The classic symptoms of diabetes are weight loss, frequent urination, unusual hunger and excessive thirst.

TREATMENT

Diabetes always needs to be managed with the guidance of a competent health care practitioner, since the complications of this condition can be life threatening. However, with professional guidance there are a number of self help techniques diabetics can use to improve their health.

DIET

The number one therapy for diabetes is an appropriate diet along with nutritional supplementation to correct any deficiencies. Losing weight can result in a reduction or even disappearance of diabetic symptoms in some cases. (But only in people who were overweight to begin with.) Losing weight is best accomplished through a calorie controlled diet in combination with physical exercise. Exercise also gives the additional benefit of helping control blood sugar. A diabetic diet should emphasize foods which produce the least elevation in blood sugar. These foods are: most fruits (with the exception of bananas and raisins); legumes (especially soybeans), whole grains (especially whole grain rye bread, wholemeal pasta and buckwheat). Sucrose (cane sugar) should be eliminated from the diet. Fructose (fruit sugar) is a good alternative. Half or more of your calories should come from unrefined carbohydrates, and a maximum of 30% of your calories from fats. This can be accomplished by reducing your consumption of animal fats, which is a particularly good idea if you have diabetes since diabetics are prone to heart disease. By the same token you should also reduce your salt intake.

Many diabetic diets designed by dieticians are based around a 'portion' or 'exchange' system to limit the consumption of carbohydrates which could cause a dangerous rise in blood sugar. If you are following such a diet and wish to modify it for any reason, you should talk to your health practitioner first. This is particularly important if you have insulin dependent diabetes.

SUPPLEMENTS

In addition to a sensible diet, you should also seek an evaluation to see if you are deficient in any vitamins or minerals. The frequent urination which is a symptom of diabetes can lead to mineral deficiencies, such as zinc. Diuretics (water pills) which are often prescribed for diabetes can worsen the condition by creating a deficiency in magnesium or potassium.

CHROMIUM

Local laboratories are unlikely to be able to test whether or not you are deficient in chromium, but a number of studies have shown chromium supplementation can benefit people with diabetes, particularly those who are elderly and have non insulin dependent diabetes. If you can tolerate brewer's yeast, you could try taking 20–30 tablets a day (or 9 g of powder). This also has the advantage of supplying you with a good amount of B vitamins. If you are allergic to yeast, 200 mcg of chromium chloride daily can be tried. This form of chromium is better absorbed along with the B vitamin niacin at 100 mg daily. Chromium supplementation has been shown to lower total cholesterol while raising HDL cholesterol (good cholesterol). It can also improve glucose tolerance. Exercise helps your body retain the chromium it needs. An excellent supplement for chromium would be Kyo-Chrome, made by Kyolic.

OTHER MINERALS

- Manganese deficiency is common in diabetics. Seek professional advice about supplementation with this mineral. It is also worthwhile seeking advice about a suitable level of supplementation for magnesium since a lack of this mineral predisposes to coronary artery spasm as well as making it harder to control diabetes.

- Potassium may also be needed as a supplement since insulin administration can cause deficiency in this mineral.

- Zinc supplementation should also be considered since it is involved in insulin production, secretion and utilization in the body. It also helps protect the beta cells in the pancreas from being destroyed and plays a vital role in immune function.

VITAMINS

- **B vitamins** are important for diabetics. Pyridoxine (Vitamin B6) supplementation has been shown to help people with diabetics who suffer from peripheral neuropathy - nerve damage which results in numbness and pain, particularly in the hands and feet. Vitamin B6 also has a protective effect against other diabetic complications. Vitamin B12 is also useful for treating diabetic neuropathy.

- **Vitamin C** supplementation is also needed by diabetics, since it helps the transport of insulin into the body's cells. A deficiency in vitamin C may be responsible for the capillary fragility in the eyes which can lead to diabetic retinopathy which, if untreated often progresses to blindness. Low levels of vitamin C can also lead to immune system depression and raised cholesterol.

- **Vitamin E** supplementation is important in diabetes since as an antioxidant it can help prevent free radical damage which can lead to atherosclerosis (narrowing and scarring of the arteries).

HERBAL REMEDIES

- **Perocarpus Marsuption** is a botanical medicine which has been traditionally used for diabetes in India. An extract from the bark of this plant contains a flavonoid epicatechin which, along with an alcohol extract of the plant have been shown to cause the beta cells of the pancreas to regenerate and function again.

- **Bitter Alelon** *(Balsam pear)* has been used as one of the traditional medicines of Africa, Asia and South America. It has known blood–sugar–lowering properties. In some people it may be suitable as a replacement for insulin. A daily dose of 50–60 ml of juice (taken orally) has shown promising results in clinical trials.

- **Blueberry Leaves** *(Vaccinium myrtillus)* is an extract of blueberry leaves which has anti-hemorrhagic and antidiabetic properties. Injections of this extract can be substituted (under professional supervision of course) for insulin. The most active ingredient of the blueberry extract appears to be the compound myrtillin. The normal injectable dose is 1 gm daily. However beneficial results from just one administration have been known to last for several weeks. Myrtillin and the other anthocyanides found in blueberry leaves are not as strong as insulin but are less toxic even if 50 times the recommended dose are administered.

- **Essiac** herbal remedy has reportedly been used to successfully treat diabetes. The herbal formula was traditionally used by North American Objibway Indians as a treatment for cancer. (For full details see section on Cancer). A French-Canadian nurse by the name of Renée Caisse (Essiac is Caisse spelled backwards) learned about the remedy. She began to use it to treat cancer. One of the people she treated had both cancer and diabetes.

He recovered from both conditions. Other anecdotal reports support the idea that this herbal remedy may help diabetics to reduce, or in some cases eliminate, their need for insulin. However, like all herbs used for the treatment of diabetes, Essiac should only be tried under professional supervision.

DIGESTIVE PROBLEMS

Problems with digestion are fairly common and are important to remedy. If your digestion and absorption of food is impaired, your general well-being is threatened.

HOW DIGESTION WORKS

The digestive process begins in the mouth where the enzyme ptyalin in saliva begins to break down starches. Once in the stomach, food is further broken down by hydrochloric acid and pepsin. Pepsin has an important role to play in breaking down proteins. As people age, production of stomach acid may tend to decline, adversely affecting the ability of pepsin to do its job, and reducing the efficiency of the digestive system.

One cause of the decline in the ability of the stomach to produce adequate amounts of hydrochloric acid is the use of antacids which neutralize stomach acid thereby stimulating your body to manufacture more to compensate. In the long term this may strain the capacity of the stomach to make acid and result in an insufficient production of hydrochloric acid. After being churned up in the stomach, food goes into the small intestine. Here, secretions from the pancreas break the food down still more. The liver also secretes bile salts and acids which break food down before the food is shunted by peristaltic contractions into the large intestine. Here, water and some minerals from the food are absorbed before the waste food mass is eliminated.

DIGESTIVE PROBLEMS

Digestive problems are many and varied. This book does not have the space to deal adequately with the more serious conditions which would need professional assistance. A reading list is supplied at the end of this book for people who suffer from some of the less common digestive problems such as coeliac disease, colitis or diverticulitis.

INDIGESTION

Indigestion (also called dyspepsia) is the name given to discomfort suffered after eating. Someone suffering from indigestion is most likely to feel full for hours after a normal meal, often accompanied by nausea and belching. Whole pieces of food may be seen in bowel movement.

CAUSE

Indigestion symptoms of this kind may be caused by failure of the stomach to produce enough acid to digest food properly. Indigestion can also be caused by emotional upset and stress. It is better to delay meals rather than eat when you are anxious or tense.

Indigestion may also be caused by excess stomach acidity. This can be temporarily relieved by taking an antacid such as sodium bicarbonate (baking soda) or natural papaya or papain, an enzyme that aids digestion. Do not take antacids which contain aluminum. If antacids help your indigestion, it is probably caused by excess stomach acidity. If antacids do not help your indigestion, try taking pepsin and betaine hydrochloride (200 mg). These tablets will supplement your natural secretion of stomach acids. Take 1–3 tablets dissolved in water before each meal.

If you take these digestive aids and find that your symptoms become markedly worse, it probably indicates that you have a problem with excess stomach acidity. Stop taking the pepsin and betaine hydrochloride **immediately**. Often 1 teaspoon of unpasteurized apple cider vinegar and 1 teaspoon of raw honey, taken in a glass of water, will aid stomach acidity safely and effectively, however, like the pepsin and betaine hydrochloride, these should not be taken by people with excess stomach acidity.

If your symptoms improve as a result of taking the betaine hydrochloride and pepsin, you probably have a problem with insufficient stomach acidity. You should seek the advice of a holistic health professional for further advice about how to improve your digestion and get your stomach functioning properly again. You should be checked for heavy metal toxicity since in some circumstances—such as when mercury is being leached from amalgam fillings and constantly swallowed with saliva—your stomach may shut down its production of hydrochloric acid in an effort to avoid absorbing the toxic mercury.

Basic self–help care for this condition includes: not drinking with meals (other than acid supplements), since water, juice or any other drink will further dilute weak stomach acid. Small meals are better than large meals. Chewing food thoroughly—try chewing a mouthful of brown rice 30 times—will also aid predigestion before it reaches the stomach.

Self-help care for someone suffering from indigestion caused by excessive hydrochloric acid production includes:

- Eating small, more frequent meals instead of large meals.
- Not eating late at night.
- Avoiding spicy foods, especially those containing chili and curry. Fatty foods should also be avoided.

Instead of taking antacids, take aloe vera juice *(see the Super Foods section for more information)*.

Some people find that drinking milk (which have actually been shown to raise production of stomach acid) and eating other dairy products as well as wheat, increase stomach problems. Keep a diary of what you eat (and how you feel) to see if you can pinpoint any allergies or seek professional help to identify foods you may be allergic to.

The following herbs may help relieve stomach pain: slippery elm and peppermint. These can be made into a tea. Use about one teaspoon of the herb for each cup of water.

Ordinary tea and coffee, as well as alcohol and smoking, can make digestive problems worse.

CONSTIPATION

Constipation is a word used to describe bowel movements which are hard and infrequent. Often a person who is constipated feels the urge to go to the toilet, but cannot produce anything, even with straining. The abdomen may feel tender and the sufferer may complain of nausea or a headache.

CAUSES

Constipation has numerous causes. They include low fibre diet, excess consumption of meat and/or dairy products, poor liver or thyroid function, inadequate fluid intake, and lack of exercise.

Constipation may also be caused by some prescription drugs. Occasionally constipation can be caused by cancer. Sudden constipation, or bleeding with bowel movements, or unexplained changes in bowel movements, should be checked by a doctor.

PREVENTION

Constipation can be prevented by eating a high fibre diet, drinking 6 to 8 glasses of water a day and getting some exercise.

Rebounding (or skipping) is especially good.

TREATMENT

The treatment of constipation is very similar to its prevention. The first thing to do is ensure a good fluid intake. Then increase your intake of high fibre foods. Eat some natural yogurt which contains the same bacteria which live in your bowel and help regulate your digestive processes. Get some exercise. If the following suggestions don't ensure you have a bowel movement every day, try a gentle laxative:

Psyllium seeds, flax seed meal (or seeds)—chew them very well before swallowing (or mix with water), and rice bran can be tried. Dosage: Take 1 teaspoonful per day.

If these don't work, consult a naturopath about a herbal laxative which can help you. Don't dose yourself with mineral oil—you'll only deplete your body of the fat soluble vitamins. A naturopath or nutritionally–aware health professional, may also be able to suggest tasty ways to constipation–proof your diet and lifestyle.

DIARRHEA

Diarrhea is the name given to runny bowel movements, which can sometimes be watery or mucousy. Long term diarrhea is dangerous since it can result in the loss of vital water and minerals from the body. If you have blood with your bowel movements, see a qualified health practitioner.

CAUSE

Diarrhoea may be caused by a bacterial or viral infection, food poisoning, allergies, emotional stress, or drugs. It is important to know what has caused diarrhea.

TREATMENT

Grated apple (without peel) and yoghurt (sprinkle a little cinnamon on), is a traditional remedy for diarrhea. The plain yoghurt with acidophilus/bifidus culture contains bacteria which help to regulate the digestive system. If you cannot keep this down and if diarrhea is accompanied by vomiting, try peppermint tea or ginger tea, taken in small sips. Use a teaspoon of dried leaves or powder for each cup of hot water and sip small amounts slowly. If you cannot keep mint tea down, seek medical help, since you may become dehydrated. Check that any medication you are offered does not contain aluminum, since this may aggravate diarrhea.

A natural alternative for avoiding disorders such as constipation, diarrhoea or candida is to replenish your healthy intestinal flora with Kyo-Dophilus or Probiata. These products are a must for those who want the ultimate in flora protection. They require no refrigerator and are great for travel. Most important of all they truly colonize in the intestinal tract.

Homeopathic remedies may also help resolve chronic diarrhoea, and fasting on water may also help. Rehydration fluids may sometimes be necessary since vital mineral balances may become disrupted.

If you live alone it's a good idea to keep an emergency stock of rehydration fluids in the medicine cabinet.

For a list of books with good information about other digestive problems, see Suggested Reading section at the end of this book.

INCONTINENCE

Urinary incontinence is one of the most common reasons why elderly people have to go into full time care. Incontinence generally means passing urine when you did not intend to and it may happen in the form of sudden leaks when coughing or laughing or running, unexpected leaks when changing position, dribbling after urination, the urge to urinate immediately and/or frequently or the total loss of control of the bladder. An erratic bladder may produce the need to urinate even after the bladder has been emptied.

It affects twice as many women as men. Unfortunately it tends to worsen with age and is aggravated by other degenerative diseases. Many people find it embarrassing to talk about, even to their doctor. In terms of social problems it can be demoralizing but people should be encouraged not to withdraw from social contact.

CAUSES

In Men and Women

- Bladder and urinary tract infections. Infections can develop if the bladder is not completely emptied. Low grade infections may be present in many cases without being noticed.

- Emotional problems, anxiety, stress and grief can produce temporary incontinence.

- Gravity is a factor in many lower body ailments. A major contributor to this is years of sitting where inert muscles offer little resistance to the gravitational pull. The constant downwards pressure combined with bad sitting postures, obesity, or extra stomach fat combine to weaken the lower abdominal, pelvic floor and pelvic girdle muscles, which places tremendous strain on organs, sometimes resulting in deposition of the bladder neck and prolapsus of the bladder, uterus and other organs.

- Drugs which may be prescribed for high blood pressure and heart disease, diuretics sedatives and tranquillizers may induce temporary incontinence. Similarly some over the counter drugs like antihistamines can affect the bladder. Also food and medicine combinations can aggravate incontinence. Check with your pharmacist or doctor.

- The presence of Alzheimer's disease, senility, strokes or other neurological disorders may impair the brain's ability to control the bladder.

- Other degenerative diseases such as diabetes, kidney or bladder stones, brain or spinal tumors, bladder cancer and Parkinson's disease are known to effect incontinence.

In Women Only

- Incontinence is often caused by the weakening of the pelvic floor muscles and the muscles of the urethra canal. The urethra canal alternately contracts when the bladder is being filled and opens to enable urine to be expelled. The pelvic floor muscles are a large group of muscles which act like a sling under the bladder, uterus, vagina, urethra and anus. Pregnancies place a load on these muscles. During the birth process, long hard labors, tears, episiotomies, and the use of forceps traumatize and stretch these muscles. Many women never do the exercises required to correct this.

- During menopause the reduced levels of estrogen which causes the thinning and shrinking of vaginal tissues may also affect the urinary organs, often temporarily. For some women this is often the first experience of incontinence.

- Cystitis can cause the urgent need to pass water, often when there is none or very little. However, leaks can occur.

Women who smoke have been found to suffer from incontinence at more than three times the rate of nonsmoking women.

TREATMENT

For Men and Women:
- The first part of treatment for incontinence is its management. Special pads, undergarments, mattress covers, neutralizing deodorants, are available to help contain or disguise the leakages. In many cases these can be supplied through the public health system. Don't withdraw from social contact. Bring yourself to talk to someone about this, your naturopath, your doctor or nurse, because it is more easily treated at onset. For those caring for an incontinent person there may be free home help services or grants available.

- Find out from your doctor or health system, self help or support groups.

- Exercises that reduce the effects of gravity—see Exercise section.

- Review your diet. See nutrition section. Among other things you need a diet high in fibre to keep bowels moving. Constipation puts a strain on weak pelvic floor muscles. Restricting your fluid intake will contribute to bladder infections due to stagnant urine and dehydration of tissues. Studies show that exercise combined with weight loss, especially loss of stomach fat, can greatly improve incontinence.

- Herbs: Cranberry juice is a natural deodorizer for urine. Some people find it also helps with incontinence. It reduces infections.

  | Buchu Tea | Oatstraw Tea |
  | Dandelion Tea | Cranberry Juice |

- The following supplements (per day) may also be of assistance:

  | Calcium, 1000 mg | Magnesium, 400 mg |
  | Potassium, 200 mg | Vitamin A, 20,000 IU |

  | Zinc, 80 mg | Vitamin E★, 200–600 IU |

  ★*(If blood pressure is high, seek professional advice.)*

  Biochemic Cell Salts: Calc Flour, Calc Phos, Mag Phos, Nat Mur

- In advanced cases there are many drugs that can treat incontinence. However, the drugs may have side effects, including irritability.

For Women Only

- The regular practice of pelvic floor exercises helps to bring back control of the weakened pelvic floor muscles which can occur during numerous and difficult pregnancies. In some cases where the muscles may be severely weakened, benefits may take a while to become apparent. However it is worth persevering as this is the most natural way to treat it.

- Pelvic floor exercise: Sit on the lavatory and tighten the anal muscle that controls bowel movements. Pass some water and try to stop the flow mid-stream by tightening the muscles of the vagina for 10 seconds. Now that you have located the muscles and got them working you can practice this sitting watching television, standing at the bus stop, lying down, upon sleeping or waking, in a store line-up. Strengthening these muscles is also a bonus for you and your partner during sex. If you faithfully try to do it every hour you will get benefits. First tighten the back passage muscles and then the front passage. A natural consequence of tightening these muscles is that your back will straighten and benefit *(see the exercises for the lower body problems under the Yoga Section).*

- Get checked for bladder infections or cystitis.

- Estrogenic herbs may be useful for mild cases during menopause *(see chapter on The Natural Approach to Menopause).*

- A pessary is a small rubber device that fits in the top of the vagina and holds prolapsed organs in place. This is a most effective solution and is helpful to elderly women who are too ill for surgery.

- If none of the above helps, surgery may be needed to correct the stretched muscles and re-position the bladder. In preparation for this a small diary noting the whens, wheres, frequency, how much, what prompts leakages, etc. is advisable so that you can effectively answer questions and obtain the best treatment. If you are contemplating surgery, you or your family should get a book from the library detailing medical diagnosis, standard tests and surgical procedures. Although a routine examination by a surgeon should not be painful, some tests can cause some pain. You need to be equipped

"There may be a few side effects!"

with all the right questions to ask why you need certain tests, or what benefits you will get from treatment. The urinary incontinence section in the book *Ourselves Growing Older* clearly explains the medical procedure.

PREVENTION

- A diet providing all nutritional needs.

- Sufficient exercise to keep muscles toned. Yoga type exercises or swimming, to strengthen lower abdominal and pelvic floor muscles.

- Break long periods of sitting with some walking around or exercise.

PROSTATE DISORDERS

The prostate is a donut-shaped gland which is situated beneath the bladder in men. It encircles the urinary outlet or urethra. Prostatic fluids are ingredients of semen.

The prostate is the most common site of disease in the male genitourinary system. The three most common diseases that occur are **Prostatitis, Benign Hypertrophy** and **Cancer.**

DEFINITIONS

Prostatitis is the most common form of disorder of this gland and it occurs in all age groups. It is an inflammatory condition often caused by bacterial infection. Due to the inflammation and swelling it can partially block the flow of urine out of the bladder. This results in distention of the bladder creating further susceptibility to infection within the bladder.

The symptoms of prostatitis include pain in the lower abdomen, back, testicles and the area between the scrotum and anus. The need to urinate frequently may accompany this - possibly with a burning sensation. Urine may be cloudy (due to pus) or contain blood. Symptoms may include fever and general unwellness.

If not treated properly, prostatitis may become chronic leading to greater difficulty in passing urine.

Benign Hypertrophy is the gradual enlargement and hardening of the prostate gland tissue. The only symptoms to be felt at first may be a feeling of congestion or discomfort in the pubic area along with a constant feeling of fullness in the bladder. But the enlarging gland usually compresses the urethra tube along which urine flows and usually what follows is difficulty in starting a urine stream and in passing urine. As the urethra tube becomes more compressed the normal urine flow may become a slow dribble. Since the bladder cannot be completely emptied, along with the discomfort comes the inconvenience of needing to urinate frequently. Disruption to the urinary flow may cause urinary tract infections and in severe cases retention may cause uremic poisoning and damage to the kidneys.

Benign Hypertrophy occurs in 30 percent of men in the 50s age group. Up to 75 percent of men may be affected, to varying degrees, by the time they reach their eighties. Early diagnosis, treatment and nutritional management is important to avoid the medical procedures needed to alleviate urine retention. This involves a catheter being inserted along the urethra and into the mouth of the bladder to drain off the urine. It will accumulate again and often surgery is advised to reduce the size of the prostate gland. Even after surgery, if the causative problems are not addressed, the prostate can enlarge again.

Cancer of the prostate is the third most common malignancy to be found in men, but it rarely occurs in men under 60 years of age. The symptoms are similar to prostatitis and include difficulty in urinating, with frequency at night and usually blood in the urine. This may be the reason why it can spread before diagnosis. The state of the prostate can be determined by a physician by examination through the anal wall. Evidence of cancer might be suggested by the presence of nodules or by the abnormal hardness of the gland.

CAUSES

Prostatitis is caused by a bacterial infection, most commonly sexually transmitted.

Benign Hypertrophy is thought to occur because of the changes in hormone levels in the prostate gland. Age and other factors trigger the decline in the male hormone testosterone which results in poor metabolism of other hormones. Because of this, testosterone changes into another hormone known as dihydrosteostorone (DHT). It is the DHT which accumulates in the prostate cells and is stored in the prostate walls causing the enlargement. Higher levels of the hormone prolactin increase the amount of testosterone absorbed by the prostate gland which may allow more DHT to be formed and stored in the prostate.

Nutritionally the average western diet (high in saturated fat and low in fibre) contributes to changes within the hormone system. Glands like the adrenals and prostate age as the body ages but the age of the body can be influenced by our living habits. The prostate gland secretions nourish sperm cells. The lack of proper nutrients in the body for manufacture of this hormone could contribute to disorders of the gland. The male reproductive system needs fresh unprocessed fats and the highest quality proteins to be healthy. Diets based on processed foods where most natural proteins and unsaturated fatty acids have been removed (breakfast cereals), heated fats and oils (fried foods) and hydrogenated fats (pastries, pies, margarines) are inadequate for this purpose.

Pesticide residues in the food we consume affect the hormone system and in particular increases DHT levels.

A deficiency of the trace mineral zinc is now thought to contribute to benign hypertrophy. Much of the soil around the world is deficient in zinc. Zinc is required for the metabolism of protein. Medical scientists have discovered that zinc has the ability to reduce the concentration of prolactin in the blood. This means that less DHT is formed in the prostate gland. Research has found that a healthy prostate gland contains more zinc than a swollen, sick one.

Residues of hormones widely used in animal farming are passed on to humans through meat and milk. These may interfere with normal hormone metabolism in the body.

Alcohol, especially beer, increases the levels of prolactin which increases DHT. Tobacco also plays a major role in the poisoning of the prostate gland.

Prostate Cancer is of course caused by a combination of factors but a high fat diet certainly contributes to it. Additionally the chemical reactions that occur when fats are heated lead to the production of free radicals which can cause cell damage. This can mean a higher risk of cancer for some people, especially if the immune system has been weakened. Coffee, strong tea, alcohol and smoking have also been linked to cancer of the prostate.

Also in the area of cancer control, Dr. John Pinto of Memorial Sloan Kettering Cancer Centre presented his research on the use of aged garlic extract with human prostate cancer cell lines. Pinto's research showed that Aged Garlic Extract was successful in blocking the growth of prostate cancer cells.

Prostate cancer occurs most often in men with a history of sexually transmitted diseases.

According to the August 1989 issue of *The Medical Times* **"the risk of prostate cancer for males after a vasectomy increases threefold."**

TREATMENT

Prostatitis

Pay attention to your nutritional intake *(see Nutrition and Health chapter)*. Infection of the prostate gland can be a major result of nutritional decline. Prolonged nutritional deficiency and infections can cause disorders of the glands and hormones. A full and well balanced diet with supplements of vitamins A, C, D, E, vitamin B complex, Kyolic Garlic and Kyolic EPA with omega 3 fatty acids to boost the immune system should help resolve any chronic infection. Also use essential fatty acids as well as other prostate protective nutrients (see benign hypertrophy below) and seek the advice of a qualified natural therapist.

Increase water intake to 6–8 glasses per day to prevent cystitis and kidney infection. If you are sexually active and have more than one partner you should first ascertain whether an infection has been passed to you by sexual contact and, if so, get the appropriate treatment. The natural therapy approach to this might include specialist herbal preparations, homeopathy and orthomolecular supplements prescribed by a professional in those fields.

Benign Hypertrophy

Good nutrition and organically grown food is important in treating prostate disorders. Reduce alcohol consumption. Stop altogether if possible. The same can be said for coffee and tea. *(see Nutrition and Health chapter)*

Zinc supplements—see below. Studies carried out with zinc sulphate shows that it can reduce prolactin levels in the bloodstream for several hours 30 minutes after being taken. A medical study in 1976 found that zinc combined with vitamin B6 was able to reduce prostate enlargements.

A secret traditionally handed down from father to son amongst peasant people to preserve the prostate is **pumpkin seeds**. Pumpkin seeds contain all the nutrients that are the building blocks for the male hormones even as men age. They supply the body with the nutrients to support normal hormone metabolism. They are high in phosphorus, magnesium, iron, B vitamins, zinc and contain some vitamin A. They contain about 30% protein and 40% fat and are a completely natural food. Their fat is rich in unsaturated fatty acids (vitamin F) which is essential for the male reproductive system. Where they are used widely prostatic hypertrophy is almost unknown. They can be freshly ground or blended with other seeds and sprinkled on food if there are chewing problems.

Cold pressed oils such as olive, safflower, flax seed and pumpkin seed will also supply essential fatty acids. Use 3 teaspoons daily.

Studies carried out some years ago on a group of patients using only essential fatty acids showed a significant reduction in residual urine, bladder inflammation, dribbling and the size of the prostate, some reduction in night time urination, a decrease in fatigue and leg pains while showing an increase in urinary flow and sexual libido.

Amino acids (components of protein) were used in a trial among a group of forty cases of prostate enlargement. The three amino acids tested—glycine, alanine and glutamic acid were given in capsule form after meals and this relieved the night time need to void in 95% of cases and completely eliminated the need to void in 72%. Urgency and frequency of urination, discomfort and delayed urination was reduced in an average of 70% of cases.

It was also discovered that edema (swelling in other parts of the body) disappeared during treatment. Edema is often a symptom of protein (amino acids) deficiency, kidney failure and the result of too much salt which retains water in the tissues. Therefore a diet rich in a source of good proteins and low in salt are a good combination for treating an enlarged prostate. Although meat is high in these amino acids, it also contains animal fat which should be reduced in favor of essential fatty acids. Get amino acids from vegetable sources like kidney beans, lentils, soybeans, nuts, seeds, chlorophyll, royal jelly and food grade brewers yeast.

Magnesium is an important mineral for treating urinary problems of prostatic origin. Men in their 40s or those older who are not affected by Benign Hypertrophy should ensure they get a magnesium rich diet to prevent being affected by it later on. Diet should include wheat germ (which should be kept in the fridge or freezer), pumpkin seeds, sunflower seeds, honey, nuts, green leafy vegetables and brown rice. As far back as the 1930s, in France, magnesium chloride tablets were used by Dr. Joseph Favier to relieve chronic cases of nocturnal urinating problems, urine retention and bladder residue. In many cases they prevented prostatic operations being required. Obtain the magnesium in a more natural form, by diet, or a well-absorbed form of supplementary magnesium, like magnesium citrate.

Drink 6 to 8 glasses of **purified water** daily. This can help in preventing bacterial infections in the urethra.

Fat soluble **vitamins** are important to the health of this gland. Vitamin A is important for the protection of tissues that line the digestive and reproductive tracts. Vitamin E deficiency creates problems for the reproductive systems of both males and females in animals and humans alike. Flax seed oil is a good source of vitamin E as well as essential fatty acids. Take up to 2 tbsp daily.

Daily supplements of vitamins and minerals should include:

Kyolic Garlic	3 per day
Zinc	80 mg
Beta Carotene	25,000 IU
Vitamin E★	600 IU
Vitamin C	1–4 grams
Vitamin B6	50 mg twice daily
Lecithin	500–1000 mg
Calcium	1000 mg
Magnesium	800 mg
Kyolic EPA	4 per day

Essential Fatty Acids   by oil supplement—see above

★Caution: This amount of vitamin E should not be taken if you have high blood pressure or a rheumatic heart condition. See the section on vitamins in the chapter on Nutrition and Health.

Other orthomolecular, or herbal preparations can be prescribed by a registered natural therapist if required.

Herbal: A simple tea can be made from parsley. Use one handful of parsley to 1 litre of water; simmer for 5–8 minutes and strain; dilute as used with 50% water and have three cups daily.

High quality ginseng is a tonic to the male reproductive system. It may be bought in tea or supplement form.

Exercise: Staying active as much as possible maintains circulation, but avoid bicycle riding due to the compression it exerts on the prostate gland. Also avoid exposure to very cold weather.

Hydrotherapy: Sitz baths may relieve congestion and are useful in improving circulation in the pelvic region. Only the lower part of the trunk is immersed. Keeping the body warm, sit in enough water to cover the buttocks. Use hot/warm sitz baths or alternate 3 minutes hot and 1 minute cold for 15 minutes.

Osteopathy/Massage: Manipulation to the spine, joints and tissues is a valuable therapy for prostatitis as it can improve nerve function and the blood flow to the pelvic basin.

Massage of the prostate gland is helpful in reducing its size. This can be carried out by a physician. However, it needs to be done regularly - once a week.

Gravity: One factor in prostate problems often overlooked is the effect of gravity on the body. As muscles generally weaken with age from poor diet, little exercise and bad posture, the internal organs tend to drop into the pelvic basin, interfering with the return flow of blood back to the heart. Constipation can contribute to this. With pelvic problems in elderly men and varicose veins in women, posture and circulation always need attention.

Prostrate Cancer: For the prevention of prostate cancer—as well as benign hypertrophy—a regular intake of zinc and unsaturated fatty acids (Kyolic

EPA and Kyolic Garlic) is very important. *(see Cancer section, earlier this chapter)*

PREVENTION OF PROSTATE DISORDERS

A healthy diet including foods rich in zinc and essential fatty acids is the best prevention of prostate problems. *(see Nutrition and Health, chapter 4)*

Sufficient exercise. *(see Breathing, Exercise and Relaxation, chapter 6)*

A minimal intake of alcohol, coffee and tea. Cut down or give up smoking.

Reduce stress. Practice relaxation techniques.

A good relationship with wife or partner. Although there is no evidence that celibacy contributes to prostate disorders, research suggests that men who are sexually active have fewer prostate problems. This may be because there are higher levels of testosterone in the body and better hormone metabolism.

SHINGLES

Shingles is caused by Herpes zoster, the virus that also causes chicken pox. Shingles is characterized by intense nerve pain in the nerve endings of the affected area. A rash of itchy blisters develops a few days later which normally lasts for five to six days. The blisters eventually dry up and drop off. However the intense pain may continue. It usually appears on the abdomen, chest or back but can appear anywhere, even on the face—which can endanger the eyes.

CAUSE

The virus that causes shingles generally lies dormant in the body for years and is triggered by stress when the immune system is depressed.

TREATMENT

- An improved diet which must include raw fruits, vegetables, brown rice, nuts and seeds.
- Juice therapy for cleansing.
- Vitamin therapy for building immune system.
- Rest and keep warm.
- Short periods of sunlight on affected area.

- Homeopathy is effective.

- A cream with an extract of cayenne *(capsicum)* called Zostrix can be prescribed by a doctor.

- Cayenne capsules which contain capsicum help relieve pain and aid healing.

- 500–1000 mg pantothenic acid *(vitamin B5)*

PREVENTION

Keeping the immune system strong is critical.

VARICOSE VEINS

Varicose veins is the name given to the condition caused when the walls of blood vessels lose their elasticity and become distended.

This damages the one way valves that help propel blood back to the heart. As a result, blood pools in the veins and they bulge. Varicosities may start in the deep veins and arteries in the calves. Blockages in those veins reroute blood to veins closer to the skin where varicosities are more easily seen. Varicose veins are often accompanied by aching, swelling, heaviness and cramps. If the deep veins are severely affected, this may result in thrombosis (clots).

CAUSES

- Insufficient exercise causing poor circulation.

- Genetic weaknesses in blood vessel walls and valves.

- Diet: mineral and vitamin deficiencies cause loss of elasticity. A low fibre diet causes straining on defecation.

- Long periods of standing or sitting—especially with crossed legs.

- Pregnancies put a strain on veins and may cut off circulation at top of legs. In addition, the hormonal changes of pregnancy soften veins.

- Obesity.

- Heavy lifting.

- Alcohol and smoking.

TREATMENT

- Increased exercise. Blood is pushed through veins by the contraction of muscles. Regular exercise prevents blood from pooling in veins. Just flexing calf muscles regularly can increase circulation. Point toes downwards and then upwards.

- A high fiber diet supplying all necessary nutrients for strengthening veins. Avoid animal protein, fried food, refined food, sugar, cheese, salt, peanuts, cigarettes, alcohol.

- A daily supplement regimen including:

  –Vitamin C plus bioflavonoids 3,000 mg daily. Vitamin C reduces clotting tendencies and strengthens blood vessels and capillaries. Women taking the Pill or Hormone Replacement Therapy should take a maximum of 500 mg of vitamin C daily. *(see the section on Vitamin C in chapter 4, Nutrition and Health)*

  – Vitamin A.

  – Brewer's Yeast or Complex B vitamin (Brewer's Yeast or unsalted food yeast also supplies protein).

  – Balanced calcium and magnesium supplement.

  – Vitamin E: 600 IU. This reduces the heavy feeling in the legs, improves blood flow and increases oxygen transport to cells. Large amounts of vitamin E should not be taken by people with rheumatic heart disease or high blood pressure. *(see section on vitamin E in chapter 4, Nutrition and Health)*

  – Zinc, for healing: 80 mg.

- Vitamin K: 200 mcg.

- Lecithin: 200 mg.

- Tissue salt calcium fluoride for tissue elasticity.

- Herbal detoxification teas.

- Massage: by hand or by gentle battery powered massager.

- When sitting, put feet up on a stool.

- A useful exercise for varicose veins is: lie on back, raise and shake right leg for up to eight seconds. Lower and rest for up to eight seconds, then repeat this with the left leg. Rest and then repeat with both legs together. Rest. Done several times a day this will allow the veins to be emptied and then refreshed with new blood which has a stimulating and contracting effect on the vein walls. People with thrombosis or clots should just raise legs level with body, i.e. put feet up on a stool.

• Never cross legs—get used to being comfortable without crossing legs.

• Women can wear support hose (tights) when standing or walking.

• Bathe legs in white oak bark herb tea (heated but not boiled) three times daily or use witch hazel compresses to relieve pain.

PREVENTION

• High fiber diet; add supplements.

• Regular exercise.

• Don't cross legs.

• Put feet up—many lower body problems are gravity related.

CHAPTER 14

THE NATURAL APPROACH TO MENOPAUSE

Menopause takes place when a woman's ovaries stop producing ova and dramatically reduce, or completely stop, producing the hormone estrogen. The result of these changes is that the menstrual periods cease, and a woman can no longer become pregnant.

Although the ovaries stop producing hormones, a woman's body can continue to manufacture estrogen in the adrenal glands. This form of estrogen—called androstenedione is converted to the estrogen 'estriol' (also called 'estrone') by the liver. In order for the liver to do this however, it must be healthy. A liver overburdened by having to process alcohol, coffee and fatty foods, may not be up to this task. As a result, hormone levels may drop more sharply than nature intended them to. Any woman who is experiencing unpleasant menopausal symptoms would do well to consult a holistic health practitioner for advice on how to support her liver. Unfortunately standard liver function tests do not diagnose milder degrees of liver function impairment—only gross damage. However, there are herbs, supplements and dietary changes which can improve liver function.

The changes which lead to menopause happen gradually over a period of 2 or 3 years (on average). The age at which the 'average' woman has her last period is 49—51. However, like the onset of menstruation, this can vary widely, with some women finishing menstruating in their late 30s (smoking is a factor associated with early menopause), while others don't stop menstruating until their late 50s.

The main indications that a woman is entering menopause are:

1. Women who are 'peri–menopausal' (experiencing the changes which lead towards menopause) experience the following alterations from their 'normal' menstrual cycle.

   Women may find their periods may:
   • gradually become further and further apart
   • gradually become lighter and/or last for a shorter time
   • become irregular
   • become heavier and longer, often with more clots

   Heavy bleeding should be medically investigated, since it can be a sign of disease. Some women who suffer from heavy periods have been helped by taking supplements of iron, zinc, vitamin B6 (as part of a vitamin B complex), vitamin A and vitamin C and bioflavonoids. Seek the advice of a nutritionally–aware health professional if you have this problem.

   While these menstrual changes are common, for about a third of women menstruation continues without significant change until their final period.

2. The other major indicator that menopause is on its way are the vasomotor effects—hot flushes and night sweats. These can vary from being barely noticeable, to mildly embarrassing, to downright distressing. Hot flushes are a common feature of women's experience in the peri-menopausal years in the Western world, but not all women experience them. A recent Swedish study found that 21% of postmenopausal women had experienced no symptoms whatsoever.

3. The third major indicator of the coming menopause is changes in vaginal tissues which may become dryer and less elastic. This may make sexual intercourse painful. In a study in which 1,750 Swedish women were surveyed about their experience of menopausal changes, only a quarter of peri-menopausal women reported some vaginal discomfort, most slight.

Of the women who had gone through a natural menopause, 39% said they felt some vaginal discomfort. Half of these women reported that their discomfort was moderate or severe.

Other problems experienced by some 'mid-life' women include depression and weight gain. Extra weight gained in the time leading up to menopause is not thought to be related to hormonal changes. Depression at this time, may however, have a physical cause in fluctuating hormone levels. This may be similar to the way that hormonal changes in the premenstrual phase of the cycle can cause emotional symptoms such as irritability or weepiness. Any physical or mental problems which coincide with menopause are of course exacerbated by nutritional imbalances, unhealthy lifestyle or unresolved personal problems.

Menopause has traditionally been seen as the 'change of life.' Menopausal changes send both a physical and psychological message to a woman that she is aging. This can impact negatively upon women's self-confidence in our society which worships youthful beauty and sexuality, but tends to denigrate the appearance of older people and refuses to acknowledge their sexuality.

Menopause and the changes which often precede it as the body readjusts from an adult lifetime of preparing to reproduce every month are as normal and natural a part of life as menstruation and pregnancy. After your body has spent 30 or more years preparing to reproduce every month, coming to the end of this era necessitates a major readjustment for your body. However, over the last thirty years or so, menopausal women have been gradually redefined by the medical profession as being 'estrogen deficient' and therefore in need of being treated with Hormone Replacement Therapy (HRT). Despite the fact that there have been no long term studies of any of the various forms of HRT to assure its safety, it has been marketed to women for a multitude of reasons. These include: relief of hot flush symptoms, reduction of the bone loss which occurs as estrogen levels drop, and as a prophylactic against heart disease.

The issues surrounding HRT are complex. Some studies have found a relationship between HRT and breast cancer. A New Zealand Government appointed panel which studied the evidence for and against using HRT in 1993, recommended against the long term use of these drugs. The panel, primarily doctors, said that studies showed long term use of HRT (8 years or longer) gave a women a least a 25% increased chance of getting breast cancer. One of the scientists whose work the panel studied, put the increased risk of breast cancer at 50% higher after just 5 years use of HRT. If you are considering taking HRT, first read *The Menopause Industry: A Guide to Medicine's Discovery of the Mid-life Woman* by Sandra Coney (first published by Penguin Books 1991). This book contains an in-depth discussion of both the risks and potential benefits of HRT.

There are a number of herbal and nutritional remedies for menopausal symptoms. If you have severe menopausal symptoms, you may want to consult a natural practitioner rather than attempting to treat yourself.

HOT FLUSHES

CAUSES

Hot flushes, or flashes, are thought to be caused by the brain attempting to stimulate hormone production. However, as the ovaries are ceasing to produce estrogen, all that happens is that blood circulation is increased, which increases body temperature. This causes the hot flushes, or sweating at night, that many peri-menopausal women experience.

Vitamin E may be used to treat hot flushes, according to Canadian gynecologist Dr. Evan Shute. High doses of vitamin E can relieve hot flush symptoms within a month.

Some doctors recommend taking 400 IU of vitamin E, preferably as Alpha Tocopherols daily to treat hot flushes. Then, if no improvement is noticed, the dose may be increased gradually over several days to 800 IU daily. If this fails to lessen the hot flush symptoms, the dosage may be gradually increased to 1200 IU (This dosage should not be exceeded). After relief of hot flush symptoms has been achieved, the dosage should gradually be reduced to 400 IU daily.

Warning: Taking high doses of vitamin E can cause high blood pressure problems if you already have rheumatic heart disease, diabetes, or high blood pressure. Make sure you have medical supervision if you wish to try vitamin E therapy for hot flushes.

Bioflavonoid supplementation has also been shown to minimize hot flushes.

Both bioflavonoids and vitamin C help strengthen capillaries, and this is thought to be part of the reason why they are effective. Bioflavonoids are also structurally similar to estrogen. Natural sources of bioflavonoids include buckwheat and the white pith of citrus fruits. If you own a wheatgrass juicer, you can buy un–hulled buckwheat from a health food store, grow it in a tray of soil and harvest and juice it when it is about 8 cm high. Diluted with pure water, this drink is high in bioflavonoids and chlorophyll, as well as other vitamins and minerals.

Another option is to try a supplementation program devised by Dr. Charles Smith in 1967. Women trying Dr. Smith's program took a supplement containing: 150 mg hesperidin complex, 50 mg hesperidin methyl chalcone; and 200 mg ascorbic acid (vitamin C). This supplement was taken six times daily. It was judged in the trial to give better relief from hot flush symptoms than calcium carbonate, the fever–reducing drug salicylamide, and an estrogen. There were however two unwelcome side effects reported by the women who used the bioflavonoid/vitamin C therapy: a slightly unpleasant odor to their perspiration, and a tendency for their sweat to stain their clothes more than usual.

If you think you could be distressed by increased perspiration odor, or staining and wish to try the program above, consider getting a health practitioner's advice about starting with lower doses. (Bear in mind, that if this therapy works for you, you should perspire a lot less, so any extra perspiration odor may be negligible.)

There are a number of herbs which are useful for menopausal women, since they contain small amounts of plant estrogen and progesterone which can safely supplement the body's naturally declining level of hormones.

Estrogenic Plants include:
- **Alfalfa** – sprouts are best

- **Red Clover** – sprouts are best

- **Soy Beans** – also best sprouted. One cup of sprouts daily is recommended.

- **Sage** – can be drunk as a cold infusion to help control hot flushes. Use 10g of dried sage leaves which have been soaked overnight in 500 ml of (purified) tepid water to which the juice of one or two lemons has been added. Then strain the mixture and keep it in the refrigerator. You can take 80–100 ml of this mixture three times a day.

If your symptoms are severe, you may take the 500ml throughout the day in divided doses. (Add a little honey or fruit juice to modify the strong 'antiseptic' taste if you want to). The 500ml daily dose should only be used for a *maximum* of six -eight weeks. Sage has an antiperspirant effect, and if used excessively will cause drying of the mucous membranes.

Please note that this herb should not be used if you have epilepsy or are pregnant.

Plants which contain Progesterone Precursors:
• **Fenugreek** – best used sprouted

• **Sarsaparilla**

• **Wild Yam**

   Consult a naturopath or herbalist about using these—or any other—herbs.

VAGINAL DRYNESS

Vaginal dryness can accompany the falling estrogen levels at menopause. Doctors will often prescribe creams containing estrogen for relief of this condition which can make sexual intercourse less enjoyable—or even painful. Unfortunately, estrogen applied inside your vagina can end up in your bloodstream, so this remedy is best avoided, if possible.

Nontoxic ways of increasing the elasticity and soothing a dry vagina include: Vitamin E—capsules may be pierced with a clean needle and the contents massaged into your vagina. A good quality beeswax and oil based ointment containing the herb calendula also aids healing. Regular sexual activity helps maintain the condition of your vagina. Use a water–based lubricant such as KY Jelly if you are also using a rubber barrier contraceptive such as a condom or diaphragm.

If you do not have a regular partner, masturbation will be just as good for keeping your vagina supple. You might like to use a pleasant cold pressed oil such as apricot kernel oil or avocado oil as a healing lubricant.

CHAPTER 15

ELECTROMAGNETIC RADIATION AND GEOPATHIC STRESS

Recent research suggests that electromagnetic stress and geopathic stress could be linked to many degenerative illnesses.

For instance, there is a two to three-fold increase in leukemia in children exposed to high levels of EMFs from power lines. This has also been shown in workers who are exposed to high electromagnetic fields in their occupations.

Concern has been expressed about electrical appliances in the home and workplace (VDUs, cell phones, etc). There may be a connection between cell phones and brain tumors.

Natural electromagnetic fields are generated by the sun, moon, earth and cosmos. The human body also produces minute electrical currents generating electromagnetic fields which are involved in cell regulation and management.

When astronauts first went into space they became disorientated and confused due to the lack of influence from the earth's magnetic field. Now pulse generators are installed in the orbiters to simulate the earth fields. Pigeons and numerous sea creatures rely on natural radiation for direction and orientation.

We are all very much connected to cosmic and earth radiation.

However there are increasing numbers and range of man-made electromagnetic fields, like those produced by high voltage power lines, lights, electric appliances such as televisions, radios, ovens, microwaves, electric heaters, electric blankets, water beds, burglar alarms, computers and office equipment. Today people are exposed to fields 200 times higher than their ancestors. The man-made fields trigger a stress response in the body and impact on the immune, endocrine, heart and circulatory systems and emotions. They have been shown to depress the production of the hormone melatonin in the pineal gland which may result in depression. They have been found to compromise the immune system and to stimulate the growth of existing cancers.

Fields from electrical appliances reduce dramatically with distance—it is recommended by the Building Biology & Ecology Institute of New Zealand to stay at least an arm's length from any electrical appliance near which you spend a lot of time. Exposure time is also very important. It is really only fields that we are near for long periods of time like overhead power lines, the alarm clock by the bedside, etc. that are of concern, as short term risk is thought to be negligible.

We are most susceptible to stress when we are sleeping, as this is when our bodies regenerate. Therefore it is at that time when we should reduce artificial fields as much as possible. Especially be aware of electric blankets, alarm clocks or cabling under the bed. As we are right underneath of electric blankets, it is important that these are turned off at the wall or even better disconnected before we go to sleep. Keep electric alarm clocks at least a meter away from your head.

Some people are very sensitive to EMF's and can suffer symptoms such as headaches, mysterious or unexplained pains, triggering off allergies and diseases such as rheumatism, arthritis and asthma. Removing the fields has in some cases resulted in 'miraculous' cures.

People who are chronically ill and not responding to treatment, may also be affected by geopathic stress brought about by disturbances in the earth's magnetic field. The disturbances are caused by fault lines and cracks in the earth's crust, underground water, wells, power lines, building activity and mining. A bio-energy and dowsing consultant should be consulted to diagnose whether electromagnetic disturbances are present, and to make recommendations.

A good check for geopathic stress is to move the bed that you have been sleeping in, and see if this simple change improves your health condition.

"You can't be God—I am!"

CHAPTER 16

METAL TOXICITY

MERCURY

Mercury toxicity is a prime contributor to a number of serious illnesses. The greatest source of most people's exposure to mercury comes from silver/ amalgam fillings in their teeth. According to Swedish corrosion scientist Dr. Jaro Pleva, PhD, new amalgam fillings contain approximately 52% mercury. After five years in the mouth, almost half of the amalgam content of the fillings will have leached out into the mouth, to be absorbed into the body. The mercury content of the fillings after five years is approximately 27% mercury. Fillings which are twenty years old have been found to contain less than 5% mercury.

This insidious exposure to mercury in our mouths becomes more frightening when you consider that the scientific community agrees that 100 micrograms of mercury daily is a dangerous dose. However the daily exposure from silver/mercury amalgam fillings can be as high as 150 micrograms.

It is possible to have amalgam fillings and not experience ill health. However, if you do have amalgam fillings and suffer from a chronic illness, the mercury you are absorbing daily could possibly be contributing to your health problems. In this case, removal of amalgam fillings is desirable. This is because saliva reacting with the metal fillings in your mouth can act like a battery to generate electric current. This effect is called 'electro-galvanism' and is responsible for the mercury leaking out of the amalgam fillings. It is also unhealthy to have an electric current so close to your brain. Some scientists believe amalgam fillings must be removed in a special order, or gross disturbances to this electric current could be detrimental.

Many people who have had their fillings removed in the correct way (and had them replaced with material to which they were not allergic) and followed an appropriate detoxification program, have found that their health problems improved.

Listed below are diseases which have been reported to improve with amalgam filling removal:

- Neurological problems—including epilepsy and multiple sclerosis, facial twitches, and muscle spasms. Mercury amalgam filling removal has also resulted in the improvement of emotional problems (unrelated to unresolved trauma) such as anxiety, depression, and irritability.

- Cardiovascular problems such as unexplained rapid heartbeat and unidentified chest pains.

- Diseases of collagen (connective tissue) such as scleroderma, lupus and arthritis.

- Immune system damage—lowered white blood cell viability and resistance to infections.

- Allergies—mercury in the body can produce unusual sensitivities to foods and chemicals.

Removal of amalgam fillings is also recommended for people suffering from cancer, since continued exposure to toxic mercury from fillings lowers the immune response and reduces recovery prospects.

Mercury toxicity (as well as aluminum and other toxic metals) also seems to play a part in Alzheimer's disease. The book *Beating Alzheimer's: A Step Towards Unlocking the Mysteries of Brain Diseases* by Tom Warren (Avery Publishing Group Inc, New York. 1991) is the author's story of his recovery from Alzheimer's disease using nutritional supplements, avoiding allergens and removal of mercury amalgam fillings from his teeth. Mr. Warren made a complete recovery from Alzheimer's (diagnosed not only by its symptoms but also a CAT scan which showed brain atrophy) and writes candidly about his experiences. Perhaps most interesting is the fact that Mr. Warren did not recover fully until he had not only removed the mercury amalgam from his teeth, but also underwent oral surgery to remove tiny fragments of amalgam lodged in his jaw!

This begs the question—if mercury amalgam fillings are so toxic that removing them can improve such serious and dreaded diseases as Alzheimer's and Multiple Sclerosis—then what is your dentist doing putting them in your teeth in the first place?

Your dentist probably filled your teeth with mercury amalgam because he or she receives information from the American Dental Association (ADA) which claims that mercury amalgam fillings are safe because the amount of amalgam which leaches from the fillings is not enough to cause disease.

Your dentist may choose to believe the ADA's propaganda because to investigate and accept the truth about mercury amalgam fillings means to take responsibility for having placed a poisonous substance in the mouths of thousands of people - some of whom may have suffered greatly as a result.

However, if your dentist—as most dentists do—refuses to acknowledge the dangers of mercury amalgam and wants to fill your teeth with it, please—for your health's sake—do not be swayed by his/her 'professional' judgement. Insist upon a safe alternative, or get another dentist who is informed about the dangers of mercury amalgam and refuses to use it.

If you have health problems which you think may be attributable to mercury amalgam poisoning, read *It's All In Your Head* by Hal Huggins and Sharon Huggins, Life Science Press, Tacoma, Washington, 1989.

This is essential reading and gives you not only the knowledge necessary to understand and remedy your health problems, but also enables you to have an informed discussion with your health practitioner or dentist. Do not begin the process of having amalgam fillings removed or replaced without reading this book.

Perhaps you no longer have teeth of your own, but a pair of false teeth? You may think that in this case you need not worry about mercury poisoning. Unfortunately, you are not completely assured of safety in this case either since a dye containing mercury may be used to color the plates of false teeth pink! The authors of *It's All In Your Head* recommend the use of uncolored plates to avoid this hazard.

LEAD

Lead builds up in body tissues over a period of time. Unfortunately we do not realize that it's happening. Most often you can't taste it, smell it or know that you're consuming it.

Acute metal poisoning is most often diagnosed in people who have worked for many years with lead products. However many people carry toxic levels in their bodies that keep diseases subclinical but slowly eats away at their health. Lead accumulates in the central nervous system, bones, and brain. Deposits form in, and damage, the liver, kidneys and heart. Lead depresses the immune system enough to impede the destruction of all those cells that turn cancerous daily so it probably contributes to some cancers. Toxic levels of lead are associated with headaches, fatigue, stomach aches, intestinal ailments and acute depression.

Common sources of lead are lead pipes, or pipes with lead solder, water, canned food in cans closed with lead solder, lead acid batteries, lead paint, dinnerware with ceramic glazes, insecticides, bonemeal and leaded gasoline. The amount of lead used in gasoline is now much lower and also the introduction of unleaded fuel has meant lower lead emissions into the air. However, due to years of high lead emissions from vehicles in most countries there are very high levels of lead in the soil (in the USA it is estimated to be 4 to 5 million metric tons) and is commonly found in garden vegetables, especially those grown or stored near roadsides. Other sources are cow's milk, calve's liver, some wines, industrial pollution and tobacco.

Chronic or acute lead poisoning manifests itself in gastrointestinal colic, headaches, constipation, anemia, loss of memory, mental disturbances to insanity, muscle weakness, impotence, paralysis and even blindness. Commonly it is diagnosed because of blue black lead line near the base of teeth or blueness of gums.

Reduce your lead level by checking canned food for any remnants of solder along the seam. Choose lead-free cans that have been welded and have no side seam. Carefully check imported canned food. Canned foods high in acid, like fruit and tomatoes, can reach very high levels of lead from cans with lead solder and become dangerous due to oxidation if stored in the refrigerator.

Use a water purifier for drinking and cooking purposes. (Boiling water does not rid it of heavy metals). Be careful about imported ceramic products. Some countries do not restrict the lead levels used in ceramics. Give up smoking. A high fibre diet with legumes, beans, eggs and onions is necessary to prevent lead build up.

A high intake of antioxidants which help to prevent toxic reactions has a neutralizing effect, e.g. vitamin E, vitamin C, selenium and zinc. Calcium is particularly important in preventing lead from depositing in the body, but it should not be taken in the form of lead-laden cow's milk, bone meal or dolomite.

HERBAL HELP

Pectin is a natural fiber found in fruits and vegetables, particularly apples. It is transformed by the digestive process into galacturonic acid which combines with lead to form an insoluble metallic salt. It cannot be reabsorbed and is eliminated from the body. Pectin can also intercept radioactive isotope strontium 90 in the digestive tract. Strontium 90, like lead can also accumulate in the bones. Pectin may also be helpful in binding to other toxic minerals and removing them from the body.

Garlic—or Kyolic odorless garlic—can also help protect your body against toxic metals.

When aged garlic extract was combined with red blood cells it prevented lead, mercury and aluminum from destroying them. When no aged garlic was added to the blood samples, these heavy metals ruptured the red blood cells.

Homeopathic Preparation CH7. This preparation contains EDTA (Ethylene Diamine Tetra-acetate), Potassium Muriaticum, Sodium Carbonicum and

Magnesium Sulphuricum. EDTA is a well known chelation substance for removing heavy metals. Dosage 15 drops 3 times daily.

Professional EDTA Chelation therapy is the most effective answer for acute lead poisoning or heavy metal toxicity.

Test kits to determine whether you are suffering from heavy metal poisoning should be available from your local health store, or naturopath.

ALUMINUM

Aluminum is the most abundant metal on the earth. Although not classified as a heavy metal, aluminum accumulates in the body and the levels in which we now consume it (on average 3 to 10 milligrams a day) may be quite toxic to the body. Even quite low levels may impair health.

It can be found in aluminum cookware and utensils, foil, baking powder, beer and drinks in aluminum cans, bleached flour, salt, tobacco smoke, parmesan and processed cheese, prescription medicines containing aluminum silicate or nicotinate, pesticides and fungicides, vegetables, milk, toothpaste, dust from aluminum manufacture, car exhausts and in processed foods as additives (aluminum bentonite, dihydroxyaluminum, aluminum phosphate, aluminum sulphate, aluminum potassium sulphate) and is absorbed by fruit drinks in foil coated waxed cartons. One of the most common ways that elderly people ingest excess aluminum is through the varying levels of aluminum salts in antacids and over the counter pain killers including buffered aspirin.

Symptoms of aluminum toxicity include gastrointestinal problems, colitis, anemia, headaches, colic, rickets, premature memory loss and aging, poor calcium absorption, softening of the bones and weak, aching muscles.

Typical western diets which are deficient in calcium, low in magnesium and high in phosphorus may also increase the absorption of toxic metals leading to osteoporosis, and the accumulation of aluminum salts in the brain. High levels of aluminum salts in the brain are linked to Alzheimer's disease. Four times the normal level have been found in Alzheimer's victims. As aluminum is excreted through the kidneys, high levels may also damage the kidneys.

It is not recommended that you use processed foods, but if you do, check the labels for aluminum additives.

A high fiber diet is necessary.

Chelation therapy is not thought to be that effective in removing the aluminum ions.

SUPPLEMENTS

A calcium magnesium formula (not dolomite)—one part magnesium to 2 parts calcium. This binds to aluminum and helps remove it from the body.

HERBAL HELP

Kelp taken in powder form up to 2 tablespoons a day or in tablets, is thought to prevent the absorption of newly ingested metals.

Pectin and garlic also offer protection against toxic metal poisoning. *(see the section on Lead Poisoning)*

CADMIUM

Cadmium is a trace metal widely used in industry. Environmental levels of cadmium are increasing. The major hazard to health is from inhalation where up to 40% of cadmium inhaled may be absorbed. Fortunately the absorption of oral doses is poor. However, cadmium is extremely toxic and accumulates in the body. Toxic levels primarily result in kidney damage.

Cadmium forms a complex with the protein metallothionein which is a protein responsible for the transportation of metals in the body. The complex is transported to the kidneys. Cadmium has a chemical similarity to zinc and because of this stimulates more production of metallothionein. The complex is stored in the kidneys and when there is a zinc deficiency replaces storage of zinc in the kidneys and liver. This can make it extremely difficult to eliminate from the body.

Cigarette smokers are most at risk. It is most commonly found in cigarette, pipe and cigar smokers, including second-hand smoke. Smoking a pack of cigarettes a day can increase your cadmium intake by up to 28 micrograms (1.4 micrograms per cigarette). If the body is functioning well it may be able to eliminate most of that but still may retain up to 4 micrograms a day. It is partly the cause of yellowing of the teeth, wrinkles and premature aging in smokers.

Other effects of cadmium exposure is the increase in thickness of capillaries, which affects circulation and may lead to vein problems. It affects the immune system, reducing T Cell production and decreasing vitamin D levels. Toxic levels may include hardening of the arteries, hypertension, anemia, joint soreness, hair loss, dry skin, reduced appetite and a poor sense of smell. Acute levels may cause emphysema, renal colic, back and leg pain, loss of calcium from bones, especially in women leading to soft or brittle bones (known as Itai Itai in Japan) rheumatoid arthritis, and testicular damage. It is also considered to be a carcinogen by some medical researchers and is especially thought to contribute to bladder cancer.

It is commonly found in plastics, nickel-cadmium batteries, drinking water, fertilizers, fungicides, pesticides, refined grains, some vending machine drinks, evaporated milk, processed food, some vegetables, oysters, kidneys, liver, rice from countries with high cadmium water levels, coffee, tea, paint, dust from industry, rubber carpeting backing, black polythene. It is produced by wear of rubber tires and unleaded gasoline exhaust fumes. Those who have worked in electroplating, engraving, jewelry making, ceramic, rubber industry, paint and fungicide manufacture and rust-proofing, may have high levels in their bodies. This can be checked by hair analysis.

SUPPLEMENTS

- Zinc

- Calcium and magnesium

- Lecithin

- Rutin

- Vitamin E

- Chlorophyll is helpful in removing cadmium from the body (alfalfa, Spirulina).

HERBAL HELP

- Garlic (Kyolic)

- Pectin

- Kelp

- Homeopathic Preparation CH7.

Chelation therapy offers the most effective way of removing toxic levels from the body.

CHAPTER 17

WATER TOXICITY

Drinking water free of contaminants is essential for health. Unfortunately, water from streams or lakes commonly contains both bacteria and dirt. This necessitates that the water be treated with some sort of disinfectant to kill germs—chlorine is a common choice. In addition, a flocculent, such as alum, is commonly used to remove dirt particles.

Unfortunately, research now shows that some of the chemicals added to municipal water supplies to prevent disease may be partly responsible for the high incidence of other serious illnesses.

CHLORINE

Chlorine is used to disinfect most municipal water supplies to prevent pathogenic organisms from causing disease. In 1904 it was discovered that chlorine could destroy the bacteria that caused typhoid, hepatitis, dysentery and cholera. This cheap, effective disinfectant, is now documented to form carcinogenic trihalomethane chemicals when it combines with humic acids from organic matter (decaying vegetation). This family of four chemicals—chloroform, bromoform, dibromochloromethane, and bromodichloromethane—is indicated by research in the USA to contribute to a possible 18 percent of rectal cancers (6,500 cases a year) and 9 percent of bladder cancers (4,200 cases a year). This is from a combination of drinking, cooking, showering and bathing in chlorinated water. In light of some of this evidence trihalomethanes are now banned from the USA.

These chlorine by-products are also suspected to raise cholesterol levels and be partially responsible for atherosclerosis by some medical authorities. As far back as 1971 Dr. Joseph M. Price, MD of Michigan, stated that "In the process of atherogenesis, chlorine is the essential agent (atherogenesis does not occur to a clinically significant degree in the absence of chlorine, regardless of diet and other contributing factors)."

FLUORIDE

The safety of adding fluoride to municipal water supplies is still being debated. The chemicals commonly used for this purpose are sodium fluoride, sodium fluorosilicate and fluorosilicic acid. Sodium fluoride is a white powder which is a by-product of the aluminum industry. It is the most expensive of the three and for that reason not as often used. Fluorosilicic acid is the cheapest and easiest compound for fluoridating water and it is a by-product of the super phosphate industry. It is derived from silicon tetrafluoride, the gas that is formed as a result of a reaction between phosphate rock and sulfuric acid. The gas is able to be collected in a gas scrubbing process using water and converted to a dilute fluorosilicic acid solution. The solution is processed to remove the silica particles leaving fluosilicic acid a solution concentrated enough to fluoridate water supplies. This solution may also contain lead, cadmium, arsenic and mercury but these concentrations are usually considered by authorities to meet safety levels.

Given the toxicity of fluoride compounds and the difficulty and expense in disposing of them it could be considered marketing genius that they find their way into drinking water supplies for financial gain. For example the uncontrolled release of silicon tetrafluoride gas would cause significant air pollution problems. From 1900 to 1940 the Aluminum Corporation of America paid out millions in damages because of stock and crop poisoning by industrial fluorine wastes.

The fluoride compounds deemed beneficial to children's teeth and added to water supplies are also used in a number of other commercial/industrial processes and are toxic enough to be packaged and marketed as rodenticides and insecticides. The addition of fluoride to one part per million in water which equates to one milligram (mg) per litre is thought to be harmless to health by many but there is increasing evidence to suggest that fluoride interferes with calcium metabolism because it binds to calcium and may even replace calcium deposits in the bones. This causes more brittle bones and is now being linked to the increasing number of hip fractures in older women. The *Journal of the American Medical Association* has published several studies showing more hip fractures in fluoridated areas.

Two British studies, one by Dr. Sheila Gibson of Scotland, have concluded that even small amounts can slow up the action of the white blood cells of the immune system. Research is still being carried out on carcinogenic trends in fluoridated and non-fluoridated American cities, but it is now believed to cause bone cancer (osteosarcoma) in young males. There is also strong evidence to suggest that it is an enzyme inhibitor and may contribute to a wide range of disorders.

Sodium Fluoride is classified as "toxic by ingestion and inhalation", "strong irritant", and fluorosilicic acid is classified as "corrosive (class 8 dangerous goods)" and is also highly corrosive to most metals. Some of the milder effects of human fluoride toxicity are flu like symptoms, nausea, vomiting, abdominal distress, diarrhea, stupor, and weakness. An ingestion of more than 10 grams sodium fluoride would be lethal.

The bottom line is that although fluoride might benefit the teeth of children under five, it is not likely to benefit elderly people. (What's more, the evidence that fluoridated water prevents cavities developing in children's teeth is fairly debatable. For example, one study carried out in New Zealand found almost identical rates of tooth decay in the teeth of children living in fluoridated and non-fluoridated areas. In fact, the cavity rate of the children who did not drink fluoridated water was marginally lower than the children who drank fluoridated water.)

For those who consider fluoride necessary, keep in mind that it is the base of many insecticides. Additionally, produce irrigated with fluoridated water means that you're already getting a good dose of it in your vegetables and other foods—so why drink it?

In the USA, in areas where water is fluoridated, an average daily dose of fluoride is between 2.5–3.0 mg with a maximum of up to 7.0 mg. Because both green and black teas are rich in fluoride, regular daily drinking can add a further 1.0–7.5 mg to your daily intake. An increased intake of calcium and magnesium may decrease the absorption of fluoride in the intestines.

ALUMINUM

Alum (aluminum sulphate) is a part of the treatment process of water in many countries. It reacts to the alkalinity in water and forms clusters with dirt, sand and bacterial organisms allowing them to be filtered out. Residues which remain in drinking water are considered safe because they can be passed out of the body by urine. But there may be a health risk to people with lowered or impaired kidney function because aluminium can build up and be deposited in the body such as in bones and in the brain. High levels of aluminium deposits in the brain have been linked to Alzheimer's disease. For further effects on health see chapter on Aluminium Toxicity.

Additionally water supplies formerly considered absolutely safe may harbor a host of microorganisms. Protozoan contamination of municipal waters is a reemerging issue. A recent study commissioned by the University of Quebec and published in *Water Science and Technology* (Vol. 27) has revealed that there are a number of micro organisms unaffected by chlorine. An environmental impact study published in Sydney newspapers revealed that one of these micro organisms cryptosporidium parvum has been found in storage systems and pipelines of the Australian, UK and USA water supplies. The tiny protozoan parasite is believed to have been responsible for a serious outbreak of gastrointestinal illness in Milwaukee USA, early in 1994, which killed 16 people. It lives inside the human digestive tract in tiny egg-like oocysts and feeds on cell nutrients. It can reproduce itself a million times a minute and when its four day life is over it is passed from the body in excrement. A healthy person may recover from cryptosporidiosis within 7 to 14 days but it could be life threatening for those with depressed immune systems. This is reason for concern for those who use treated water supplies from heavily contaminated sources. In some British cities the water you drink has passed through other people 16 times.

To remove the aforementioned chemicals used in the treatment and disinfection process of municipal water, and any pathogenic organisms that slip through the process, a home filter is necessary. Some municipal water treatment plants can only guarantee filtration to 50 microns.

Activated carbon filters remove chlorine and its carcinogenic by-products, sulphur (bad taste/odors) and pesticides. Metals like lead and aluminium salts can also be removed by this method. Filtration to a certified one micron is desirable. This filter will remove giardia cysts (which measure between 7–10 microns) cryptosporidium oocysts (which measure between 3–6 microns) and asbestos fibres a contaminant from concrete/asbestos pipes. A filter with a larger pore size could be used and water boiled for 2–3 minutes to kill any bacteria. You need to boil water for 10 minutes to get rid of cryposporidium. Killing or removing any bacteria might be particularly important if you have a weakened immune system, are recovering from illness or have a tendency towards stomach upsets and diarrhea. The effectiveness of activated carbon filters vary with the type and amount of carbon used and the design of the filter. It is essential to adhere to the manufacturer's instructions when using filters and change the filter unit as often as they advise. Activated carbon with its trapped contaminates is a rich medium for bacteria to grow in and when it becomes saturated and left unchanged your filtered water may contain a cocktail of bacteria. Bacteriostatic filters are now available which are impregnated with silver to impede the growth of bacteria. There is the risk of ingesting silver which is considered by some to be a metal safe for human consumption, like gold, and by others to be poisonous and harmful. Check also for the possible contamination from aluminum used in the housing of some filters. Activated carbon does not remove fluoride. Special filters now available from some water purification companies that remove the above undesirable substances plus fluoride, heavy metals and nitrates but do not strip the water of essential minerals. These may not cost more but because the filters remove so much they need to be changed more often so are more expensive to maintain. In most cases activated carbon filters leave the desired mineral salts in the water.

Reverse Osmosis filters will remove chlorine, fluoride, iron, lead, aluminum and other metals and giardia, especially if a carbon filter is combined in the unit to remove organic compounds and other particles.

Check that yours removes trihalomethane chemicals like chloroform. Strong water pressure is needed for reverse osmosis and unfortunately they waste water. As little as 10–25 percent of water may be retained, the rest is wasted. There is also a similar problem with bacteria growth and some reverse osmosis membranes are degraded by chlorine if they are not combined with a carbon filter to remove it. A cellulose triacetate membrane stands up to chlorine better. Reverse Osmosis can be so effective that even desirable minerals like calcium and magnesium are removed and a mineral free water created. Ensure that your mineral intake is adequate and consider supplements if you have signs of osteoporosis.

Ion Exchange filters remove metals, fluoride and dissolved salts and minerals. When they are combined with a carbon filter they also remove organic matter but they do not remove harmful pathogens. The resin of ion exchange filters, like activated carbon, may become saturated and need changing. They also create a mineral free water.

Bottled waters are free of chlorine, aluminum and normally fluoride (although fluoride does occur naturally in rocks and some waters may contain a little). Bottled waters are a rich source of minerals, a breakdown of which can be obtained from the label on the bottle. Both 'Evian' and 'Perrier' are highly regarded mineral waters, although expensive in some countries. They are also both natural spring waters which is the best type of bottled water to drink. Water claiming to be mineral water, may have a high mineral content but may be drawn from a ground bore. In some places bore water is contaminated by pesticide residues and contains nitrates. It is best to check the labels carefully for the source and err on the side of caution unless there are conclusive studies on localized bottled waters. In addition, in the USA, due to a lack of regulations about bottled water, some 'mineral water' is actually tap water which has been run through a simple taste and odor filter—and may still be chock full of other undesirable contaminants.

Simply boiling water is not an effective means of treating water as it will not remove chlorine. If you leave the lid off, some of the 'free chlorine' gas will escape. Chlorine which has been taken up by organic matter, and other compounds will not be removed. In fact boiling may concentrate rather than remove certain components.

Disinfection of the water supply of your entire home may be desirable if you are recovering from a serious illness like cancer. Installing an ultra violet water sterilizer system with a giardia safe filter would ensure that your water supply is free of viruses and pathogenic bacteria.

If you use an untreated water supply like river, lake, spring or bore, the best solution is to disinfect all the water as it enters your house. This can be done by ultra violet disinfection. Filtration, even to a 0.2 micron, may not remove all the pathogenic bacteria in untreated water. Many untreated water sources are potentially at risk from chemical and heavy metal pollution. There is increasing contamination of these sources by nitrates from heavy use of agricultural fertilizers which filter through the soil and into water tables. Nitrates are thought to be responsible for poisoning babies (blue baby syndrome). You can have your water checked for a chemical and biological analysis by a laboratory, water purification company or local council. A biological analysis can reveal the level of coliforms which indicate contamination by excrement of some sort. Their presence may also indicate other more serious disease carrying pathogens. Water can also be treated for other problems like excess iron (red/brown water) and low pH and high acidity levels (corrosion).

DISTILLED WATER

Distillation is the most cost effective and efficient way of obtaining pure water. It is about 99.9% pure. This process involves vaporizing water by boiling it. In the process, solids are removed including chemicals, metals, bacteria and viruses. The steam, which is pure H_2O is then condensed and cooled to become water.

Drinking distilled water allows the body to absorb and remove inorganic minerals, leaching them out of the body. The human body is about 60% water, and is designed to be free of inorganic solids. The more pure the water you drink, the more it is able to absorb these inorganic minerals and remove them. Our bodies can use up to three liters of water daily, depending upon the rate of elimination through the skin, lungs and kidneys. Hot water increases the elimination of water through the skin.

It has been suggested that distilled water can demineralize the body, however, the amount of organic minerals—which are the type of minerals the body uses—that we obtain from water is minuscule. Organic minerals come chiefly from the vegetables we eat.

One caution with distilled water is that it can absorb pollutants from the air, or the container you store it in. Always keep it in a sealed container, in the refrigerator, and in a good quality container designed for storing water.

CHAPTER 18

ADDICTIVE SUBSTANCES

SMOKING

The dangers of smoking are well publicized. Smoking is the main cause of lung cancer and implicated in heart disease, diabetes and other degenerative diseases. Included in the 3,800 chemicals in tobacco smoke are 43 chemicals which are known carcinogens, carbon monoxide, nicotine, radioactive compounds, hydrogen cyanide and DDT, as well as toxic metals like arsenic and nickel.

The chemicals inhaled by smokers contribute to other cancers like larynx, mouth, esophagus, pharynx, bladder, kidney, pancreas and possibly stomach cancer.

Each time a smoker inhales, these chemicals touch the cells inside the passages leading to the lungs and in the lungs. These poisons cause cells to mutate. Sooner or later one mutated cell evades the immune system and divides and eventually forms a cancerous tumour.

Lung cancer is usually discovered too late to bring a cure to most victims. Most people who get lung cancer eventually die from it within five years of being diagnosed. The cancer keeps growing until the lung cannot function.

Smoking is responsible for about one quarter of deaths from diseases of the heart and blood vessels because it causes narrowing of the arteries.

Carbon monoxide from cigarettes replace oxygen in the bloodstream making oxygen less available for vital functions.

Smoking and aging is a dangerous combination.

Chronic sinus problems, frequent colds, flus, chest infections, constant phlegm, and nagging coughs are the hallmarks of the deterioration of health that smoking brings.

Smokers are a danger to themselves and also to family and friends. Elderly people may set a bad example to grandchildren and cause them to be passive smokers when visiting. Second-hand smoke is released into the air by cigarettes and pollutes the air with the 3,800 chemicals found in cigarettes. Nonsmokers who are constantly exposed to second-hand smoke inhale the equivalent of five cigarettes per day.

One third of adults in the U.K. smoke and half of them want to give up. A heavy smoker has a one out of three chance of dying before retirement. On average that is 23 years earlier than if they had not smoked. The occasional hardy old soul can smoke all their life without illness, but most smokers do not realize how painful their last breath can be.

Whether smoking is initially an urge that creates a physical craving, or the physical craving that creates the urge, nicotine is a form of drug dependence, no less dangerous than other addictions.

GIVING UP

Decide on your reasons to stop smoking. Take it in steps, prepare to stop, stop, and work at staying stopped. Giving up requires total commitment to going through all the withdrawal symptoms, then getting the benefit on the other side. It takes courage to give up but it also takes courage to face cancer. Decide where your courage lies.

If you do not think you can give up 'cold turkey' the Cancer Society recommends a program of 2 to 3 weeks for cutting down and then cutting out cigarettes. First cut out the first cigarette of the day, then the second, and so on. Try to go longer between cigarettes. Cut out the most enjoyable cigarettes of the day—the ones with tea and coffee, the one after dinner, the one before bed, until you are left with one a day—then cut that one out.

Alternatively limit yourself to cigarettes only after meals and pick a day to give up completely. If you do cut down, be careful. It is easy to think that one more won't matter, and another, and another. The greater the number of cigarettes smoked each day, the greater the risk of lung diseases and/or cancer. The only safe cigarette is the unlit one.

Coincide giving up with changing your normal routine (perhaps a holiday) and more healthier eating habits. Take up regular walks and deep breathing. Fresh air soon becomes preferable to cigarette smoke.

Try positive affirmations taped around your house; e.g. "I am a nonsmoker"; "Breathing fresh, clean air is the most important thing I can do for my health". You must accept and believe you are a nonsmoker.

The first three days without cigarettes are the worst. Your body is so used to its regular 'fix' of nicotine that it rebels when none is forthcoming. Side effects can range from tension, anxiety, irritability and headaches to depression. If you beat the first three days, you almost have it under control. After the first two weeks, although the craving will continue for a couple of months, they will no longer consume you. If you give in to the craving and have just one cigarette, it increases the intensity of cravings.

Unless you have done irreparable damage to your lungs and heart, your body should be able to repair most of the damage. A comprehensive health program including good nutrition, herbs, relaxation and exercise will aid your body to heal itself. The risk to your health decreases the moment you give up smoking.

You will begin to feel the benefits—less phlegm, coughing spells (although coughing will continue until your lungs are cleared of residue), your breathing will be easier and you will have more oxygen in your body and more energy. Yellow stains on your fingers will fade and your teeth can be cleaned by a dentist. Your clothes will no longer reek of smoke and you will no longer have to suffer the distaste of others when you have to light up. You will contribute to less pollution.

Deal with any craving for food by continuing to take supplements, eating sensibly, snack on vegetable sticks and dried fruit or other healthy snacks. Replace caffeine with relaxing herbal teas, like camomile, yarrow, lemon balm or peppermint tea. A few sweets might help with cravings but don't get hooked on large amounts of sugar—it is just a lesser poison.

SUPPLEMENTS

A daily intake of the following supplements will assist and support the immune system:

- Beta Carotene: 25,000 IU

- Vitamin B Complex: 100 mg

- Vitamin C with Bioflavonoids: 3–5 grams

- Kyolic EPA

- Kyo-Green

- Kyo-Dophilus

- Kyolic

- Probiata

- Co Enzyme Q10: 30 mg

- L Methionine, available as liver support

- L Cysteine, take as directed. If taken singly, 400 mg of each

- Vitamin E; 1200–800 IU (increase slowly)

   (if blood pressure is high, seek professional advice)

Sipping fresh lemon juice will alleviate craving. Avoid stress and learn relaxation techniques.

Information on the effects of smoking supplied by the Cancer Society.

TEA AND COFFEE

A QUICK PICK–ME–UP OR A HEALTH HAZARD?

Tea and coffee are probably the most widely used drugs in the world. It's practically universal in our culture for people who have to leave early in the morning to go out to work to 'wake themselves up' with a cup of coffee or tea. Unfortunately, the same substances that give a morning 'cuppa' its 'get up and go' effect which make it such an attractive early morning stimulant, may also endanger your health.

The family of chemicals responsible for the stimulant effect of tea and coffee is known as the methylxanthines. Caffeine is found in coffee, while theobromines, which are very similar to caffeine, are found in chocolate and cola drinks. Tea contains a substance called theophylline.

The word caffeine is also used as a general term for the methylxanthine family.

A cup of instant coffee contains between 75 to 100 mg of caffeine; freshly ground coffee contains between 100 to 150 mg of caffeine.

A cup of tea contains anywhere from 50 to 100 mg of caffeine.

Drinks which are marketed to children and young adults score lowest on the caffeine scale—but are highest in the sugar. A mug of cocoa, and the average cola drink, both contain about 50 mg caffeine. However, these kinds of products contribute to young people becoming addicted to caffeine.

Caffeine is our society's most commonly used and abused drug—and one that is rarely recognized as such.

Caffeine, and the other members of the methylxanthine family, act upon the brain and nervous system. Caffeine affects different parts of the body differently—for example it constricts the blood vessels in the brain, reducing oxygen supply to the brain. Caffeine can also cause nervousness, anxiety and irritability.

Caffeine also opens blood vessels to the heart and increases heart rate and blood pressure. In sensitive people, caffeine can cause heart palpitations.

Caffeine raises the body's metabolic rate, but it is not a good drink for people wishing to lose weight, since it causes the liver to release additional sugar into the bloodstream. This extra sugar triggers the release of insulin which increases appetite. The net result of all these changes is normally weight gain, rather than weight loss.

Caffeine contained in foods and beverages also has an adverse effect on your digestive system. It can increase stomach acid and cause indigestion, bowel problems and diarrhea.

Perhaps one of the most serious effects of caffeine is that its diuretic effect can result in deficiency of important vitamins and minerals which are lost through the urine. Caffeine can reduce iron absorption by up to 80%. This is a particular concern for children and older people who are at risk of iron deficiency. Women who have not yet passed the menopause are also at risk of iron deficiency anaemia and there is evidence that high coffee consumption is linked with endometriosis (a painful condition in which the lining of the womb—or endometrium—becomes attached to other organs in the pelvic cavity such as the intestines.) Coffee consumption has also been linked to fibrocystic breast disease and osteoporosis.

Consuming caffeine can also result in reducing the availability of zinc and vitamin C—both essential for maintaining a healthy immune system.

If you consume more than 250 mg of caffeine a day—just two cups of filter coffee—you are at risk of becoming addicted to caffeine. However, as people age, the body's response to drugs changes. You may well find that as you celebrate more birthdays, you begin to have problems with the caffeine levels you could tolerate when you were younger.

Signs of caffeine addiction problems include: inability or difficulty with getting moving in the morning without your customary cup and getting headaches if you don't have a cup of tea or coffee when you usually do.

If you think you are addicted to caffeine and want to end the addiction, cutting back gradually is better than going cold turkey. If you suddenly deprive your body of the caffeine it is accustomed to, you risk migraine headache as well as mild depression, irritability, sleepiness, as well as elevated or irregular heartbeat.

These symptoms, particularly the headache, may be so severe you may decide that giving up just isn't worth the pain.

Drinking plenty of pure water will assist you to flush toxins from your system. Herbal teas and coffee substitutes such as 'Inca' can satisfy your desire for a hot drink without the caffeine.

SUGAR

Living in the 1990s virtually everyone has heard that sugar is bad for your health, and that it should be reduced—or eliminated from the diet. The fact that refined sugar contains a lot of calories and can also lead to tooth decay is well known. However even if you always brush your teeth as soon as you eat a sugary food, and have the good fortune not to gain weight easily, there are other good reasons not to eat sugar.

Other harmful effects of sugar include:

- Sugar depresses the function of the immune system
- The body's store of Vitamin B1 is depleted by eating sugar
- Sugar acts as a gastric irritant when it makes up 10% or more of the stomach contents—a high consumption of sugar could make the development of gastric ulcers more likely
- Eating refined sugar stimulates the pancreas to work overtime to produce insulin to convert the excess sugar into fat. The extra insulin then forces blood sugar levels lower than normal and hypoglycemia can result. Chronic hypoglycemia produced by habitual 'sugar abuse' may be a precursor to adult-onset diabetes
- Simple sugar (glucose) can be converted by the body into triglycerides resulting in elevated blood fats.

CHAPTER 19

NATURAL VISION IMPROVEMENT

Most people expect that their sight will deteriorate as a natural part of the aging process. Luckily for those of us who don't want to acquire reading glasses by the grand old age of forty or fifty, progressive deterioration of our eyesight need not happen.

Good nutrition can reduce the risk of failing eyesight because of physical problems such as cataracts. (See below). Even more encouraging is the news that visual problems such as astigmatism (blurred vision at a particular angle) or myopia (nearsightedness) may be successfully treated using the techniques developed by natural vision improvement teachers. Conscientious and creative use of natural vision techniques has freed many people from having to wear the prescription lenses that they have had to wear all their adult lives.

This chapter, of course, is necessarily brief, and so if you do have problems with your vision, you will need to obtain one of the books about Natural Vision Improvement listed in the reading list at the back of this book. There should also be teachers of natural vision improvement in your area—if you have trouble locating a teacher, ask at your local health store.

The basics of natural vision improvement courses are eye exercises or visual games designed to strengthen the muscles around the eyes, and re-educate them towards the fluid coordination of well adjusted eyes. Most natural vision improvement programs also include as a central philosophy the idea that the art of seeing encompasses much more than the physical apparatus of the eye. In *Natural Vision Improvement,* Janet Goodman describes natural vision as "mental attention, imagination, and memory", as well as "aliveness." Clearly at any time we have the choice to foster and celebrate the gift of vision which we are privileged enough to possess, or we can withdraw our energy from our sense of sight.

If you are like most people, you may well have experienced an accident in which for example, you have walked into an object which you should have been able to see easily and therefore avoided. Assuming at the time that your vision was normal, and that if you usually wore corrective lenses, you were wearing them—such an accident could not be accounted for by the fact that there was something wrong with your eyes. Rather, a more likely explanation is that you were preoccupied with some problem, withdrawing your mental energy from the task of seeing the things around you, to imagining a situation which might not then exist except inside your head.

When you habitually withdraw your energy from the task of observing what is happening around you, for whatever reason—whether you are constantly preoccupied with problems or exciting ideas; or perhaps to avoid seeing unpleasant things which are happening in your environment—you are at risk of developing problems with your vision.

If you are lucky enough to possess good eyesight, it is important to treasure this gift. You can improve and maintain your eyesight in simple ways. The first of these is making sure you always read or do written work in a well-lit, but not glaring, environment while you are seated comfortably.

Also make sure that you do not tire your eyes by subjecting them to rigid staring patterns. While you are typing or doing other concentrated work, allow your eyes to take breaks from the screen and look out and around to other objects in the room.

A simple exercise called 'tromboning' can also help train your eyes to work together if there is some disparity in the vision of each eye. Simply hold your index finger—or a pencil—about a hand's length away in front your nose and move it slowly forwards and backwards in front of your eyes trying to keep the finger or pencil in focus as much of the time as possible.

Your nutrition can also help to protect your eyesight. A study undertaken at the State University of New York (Christina Leske et al, *Archives of Ophthalmology*, February 1991) showed that older people who used multivitamin supplements had a 37% lower incidence of developing vision–threatening cataracts. In another study the Human Nutrition Research Centre on Aging of Boston showed that a generous supply of vitamins is necessary to prevent cataracts. In this case the researchers found that older people who ate fewer than three and a half servings of fruit and vegetables per day were almost six times more likely to have cataracts.

Finally, remember to make the most of your vision. The world may not be a bed of roses, but it is nonetheless still full of visual beauty upon which to feast your eyes. Take time out to enjoy watching a rosy sunset, fiery autumn leaves, a magnificent spring green tree, inspiring architecture, a child's smile. These are probably the best incentives you could wish for to continue to look after your vision.

HUMOR AND HEALTH

What's funny about the question of life and death? Just about everything. For example, there were these three gentlemen of advancing years discussing the demise of their friend. "So, what did he die of?" asked the first. "Was it cancer?" "No," replied his friend. "Was it a heart attack?" asked the other. "No," came the reply. "A stroke then?" came the question. "No," the friend answered. "He just caught cold one day and died." "Well," replied the first friend, "at least it was nothing serious."

We tend to approach questions that this book tries to address, with utmost gravity. For these are **'Questions of Life and Death.'** And who is to say that we should treat these kinds of questions…light-heartedly? These are, after all, **'Serious Matters.'**

Fact is, the lighter you treat these serious matters, the better off you become. Years ago, before words like 'stress' and 'Type A' entered our common vocabulary, we all knew intuitively that you'd live longer if you just 'took it easy.' In fact "take it easy" is still a common comment in many parts of America when taking someone's leave. It means "I hope you will have a long life." A nice parting gesture. When Mr. Science proved that Type A people had shorter life-spans, it gave new legitimacy to the people who had been taking it easy all their lives and who used to be called lazy by the Type A people.

The yogis demonstrated that you could still be a Type B (the people who took things easy) and still get things done. But only if you could learn how to program your brain to produce Theta and Alpha waves, the same waves they produced in their brains when they were meditating. However, since most western people didn't have the time to meditate, at least every day, they took self improvement courses and very ardently tried to learn how to produce Theta and Alpha waves. In fact, many of them stressed out learning how to relax, which of course defeated the whole point of the exercise. They had signs all over their homes that read **'Force Yourself to Relax.'** And many of them died trying.

The ones who didn't give up decided that there must be a better way, and right then and there chose humor as a way to relax. It wasn't that they knew the humor was a way to relax right from the start. It was only through some of their self improvement courses that they learned that laughter promoted the release of endorphins from the brain into the bloodstream and that this was a good thing. The trouble was that there wasn't that much around to laugh about, what with wars and starvation and the ozone thing happening.

And Seinfeld hadn't started yet.

So they started looking around for things to laugh at or with or about. The New Yorker Magazine's cartoons were always good for a knowing 'in group' kind of chuckle, and Leslie Neilson was good for the occasional guffaw. Pretty soon, the ones who 'got' that laughter was fun began to see the lighter side of just about everything, and were of course the first to be exiled from mainstream institutions, including their job.

But humor was catching on fast, nevertheless. In Boston several radical lesbian women's groups were secretly hiring smart-alec humor types from New York to come up and teach them 'how to do humor' on an every-other-weekend basis. Large high tech corporations were employing Marcel Marceau to give expensive retreats, while in Washington the FBI hired a professional pie-thrower from NY's East Village to come and show them how to take life with a 'grain of salt.'

In a matter of 17 hectic months the now notorious 'humor drain' had depleted New York City of most of its first rate comedic talent, and there were hardly any stand ups to be found anywhere in the City. This spawned several protests down Broadway involving untold thousands of people. The biggest one happened on a cold December 31st. It would have been successful if only it had not been unfortunately confused with the Happy New Year crowd with which it at first mingled before the two groups managed to extricate themselves, (shortly after the New Year began). Nevertheless people around the world rejoiced that NY's comedic talent was at last coming to the rescue of serious people everywhere.

In fact, when Seinfeld did at first appear, and this is a little known fact, he was initially hailed as 'The Messiah.' It was only after his book appeared that people realized that he wasn't that funny after all and that they may have been laughing at the delivery rather than the jokes themselves.

And everyone knows that Norman Cousins, no relation to Norman Invasion, healed himself of a debilitating illness by hiring Marx Brothers videos while he was in a New York hospital wasting away. He literally laughed his way to wellness, and riches, after he wrote a book about his experiences. I admired his approach, but was still somewhat disappointed in the book because even though it was called *Anatomy of An Illness*, there weren't any dirty pictures it.

THE CHILD WITHIN

Many teachers, both popular and esoteric, encourage their students to 'access the child within' as a way of retaining the vigor and the optimism of youth. The problem is, though, that the child within often has been traumatized or put down, discouraged or punished for his/her natural exuberance and love of life. The child then learns the 'virtue' of laziness, the calcification process in which we incrementally slide into patterns which get progressively more difficult to change as we age.

One of the most admirable aspects of youth is the natural insatiability of the learning process. How does this get corrupted and more to the point, how does it get redeemed in later years?

Corruption of the learning process happens gradually as our learning is disparaged by authorities who themselves have a stake in the status quo, and for whom natural curiosity, new ideas and information are perceived as a threat to their stake. As children we get the double message that learning is encouraged while at the same time "don't learn too much," "don't get too smart," or "I don't want to talk about it." Eventually this message is assimilated and people learn the subtle art of self censorship as they get rewarded for approved learning and punished for unapproved learning.

All this is defended by the defenders of the status quo as helping the cause of 'social cohesion.' However in the end, a cohesiveness largely based on reward for lying, self attenuation, fitting in, not rocking the boat, etc. may not be worth the effort and is certainly deficient in promoting sustainability. Both short term and long term prognosis for our contemporary 'civilization' is not very optimistic. Is this the kind of system you would buy into if you really had not been repressed?

When the inner (or outer) child gets repressed, the result is compensatory behavior. This means that we create behavior patterns to compensate for our feelings of hurt, anger, frustration and anxiety. Gradually we develop behavioral calcification, a cementing of attitudes, many of which are completely antithetical to the life force itself, and promote slow suicide, despair, negativity, quietism, and accommodation with the death urge.

"I'd love to change but I can't seem to get around to it," becomes the watchword of people who believe that change, however positive, is too threatening to contemplate seriously, much less assimilate. In such a situation, accessing the child within may be accessing a child who became the defensive adult too afraid or too angry or too depressed to act on good information.

So how do we redeem the inner child who still retains the sense of wonder and who is not yet paralysed by repression?

- Say a prayer for what you want. But be careful because inasmuch as all prayers are answered be mindful of what you pray for. The mind is a powerful instrument and can set up the conditions for the success of your prayer. If you believe that prayer does not work, rest assured that your prayer probably will not work for you.

- Adopt the philosophy of harmlessness. This is like the Hippocratic Oath— "above all do no harm." Doctors used to take this oath, before they sold out to the pharmaceutical industry. When you begin to enter harmlessness you begin to peel away some of the garbage you've bought into as they years have gone by. This garbage is your own personal collection of lies that you have tried to convince yourself were true in order to gain the rewards of parental approval, career advancement, peer/spouse approval, etc. They all involve your having to turn yourself off to the harm you have been causing yourself, others and the planet generally. Many people think that 'the truth hurts.' It does, sometimes, but lies hurt more.

- Remember that the truth shall set you free... but first it will piss you off. Use the breath and any other help you can get to deal with your anger when you realize how much you have lied to yourself and how much you have been lied to. The actual amount is staggering—so much that it has never been quantified.

- Respect the truth and be faithful to it. Contrary to popular belief the truth is not what people agree it is. It is what you, in your heart of hearts, know that it is. Often the truth lies hidden, afraid to come out to face the ridicule of all those people who are experts or who 'know better' or who simply have the authority to influence others to agree with them. Be strong. You will need the strength of a warrior to do battle with the forces of darkness, some of which have found a comfortable home inside your own head.

- Every so often take a vacation from self improvement. Indulge yourself. Pig out. Have a beer with the guys. Eat some ice cream. Ask someone famous for an autograph. Watch a sunrise. Paint a picture. The key to redeeming the child within is enjoying life. Remember?

WHAT IS YOUR REALITY?

Everyone likes to believe that the reality that they see and operate in is the only reality that there is. Most people think that people who operate in different spaces with different referents and different beliefs in what is 'real' are either deviant (at best) or mentally unbalanced.

This is one of the most important ways by which social cohesion is maintained. This is the foundation stone of 'us' and 'them'— the linchpin for group 'solidarity.'

This is the consciousness 'womb' to which we return day after day as we awaken from another reality where the subconscious rules, and where things can become as frightening as they are commensurately unexpected.

The security drive is a part of us all, even the most adventurous. But with too much of it we cling to the apron strings of the totally predictable; we become insufferably conservative and fearful of change and we cleave to the dictates of the group mind or the totalitarian impulses of the maximum leader. We inch our way around the crawl space of consciousness, but it's very dark and we make no progress.

But for most of us this is *'Reality.'* Why? Simply, and sadly, because this is the reality of all of those around us from whom we took our cues. This was the reality of our parents and their parents before them. This is the reality of a society that seems obsessed with palliative materialism, the insane and futile pseudo fulfillment with the products of factories and shopping malls.

But we permit the seduction, for it appears incrementally, and it comes with the rewards of compliance and the punishments of rebellion. Thus we forego the challenges of the unpredictable, preferring to hide out and bear down, conforming to a society devoted to the death urge.

But wait. This is for 'others'—not for the gentle reader (much less the gentle authors). But is it? To what extent exactly is your 'reality' maintained or transformed by others?

And exactly how is your life expectancy determined by others?

The contention of this book is that our life expectancy is to some extent— exactly how much is unknown—determined by the expectation of others. Case in point (from Gary Courtenay): A woman goes to a doctor with a complaint. The doctor finds 'inoperable' cancer and tells the patient she has three months to live. The patient dies in exactly three months. An autopsy reveals no cancer anywhere.

Take the Aboriginal technique of 'pointing the bone' to cause illness or death. The Hawaiian Kahunas used something similar, thoroughly explored in Max Freedom Long's book *The Secret Science Behind Miracles inter alia.*

To what extent have you 'bought into' the reality of others to determine your own life-span? To answer this question, please bear in mind that a thorough and complete exploration of this question involves some serious self examination. Not for the faint hearted or those who are 'set in their ways.' For to fully answer this question requires the participant to be completely honest, to recollect the minutiae, the seemingly insignificant details of one's early (and later) programming, the little 'cues,' the subtext of the family politics. It requires one to look at so-called 'heredity' and how it works to hypnotize people into believing that if their mother got breast cancer, they will too. Or, on the more positive side, if their father lived to 100, they will, too.

Because the fact is, what you think has a great deal to do with how long and how well you will live. Nothing is 'regardless of what you think.' And every thought matters somehow to someone, especially you.

Life and reality turns out to be a mass exercise in self hypnosis. Freedom turns out to be the extent to which you learn to become conscious, to escape from the hypnotic programs, even the ones you make for yourself. Especially the ones you make for yourself.

This is the secret of 'affirmations.' They are nothing more or less than your chance to gain some semblance of control over the information you utilize to program yourself.

Here are some affirmations the authors have used to effectuate some positive change in their lives, and hopefully to enhance their life-span:

- I deserve love.
- I no longer have any need to harm myself in any way.
- I give and receive freely.
- I am now an enlightened being.
- My life force is always growing in strength.

SPIRITUALITY, CONSCIOUSNESS, GRIEF AND DYING

Life upon this planet Earth is an adventure. Sometime during this journey most of us are moved to ask the question—**who am I** ?

It seems that many of us have an inner knowing (intuition) that we are in fact **spirit**. The 'I am,' is really not of this physical world, but a point of individual consciousness born from what we call **god**. As one respected scientist said, "As you look into the Universe, it all appears as one great thought manifesting itself."

In her book *You Can Heal Yourself* Louise Hay describes this very well in the following:

> "In the Infinity where I AM,
> All is Perfect, Whole and Complete.
> I recognize my body as a good Friend.
> Each Cell in my body has Divine Intelligence.
> I listen to what It tells me and know that its advice is valid.
> I am always safe and Divinely protected and guided.
> I choose to be healthy and free.
> All is well in my world."

Once we begin to understand the spiritual nature of who **I am**, our attitude to our journey on this planet changes.

Firstly we become more empowered and able to manifest our own preferred reality. Secondly, we begin to flow with the movement of life called time, blending into and becoming one with the one constant factor in our lives, eternal change.

It is here that the excitement of living begins. Nothing need be called boring ever again. We need never again be afraid. Change becomes something to embrace. Like a child we can play the game of life, using our imagination to the full, delighting in the involvement with life.

How does this acceptance of change influence my life, you may ask?

It releases the need to hold on to the past and to accept the inevitable losses that occur in life be they material possessions or personal relationships. The grief at the loss of a loved one, especially after many years of shared experience, becomes a process to embrace and let go, as a natural and inevitable event. The pain felt is a part of living, a part of being Human. It is an acknowledgment of the memories of the joy and pleasure shared.

How do we let go and flow with change?

"I cross the bridges with joy and ease."

This positive affirmation is needed to replace the habit of thinking that arose from our conditioning and beliefs. You are much more than your conditioned Mind. You direct your mind which can be retrained to become your willing partner to a greater and freer life. It will respond to your desire and instruction. There is an incredible power and intelligence within you constantly responding to your thoughts and words. Align yourself with this, it is **I am**.

Do not think of your mind as in control. **You** are in control.

I am is the master of the mind, your passion for love and belief in yourself is the key.

You can change the thoughts of your mind, by the use of the words you use and the desires **you choose**!

Once you master the understanding of who you are, then you will be able to let go of the old thought patterns, the beliefs relating to grief of the passing of the old, and the rebirth of the **new**.

Do not take yesterday into tomorrow, for then it is not new.

The only moment that you have control over is **now**!

Use this tool, learn to live in the now, and witness the changes in your experience of life.

Always remember that your efforts to let go of your habit of holding on to the past, will take time to change. Allow yourself this space, practice diligently, and you will accept these changes with dignity and passion.

The way in which we see the world is governed by the attitudes we have learned, these are habits also and can be changed.

An excellent way to understand the way in which attitudes influence our response to the occurrences in our lives, is to recognize attitudes as filters through which we (**I am**) view the world and its events. Filters may be anger, fear, guilt, poor self esteem, resentment and the habit of holding on to the past. We all have attitudes, they are a necessary part of our mental function. The more they are out of tune with the reality that we live in, the more they will create for us unnecessary stress and suffering. "From the point of view of who **I am**, I now recognize and choose to reevaluate my attitudes and change those that do not serve me well. I choose to create new attitudes that are in harmony with the ever changing nature of life."

All things in this dimension live and die. So it is that relationships, occupations, ideas, beliefs, and even atoms, come and go. Day becomes night, spring becomes summer, a life is born and a life dies. But do they really? I think not, they just change. Like the butterfly, with its cycle of metamorphosis, eternal motion.

Every day then is a new beginning, a rebirth, after a night of rest and repose, even the dying process itself is only another part of this great spiritual journey. How different is our response to the events of life **if we simply change our perspective of reality**. How much more easily can we let go and let God share its life with us for a short time.

"Life is an adventure to be lived, not a problem to be solved."

TOWARDS 'SUPER IMMUNITY'

- If it is indeed true that every cell in our body is replaced at least once every seven years then it stands to reason that the more vital (read: **alive**) the nutrients taken into the cell, the healthier that cell will be.

- Dead matter is by definition devoid of the 'life force' which for the purposes of simple definition is the bio electricity that permeates and surrounds all living things. Artificial food is dead food and by definition cannot promote or support life.

- The more refined the food, the less 'life force' there is within it. Therefore, as a rule of thumb, eat foods that are less refined, preferably raw foods, sprouts, wheat grass juice, salads, carrot and vegetable juice, etc. Wheat, for example, can be eaten as wheat berries, boiled as a hot cereal. Whole grains are to be preferred over processed. Raw comb honey or maple syrup rather than white (or brown) sugar.

- Natural medicine, acupuncture, homeopathy and even folk medicine whose wisdom is time tested—and has been found to work—is usually more reliable than allopathic medicine that is corporate driven and newer than yesterday. Some alternatives do not work for everyone. Therefore pick and choose according to what works for you. If you're sick, give your system all the help it needs to heal. If you're well, see a Chinese herbalist/ acupuncturist to help you maintain your health. Most wise doctors now recommend antibiotics as a last resort, otherwise you risk the chance that they won't work and will make you worse. These wise doctors will prescribe antibiotics only after your condition has been diagnosed by a reputable laboratory to be bacterial in nature. Most naturopaths prescribe probiotics to help you increase the strength of your immune system.

- Controlled fasting, sauna and moderate exercise work to detoxify the body and promote its elasticity. Disease usually happens slowly as a result of the toxic overload the body is forced to carry. Meat is especially implicated here as it is very difficult for the human alimentary tract to properly digest and often putrefies inside the intestine. Two of the authors recommend a vegetarian diet; and two recommend a diet in which red meat, fowl and fish play a limited part.

- Thanks to the mineral depletion of the soils of many farms, the authors recommend mineral and vitamin supplementation. It is virtually impossible to get a 'balanced' meal today with all the nutrients you need. We all live in a toxic world in which our vital organs are coming under increasing amounts of stress from environmental poisons. Vitamin supplementation has become increasingly important to maintain adequate health. Please consult your heath professional before taking supplements.

- Yoga and other relaxation exercises should be undertaken with the knowledge that they have been shown to contribute toward a more balanced human ecology. Yoga breathing, for example, can help improve the oxygenation and distribution of energy within the body. Oxygen levels in the atmosphere are at their lowest levels in recorded history. The human body was originally adapted to a 30 percent O2 environment, according to the latest evidence. We are now less than 20 percent, in some areas considerably less. In the absence of a concerted effort to halt the disintegration of the ecosphere, the individual must make an all out effort to try to compensate for the effects of our contemporary plagues.

- There are several 'longevity herbs' that have been known to esoteric medicine for thousands of years. The authors encourage the reader to investigate these herbs at herbal retailers or local herbal practitioners.

- There are several 'super foods' that promote Super Immunity. The authors encourage the reader to experiment with these foods and gauge the results him/herself. If you feel better, try not to be discouraged by those for whom this is merely 'anecdotal evidence.'

- Sleep is one of those things that people are not getting enough of in their headlong rush to successful careers—or just economic survival. The authors can attest to the life sapping effects of too little sleep and conversely the life giving effects of the right amount of sleep. The authors encourage the reader to enjoy his or her sleep time, to use one's dreams to process daily problems, and to access some of the higher dimensions.

SUGGESTED READING

ALZHEIMER'S

Beating Alzheimer's by Tom Warren. Avery 1991.

CANCER

How I Conquered Cancer Naturally by Eydie Mae with Chris Loeffler. Originally published by Harvest House Publishers, Oregon, USA. 1975. Now published by Avery Publishing Group, New York.

Beating The Odds: Alternative Treatments That Have Worked Miracles Against Cancer by Albert Marchetti. Contemporary Books, Chicago, 1989.

Beating Cancer: My Way by Bill Hall, Waihi, New Zealand, 1991.

Burden of Proof: Surviving Cancer, AIDS and Most Diseases Whakatane, New Zealand, International Publishing. 1992.

How to Be A Healthy Patient by Stephen Faulder, Headway-Stoddard Stratton, 1991.

Love, Medicine and Miracles by Bernie Siegal. Published by Arrow.

Getting Well Again and *The Healing Journey* by Carl Simonton, MD. Bantam.

USA.

You Can Conquer Cancer by Dr. Ian Gawler, Hill of Content Publishing, Melbourne.

A Simple Guide to Better Health and *Why Be Scared of Cancer?* by Dr. Eva Hill, published by G.W. Moore, Auckland.

A Cancer Therapy: The Results of Fifty Cases by Dr. Max Gerson. Published by The Gerson Institute, USA.

Heal Cancer: Choose Your Own Survival Path by Cilento and Chamberlain. Published by Hill of Content, Melbourne.

Options: The Alternative Cancer Therapy Book by Richard Walters.

Vitamins in Cancer Prevention and Treatment by Prasad Kedar, Inner Traditions, USA.

The Cancer Survivors and How They Did It by Judith Glassman. Dial Press, New York. 1983.

A Gentle Way With Cancer by Brenda Kidman. Century Publishing, London.

How to Fight Cancer and Win by William L. Fischer. Alive Books, Vacouver, Canada.

The Healing of Cancer: The Cures, the Cover-ups and the Solution Now! by Barry Lynes. Published by Marcus Books, Canada.

The Cancer Industry: The Classic Expose on the Cancer Establishment by Ralph Moss. Paragon House, New York.

CHELATION THERAPY

The Chelation Answer by Morton Walker DPM. Second Opinion Publishing, Georgia, USA. 1994.

"The Chelation Way: The Complete Book of Chelation Therapy by Dr. Morton Walker. Avery Publishing Group Inc, New York. 1990.

DIGESTIVE PROBLEMS

Nutritional Medicine: The Drug Free Guide to Better Family Health by Dr Stephen Davies and Dr. Alan Stewart, Pan Books.

Encyclopedia of Natural Medicines by Michael T. Murray, ND, and Joseph E. Pizzorno, ND. Prima Publishing, P.O.Box 1260 mp, Rocklin, California, 95677.

The Family Library Guide to Natural Therapies by Nancy Beckham, Family Library, Australia.

MEDICAL TESTS

The Patient's Guide to Medical Tests (2nd Edition) by Dr. Edward Pinckney and Cathy Pinckney. (This book was first published as *The Encyclopedia of Medical Tests*).

It's Your Body—Know What the Doctor Ordered: Your Complete Guide to Medical Testing by Marion Laffey Fox and Dr. Truman G. Schnabel.

MENOPAUSE

The Menopause Industry: A Guide to Medicine's Discovery of the Mid-Life Woman by Sandra Coney, first published by Penguin Books in 1991.

NUTRITION

Nutritional Medicine: The Drug Free Guide to Better Family Health by Dr. Stephen Davies and Dr. Alan Stewart (first published by Pan Books, 1987)

Laurel's Kitchen: A Handbook for Vegetarian Cookery and Nutrition by Laurel Robertson, Carol Flinders and Bronwen Godfrey. First Published 1976, Nilgiri Press, subsequently produced in paperback by Bantam Books.

Diet for a Small Planet by Frances Moore Lappé, Balantine Books, New York.

Prescription for Longevity: Eating Right for a Long Life by James Scala PhD, published by Plume Books, 1992.

The Gradual Vegetarian: The Step by Step Way to Start Eating the Right Stuff

Today by Lisa Tracy 1985 Dell Publishing. This book contains over 200 recipes.

Sugar Blues by William Dufty. Published by Warner Books.

Diet for the Atomic Age: How to Protect Yourself From Low-Level Radiation by Sara Shannon. Avery Publishing Group, New York.

Essential Supplements for Women: What Every Woman Should Know About Vitamins, Minerals, Enzymes, and Amino Acids by Carolyn Reuben, CA, and Joan Priestly, MD. A Perigee Book.

STRESS

Successful Stress Control. The Natural Way by David Hoffman. Thorson's Publishers Inc, Vermont. 1987.

GENERAL

Back to Eden by Jethro Kloss, Back to Eden Books, California.

New Start: New Health, New Energy, New Joy by Vernon W. Foster, MD, Woodbridge Press, California.

Fit For Life and *Fit for Life II* by Harvey and Marilyn Diamond. Warner Books.

Be Well Naturally: A Complete Guide for New Zealand Women of Any Age by Lynda Wharton, Penguin Books.

The Bee Hive Product Bible by Royden Brown, Avery Publishing Group, New York.

Racketeering in Medicine: The Suppression of Alternatives by James Carter. Hampton Roads Publishing Company.

For Health or Profit? : Medicine, the Pharmaceutical Industry and the State in New Zealand Edited by Peter Davis, Oxford University Press, Auckland.

AUTHOR PROFILES

GARY COURTENAY, ND

Gary began his career as a Natural Therapist in 1962.

He was the first student to be trained in New Zealand under the Association of Naturopaths, which was at that time the main professional organization. The Association was started by Murdoch Ross and David Duggan and consisted of a small group of dedicated men and women who had a vision for the future of Natural medicine. His tutor was Roy Powell with whom he worked as a student/assistant. At the same time completing a course from the British Guild of Drugless Therapists. In 1963 on passing their examination, he gained the first Diploma of Naturopathy from the New Zealand Healing Association.

In 1964 he passed the examination for both the New Zealand Association of Naturopaths and the British Guild of Drugless therapists and became a fully qualified member of both organizations. He began practice in Cromwell Street, Mt Eden, and remained there until 1968 when he, upon the urging of Marjorie Spears, a health store proprietor in Nelson, moved to Nelson to begin the first Naturopathic practice there.

In 1972, under the direction of David Duggan and the Association of

Naturopaths, Gary opened the first college for training Naturopaths in New Zealand and conducted a class of 10 students, most of whom are in practice today.

In 1977, with a family of 5 children, he moved to Australia, where he eventually settled in Melbourne. In 1983 he started a practice and meditation centre and a couple of years later joined with Colin Charnley, ND DO DC, Naturopath, Chiropractor, and Acupuncturist, who was one of the students that he trained in 1972. He remained in practice at Parkdale, Melbourne, until 1990, when he returned to New Zealand.

Since returning to New Zealand he has established a busy practice at Browns Bay, is President of the Homoeobotanical Institute and was the founding President of the Task Force of the Charter of Health Practitioners which began in December 1993.

He now holds the position of President of the Natural Medicine Board of the Charter and is an active committee member of the Association of Natural Therapists and the New Zealand Healing Association. He has also formed the Society of Natural Therapists and Researchers Inc. This body is an affiliate signatory to the Charter of Health Practitioners and accredits practitioners for Charter.

His latest contribution to natural medicine is in establishing a college of Clinical Nutrition in New Zealand. This is a post graduate course created by Henry Osieki, B.Sc., of Australia, a brilliant biochemist who has created a scientific base for clinical nutrition. This course is designed for naturopaths, pharmacists, nurses and doctors.

KATHERINE JOYCE SMITH, CHS

Katherine is the author of *Super Foods* and other books on health and nutrition. She is a practicing Medical Herbalist, living in Aukland, New Zealand.